W9-BBH-586

John Locke and Children's Books in Eighteenth-Century England

Blake inv & s

The Dog.

Pub.d June 18. 1805 by R Phillips N 6, Bridge Street Black Friers.

John Locke and Children's Books in Eighteenth-Century England

•

Samuel F. Pickering, Jr.

THE UNIVERSITY OF TENNESSEE PRESS

KNOXVILLE

Manufactured in the United States of America. First edition.

Clothbound editions of University of Tennessee Press
books are printed on paper designed for an effective life
of at least 300 years, and binding materials
are chosen for strength and durability.

Frontispiece: From William Hayley, *Ballads*.
By permission of the British Library.

Library of Congress Cataloging in Publication Data

Pickering, Samuel F 1941–
John Locke and children's books in eighteenth-century England.

Bibliography: p.
Includes index.
1. Children's literature, English—History and criticism. 2. Locke, John, 1632–1704—Influence.
I. Title.
PN1009.Z6P5 820′.9′9282 80-24899
ISBN 0-87049-290-X

For my parents and grandmother
with deep affection

Contents

Illustrations

THE ILLUSTRATIONS IN THE TEXT ARE THE SAME SIZES AS THE ORIGINALS.

Preface

This study has two roots: the first is sentimental and the second, scholarly. My happiest memories are made of books, particularly the small volumes I read as a child. Like oatmeal on a cold winter's morning, they have stuck with me although I have long since trudged over the hills and far away. To recapture the delight of that first reading is the dream of many academics, and when given the opportunity, I settled in the British Library and began examining books written for children in the eighteenth century. I approached children's books from the perspective of my earlier study of evangelicalism and the novel. Instead of finding religion on every page, however, I discovered the ideas of John Locke. For the eighteenth-century British educator, Locke provided a theoretical umbrella for all seasons. Even when the rude brow of Rousseau loured on the horizon, educators simply raised the Lockean shield and pressed onward. For the eighteenth-century Englishman, Locke was, as Mrs. Trimmer labeled him, "our great philosopher."[1]

My approach is historical. Critical methodologies are ultimately matters of taste. My feeling about much contemporary structuralist and phenomenological criticism resembles that felt by a rude son of Neptune in *The Adventures of a Bank-Note* (1771) when he was informed that gentlemen of taste admired a rouged and befrizzled lady of fashion. "Taste!" exclaimed the sea captain, "a queer taste indeed: for my part, I had rather taste a piece of salt beef that has made two voyages to the East Indies, than taste that paint and putty of hers; why, it would set the chain-pump of my bowels a-going, and not only bring up all my bilge-water, but send my pluck overboard, through the scupper-holes."[2]

This book is not all-inclusive. Many scholarly paths were carved through the wilderness of children's books by F.J. Harvey Darton in his pioneer study, *Children's Books in England.* Where Darton has cleared away the underbrush, I have not felt obliged to trail behind. Moreover, I have given short shrift to Perrault's fairy tales and to nursery rhymes. Much light has been shed on these subjects by Iona and Peter Opie's *The Classic Fairy Tale* and *The Oxford Dictionary of Nursery Rhymes,* Max Lüthi's *Once Upon A Time on the Nature of Fairy Tales,* Bruno Bettelheim's *The Uses of Enchantment,* and Roger Sale's *Fairy Tales and After.* I can do no better than refer readers to these books. For my own part, however, I hope that my explorations, like those of Sir John Mandeville, will prove interesting. Unlike Mandeville, I have not met those remarkable big-footed, one-legged Ethiopians who could run faster than deer and who, when the sun burned down or storms streaked across the plains, stretched out on their backs and raised their "foot" above them like a date palm.[3] Still, I have read some odd things which I think will prove interesting not only to students of literature and education but also to that nonacademic reader for whom children's books hold sweet pleasures.

In some ways books resemble flowers. Seeing blossoms in the spring, the reader is often unaware of the care the cuttings received in the winter. I owe debts of gratitude to many people who knowingly and unknowingly helped my book "to shoot." If my book resembles a black-eyed Susan more than it does a rose, the fault is mine, not theirs. At Dartmouth, Jay Parini was sympathetic to my problems and made helpful suggestions. Carlos Baker, E.D.H. Johnson, and Louis Landa at Princeton have always encouraged me. Busy with their many projects, John Sutherland of University College, London, and George Core at the *Sewanee Review* have been good examples, spurring me to work when I might have dozed through a term. James Axtell at William and Mary graciously answered my questions about John Locke. J. Paul Hunter of Emory University twice read this study in manuscript; without his thoughtful readings and many fine suggestions, I would have committed a chorus of howlers. I am also grateful for the help extended to me by librarians at the American Antiquarian Society, Baker Library of Dartmouth College, the Bodleian, the British Library, the Guildhall Library, the Printing Library of St. Bride Institute, the Victoria and Albert Museum, and Dr. Williams's Library. Last, I wish to thank the American Council of Learned Societies, The University of Connecticut Research Foundation, Dartmouth College, and the National Endowment for the Humanities for helping sponsor my research.

Storrs, Connecticut
September 1979

Samuel F. Pickering, Jr.

John Locke
and Children's Books
in Eighteenth-Century
England

•

CHAPTER ONE

Our First Philosopher and the Animal Creation

Many of the most memorable characters in modern British and American children's books are animals. Without their animal personae, contemporary children's books would almost appear underpopulated. Along the bookshelf Mrs. Tiggy-Winkle washes clothes and Squirrel Nutkin dances like a sunbeam before Old Brown. Despite their father's unhappy transformation into a pie, Peter Rabbit and the Flopsy Bunnies sample Mr. McGregor's lettuce while Ginger and Pickles do a thriving, if not profitable, business in sugar, snuff, and galoshes. Near by, Uncle Wiggily Longears putts slowly along, nibbling on his turnip steering wheel and keeping an ear cocked for the roar of "Toad, the terror." Across the shelf is Pooh Corner; beyond that, an open space from which echoes the laughing taunt, "Bred and bawn in a briar-patch, Brer Fox—bred and bawn in a briar-patch."[1] Books for children have not always been filled with such marvelously human animals. If these crawling, flying, and hopping characters had been written into books for children in the eighteenth century, they would have found themselves in a less anthropomorphic and sentimental world.

According to Harvey Darton, children's books did not stand out "as a clear but subordinate branch of English literature until the middle of the eighteenth century." Until John Newbery's publishing success, children's books had consisted mostly of ephemeral chapbooks and ballads and a few "Godly books." By the beginning of the nineteenth century, however, the trade in children's books was thriving, as many publishers, including John Marshall, J. Harris, Stockdale, Rivington, Longman, and J. Johnson, devoted much of their energies to children's books. Many factors lay behind the creation and rapid expansion of this trade. The "commercial prosperity," as Mrs. West put it, had increased the size of the middle class and contributed to social mobility within Britain itself. As large numbers of people climbed above penury and achieved modest financial security, they were better able to afford books for their children. Because the future seemed to promise more than laborious poverty, they wanted books which their children could use as educational stepping-stones to climb higher in society. Later, with the rapid growth of Sunday schools in the 1780s and 1790s, popular education began, and a new reading public of some five hundred thousand Sunday scholars was created.[2]

In his *Memoirs* (1792), James Lackington, a successful London publisher, wrote that the "sale of books in general" had "increased prodigiously within the last twenty years" and estimated that "more than four times" the number of books were sold in 1790 than were sold twenty years earlier. "The poorer sort of farmers, and even the poor country people," Lackington wrote, who had once spent their winter evenings in telling stories about witches, ghosts, and hobgoblins, now listened to their sons and daughters read tales and romances. Book clubs, circulating libraries, and Sunday schools all contributed, Lackington thought, to the "rapid increase of the sale of books." To some extent the children's book industry helped create the general boom in publishing. It was "worth remarking," Lackington noted, that "the introducing histories, romances, stories, poems, etc. into schools" had been "a very great means of diffusing a general taste for reading among all ranks of people." Formerly, when their reading was restricted to the Bible, children did "not make so early a progress in reading." Now that they were "pleased and entertained as well as instructed," many developed a "relish for books" which would "last as long as life."[3]

If commercial prosperity made the expansion of the book trade possible, the writings of John Locke provided publishers and educators with a wealth of general and particular educational matter. No other Englishman had written so broadly and so reasonably on education. Previous seventeenth-century writers had limited the applicability of their works by appealing to select social classes or particular religious groups. Henry Peacham, for example, wrote *The Compleat Gentleman* (1622) for the nobility alone, a small group. And although he praised those ancients who by hard work and talent had risen from "meanesse of birth and beginning" to outstanding positions in their societies, he had little sympathy for upwardly mobile groups in his own country. He attacked people "who by Mechanicke and base meanes" had "raked up a masse of wealth" and he argued that "like a plague" infecting the whole world "every undeserving and base Peasant" was "ayming at Nobilitie." "The exercise of Merchandise," he asserted, was "accounted base" while those who labored "for their livelihood and gaine" had "no share at all in Nobilitie or Gentry." Even if parents whose occupations were "much derogatory from Nobilitie" were not put off by Peacham's single-minded appeal to "the Nobler Orbes" and read *The Compleat Gentleman* diligently, they discovered that much of the book's contents were not suited to the practical world of "Merchandise" in which their sons would struggle. Peacham did not clutter his pages with educational goods which a rising tradesman would find useful. Instead, he stocked the arts and graces and the more exotic knowledge necessary to furbishing a nobleman as an accomplished courtier. Typically, he included a chapter "*of Armorie and Blazonrie.*" "It is mete that a Noble or Gentleman who beareth Armes, and is well descended," he instructed, "bee not only able to blazon his owne proper Coate; derive by pedegree the descent of his family from the originall, know such matches and allies as are joyned to him in blood: but also of his Prince, the Nobilitie, and Gentry where he liveth." Before middle-class parents who tried to winnow Peacham's book in hopes of separating practically useful educational information from socially irrelevant material stood another formidable obstacle. *The Compleat Gentleman* contained a vast number of references to classical literature and quotations in Greek and Latin, which would have baffled all readers lacking a classical education.[4]

Locke did not limit his readership. *Some Thoughts Concerning Education* (1693) was written in clear, simple prose and did not contain quotations in Greek or Latin and obscure references to classical literature. Locke, Bolingbroke wrote in *Letters or essays addressed to Alexander Pope, Esq.*, "appealed to the experience and conscious knowledge of every one, and rendered all he advanced intelligible." In *An Essay Upon Study* (1731), John Clarke, master of the grammar school in Hull, stated that Locke's works were "the best fitted" of all that he knew "in any Language . . . to improve the Understanding." "For Style," Clarke continued, they were "inferiour to nothing in our English Tongue." "A rich and noble Vein of fine Sense, and strong Reasoning" ran "through them all without exception; in as Masterly Language, every where just and clear, and as well adapted to the Nature of the Subject or Design, as is perhaps any where else to be met with." *Some Thoughts* was filled with useful material on day-to-day educational practice. Much of its content appeared applicable not merely to the "Gentleman's Son" for whom it was ostensibly written but to the children of parents in all walks of life. Locke was a popularizer. He took educational suggestions dangling loosely from many works and wove them into what the eighteenth century saw as a magic carpet. Not only would it carry children upward, but it was available to everyone, not simply princes lounging amid frankincense and myrrh but shopkeepers' sons rummaging through sugar and salt. Locke convinced parents, especially those in the rapidly expanding middle class, that childhood education shaped both the moral and the economic man. From him they learned how to develop a child's personality so that instead of being prepared merely to carry himself with grace among the lords of the land or to meet his maker, as religious writers had it, he would be fit for ordinary daily life and be able to face its many physical, mental, and moral challenges. In order to help her rear their son Billy, Richardson's Mr. B. gave Pamela "Mr. Locke's *Treatise* on Education." With the carelessness which marked a man educated by the less thorough and practical methods of an earlier time, Mr. B. explained that he had "not read it through" and had only "dipp'd into it here and there." But he thought, he said, from seeing the "Name of the Author" that Pamela could not have "a better Directory." Not to the manner born as was Mr. B., Pamela believed that factors other than birth would greatly influence Billy's future chances in life. Consequently, she read Locke with absorbing interest and like many middle-class parents was convinced by him that a good education would be crucial to her son's success. From Locke she learned over a "thousand" rules. Moreover, she wrote Mr. B. a series of instructive letters describing Locke's "excellent Book" and filling over sixty pages of the fourth volume of Richardson's novel.[5]

Before the reign of Queen Anne, the *Guardian of Education* stated in 1802, there were "very few" books written for children. "*The first period of Infantine and Juvenile Literature*" began, the journal declared, after Mr. Locke popularized "the idea of uniting amusement with instruction." In *Some Thoughts Concerning Education* and his closely related *Essay Concerning Human Understanding* (1690), Locke also provided the eighteenth century with what seemed to be a scientific basis for the study of human development and an explanation of the crucial formative influence of education. According to Locke, the "great Thing to be minded in Education" was "what *Habits*" were settled. Since nine men out of ten, he held, were formed "Good or Evil, useful or not, by their Education," life for the orthodox Lockean became not so much virtue rewarded as good habits rewarded, and the most important duty owed to children was establishing them in sound habits of mind and body based on right principles. The child was not a diminutive adult. Instead, he was the father of the man, as Locke contended that the "little, and almost insensible Impressions on our tender Infancies" had "very important and lasting Consequences." There were no innate ideas or principles in the mind, and a child's mind, he stated, initially resembled an "empty cabinet" or a "white paper void of all characters." "*Experience*" on which knowledge was founded furnished the cabinet with ideas through "SENSATION" and "REFLECTION." The "great source of most of the *ideas* we have," Locke taught, was the senses. Observing "*external sensible objects,*" the senses conveyed into the mind "distinct *perceptions* of things," according to the various ways "those objects" affected them. Thus, through observation, children picked up their ideas of yellow, white, hot, cold, soft, hard, bitter, and sweet. The "other fountain," Locke stressed, "from which experience" furnished the understanding with ideas was reflection, "*the perception of the operations of our own minds* within us, as it is employed about the *ideas* it has got." In time, Locke said, the mind reflected on "its own *operations* about the *ideas* got by *sensation*" and thereby stored itself "with a new set of *ideas.*" These ideas, which could "not be had from things without," Locke explained, were such things as doubting, believing, reasoning, knowing, willing, and "all the different actings of our minds; which we, being conscious of and observing in ourselves" received into our understandings. This second source of ideas, Locke emphasized, was wholly within introspective man and although it did not resemble sensation, it could reasonably be called "internal sense." From these simple ideas, the mind built complex ideas. This was done in three ways: first, by uniting simple ideas, a process which led to concepts such as beauty, gratitude, a man, an army; second, by comparing ideas, thereby getting "*ideas* of relations"; and third, by breaking apart ideas which became joined and developing the ability to abstract.[6]

As an extension of this theory of understanding, Locke taught that men came "to be furnished with fewer or more simple *ideas* from without, according as the *objects* they converse with afford greater or less variety; and from the operation of their own minds within, according as they more or less *reflect* on them." By controlling the objects which impressed a child's senses, by instigating his reflection, so far as was possible, and by directing the building of complex ideas, Lockean educators believed that a child could be shaped or educated. Locke's denial of innate ideas made a child the product of his education. All experience now had to be scrutinized carefully, because learning made a child not merely of this world but also of the next world. "Nothing," Locke emphasized in *Some Thoughts,* "that may form Children's Minds, is to be over-look'd and neglected, and whatsoever introduces Habits, and settles Customs in them, deserves the Care and Attention of their Governours."[7]

Educators linked Locke's theory of the origin of ideas to his theory of the association of ideas. The latter explained the growth of habits and lent weight to the belief in the necessity of a highly structured early education. There was scarcely anyone, Locke wrote, who had not observed something "odd" or "extravagant" in "the opinions, reasonings, and actions of other men." These oddities were caused by the association of ideas. Although some ideas had "a natural correspondence and connexion," others, he explained, "not at all of kin" came to be so united in men's minds by education, chance, or circumstance that it was difficult to separate them. When one came into the understanding, "its associate" appeared with it, and if there were more than two "thus united, the whole gang, always inseparable," appeared together. Since custom settled these "habits of thinking in the understanding," Locke advised "those who have children or the charge of their education . . . diligently to watch and carefully to prevent the undue connexion of *ideas* in the minds of young people." Just as important for children's books and practical education was the "due" connection of ideas. By careful attention to Locke's theories, educators saw how right behavior could be "woven into the very Principles of his [a child's] Nature." "The *Associations* or Knots of *Ideas,*" Philander argued in Fordyce's *Dialogues Concerning Education* (1745), determined "*right* or *wrong Taste,*" were the origin of "Passions" and "Conduct," and were "the Spring of our Happiness or Misery in Life." Therefore, he continued, settling "just *Associations* in the Minds of Youth" and breaking "wrong ones" was "an Affair of the utmost Importance in *Education.*" "Doing this aright," he emphasized, was "the grand Art or Engine of *moral Culture.*" "Without an adequate knowledge of the power of association," Catharine Macaulay Graham wrote in *Letters On Education* (1790), a tutor would not be able "to fashion the mind of his pupil."[8]

It seems almost impossible to exaggerate the influence of Locke's writings upon eighteenth-century thought in general and upon educational thought in particular. "Locke, beyond any other writer," Gerald Cragg wrote, "was to be the moving spirit of the eighteenth century. He summed up all that the previous period had achieved. He anticipated all that the new generation would attempt. In every branch of intellectual endeavour his influence was supreme." According to Lawrence Cremin, Locke and Newton were "intellectual prisms" through which "innovative ideas" were diffused to the larger public. By 1704, John Yolton argued, Locke's "epistemological, moral, and religious doctrines" had been so "thoroughly disseminated both in England and abroad" and had been "so much discussed, criticized, and praised" that "no responsible thinker in the eighteenth century could afford to omit reference to Locke." Of *Some Thoughts,* Richard Aaron wrote simply, "few other English books have influenced educational thought so deeply."[9]

In eighteenth-century England, the educational writings of "the great Mr. *Locke*" were practically biblical. Everyone interested in education read the texts, and almost all were true believers. In *Sermons on The Religious Education of Children* (1732), Philip Doddridge cited Locke and Solomon to prove that men were formed by their educations. *Some*

Thoughts itself appeared in at least twenty-five English, sixteen French, three German, six Italian, one Swedish, and two Dutch editions during the century. As with the Bible, most readers read Locke's educational writings for truth and wisdom rather than for controversy. Readers wanted to learn correct, practical educational methods, and few educators probed deeply or questioned Locke's ideas. William Warburton, the bishop of Gloucester, wrote in 1759 that Locke was "universal." Under the heading *education,* Ephraim Chambers's *Cyclopaedia: Or, An Universal Dictionary Of Arts and Sciences* (1728) stated, "Mr. *Lock*'s excellent Treatise of *Education,* is known to every Body." In her gardens at Richmond, Queen Caroline placed busts of Locke, Newton, Clarke, and Wollaston because "they were the *Glory* of their *Country,* and stamp'd a Dignity on Human Nature."[10]

Throughout the eighteenth century, writers on education paid tribute to and popularized Locke's ideas. Locke's most influential follower, Isaac Watts, stated in his *Philosophical Essays* (1733) that Locke's treatises on government and education had "laid the Foundations of *true Liberty, and the Rules of Just Restraint for the younger and elder Years of Man*" while his essay on the understanding had "*diffused fairer Light through the World in numerous Affairs of Science and of human Life*" and contained "*many Truths*" which were "*worthy of Letters of Gold.*" In *The Christian School-Master* (1709), James Talbott urged the founders of charity schools to pay particular attention to the education of young children, saying that since children's minds resembled "blank Paper, or smooth Wax . . . capable of any Impression" it was "of the greatest Importance" that they be marked by true religion. In *An Essay Upon The Education of Youth In Grammar-Schools* (1720), John Clarke stressed the importance of Locke's theory of the origin of ideas. Children were "Strangers in the World, where," he wrote, "the first Acquaintance they make is with sensible Objects: Those must store the yet empty Cabinet of the Mind with Variety of Ideas, as the Foundation and Materials of their future Knowledge." The only book on education "worth the Perusal," Clarke continued, was "*Mr. Locke's.*" Eleven years later, in *An Essay Upon Study,* Clarke paid an extraordinary tribute to Locke and Newton. "The Study of the Liberal Sciences," Clarke wrote,

> purges and purifies the mind, improves and strengthens its rational faculties, and thereby prepares it for the ready apprehension and reception of the great Truths of Religion. But the sciences of all others the most conducive to this noble purpose, are Logick, Mathematicks, and natural Philosophy, which in the last Century were wonderfully advanced here in England, by two of the brightest and ablest Genius's, that ever appeared in the World. I mean the Great LOCKE and the Incomparable NEWTON. Whose Memory will be an Honour to their Native Country, whilst Learning and Good Sense have any Place amongst the Sons of Men. The former has by precept and example both, taught the World, how to reason justly and exactly, and contributed more than all the Philosophers before him put together, to the clearing of Mens Minds, and qualifying them for the easy and expeditious attainment of solid useful knowledge. And the latter has been as happy in his Province by carrying the Mathematics, to a height vastly beyond what they had attained to before his time.[11]

By the 1730s, Locke's educational ideas had been absorbed into the thought of the century. In *British Education: Or, The Source of the Disorders of Great Britain* (1756), Thomas Sheridan praised Locke and Milton as "two eminent physicians" and stated that "the power of the first impressions made upon the minds of men, and the influence they have upon their conduct ever after, is a beaten topic: holy writ." In *Dialogues On The Uses Of Foreign Travel* (1764), Richard Hurd constructed imaginary conversations between Shaftesbury and Locke. "No man," he explained, was "more able, than Mr. LOCKE" to "give us Lectures on the good old chapter of *Education*; which many others indeed have discussed; but none with such good sense and with so constant an eye to the use and business of the world." In the *Dialogues,* Hurd's Locke stressed the formative importance of early education. There may have been a few people, he granted, "whose superior industry in advanced age" atoned "for the defects of their education," but "in general," he added, "the *Man* depends entirely on the *Boy*" and was "all his life long, what the impressions, he received in his early youth" made him.[12]

In his life of Locke (trans. 1706), Jean LeClerc said he did not write "a Panegyrick on Mr. Locke" because Locke's works were "read in several Languages" and would be "an eternal Monument of his vast Genius, sharp Wit, and exact Judgment." By the second half of the eighteenth century, Locke's educational influence was monumental. As the *Gentleman's Magazine* described Queen Caroline's gardens at Richmond as a "rural *Temple* sacred to *Learning and Virtue,*" so writers on education treated Locke's works as sacrosanct. They felt obliged to genuflect to Locke himself. References to Locke added authority to educational studies, and books published on education often contained ceremonial tributes to Locke and his ideas. Typically, in *An Essay Upon Education* (1772), James Whitchurch paid formal obeisance to Locke as "an Author, to whom the Learned must ever acknowledge themselves highly indebted, and whose Name can never be mentioned without a secret Veneration, and Respect; his Assertions being the result of intense Thought, strict Enquiry, a clear and penetrating Judgment."[13]

One of the most important threads to be woven into the fabric of character, Locke taught in *Some Thoughts,* was kindness to animals. Children, he observed, "when they have got Possession of any poor Creature" were "apt to use it ill," tormenting and treating it "very roughly" and "with a seeming kind of Pleasure." Children should be closely watched, he stressed, to see if they were inclined "to any such *Cruelty.*" If they were, then parents should teach them "the contrary Usage. For the Custom of Tormenting and Killing of Beasts, will, by Degrees, harden their Minds even towards Men; and they who delight in the Suffering and Destruction of inferior Creatures, will not be apt to be very compassionate, or benign to those of their own kind." From "the beginning," he continued, children should "be bred up in an Abhorrence of *killing,* or tormenting any living Creature; and be taught not to *spoil* or destroy any thing, unless it be for the Preservation or Advantage of some other, that is Nobler." Until the end of the eighteenth century, Locke's emphasis upon the danger of cruelty to animals influenced the depiction of animals in children's books. Drawing upon Locke's ideas, writers of children's books used animals as didactic devices to lead children away from cruelty and to benevolence.[14]

The use of animals as vehicles for instruction was, of course, not unique to the eighteenth century. Aesop's *Fables* has been in print in Britain since Caxton's translation in 1484 and had appeared in "two lines of descent," both as a book for fashionable society and as a school text.

In the eighteenth century itself, L'Estrange's and Croxall's editions, 1691 and 1722 respectively, were widely circulated in expensive volumes, while John Newbery's sixpenny *Aesop* went through many editions in the middle of the century. Later, Francis Newbery published a version which reached a thirteenth edition by 1787; and in the 1780s, Mrs. Teachwell (Lady Ellenor Fenn) wrote a series of cheap primers based on Aesop for the publisher John Marshall. In *Some Thoughts,* Locke himself praised the *Fables,* saying that they were almost "the only Book" he knew "fit for Children." In 1703 Locke's English-Latin edition for students was published as *Aesop's Fables, in English & Latin, Interlineary, For the Benefit of those who Not having a Master, would learn Either of These Tongues.* Although writers like Mrs. Teachwell and publishers like Newbery made the language of the *Fables* palatable for young children, the contents of the *Fables* changed little in the eighteenth century. According to Darton, they were essentially the "Legacy of the Middle Ages." As such, they reveal less about eighteenth-century attitudes and children's books than books written originally during the century.[15]

The first publisher, the *Guardian of Education* declared, to furnish "a great supply of engaging books" for children was John Newbery, perhaps the most attractive character in the eighteenth-century publishing world. Born in Berkshire in 1713, he became an assistant to William Carnan, a printer in Reading, when he was sixteen years old. Carnan having died in 1737, Newbery climbed the shop assistant's time-honored ladder above stairs and married his widow. After having enjoyed much success in Reading, in 1743 Newbery moved to London, where he was soon wheeling and dealing in books and patent medicines. Nicknamed Jack Whirler by Samuel Johnson, Newbery was an energetic, self-advertising entrepreneur. Blending batches of good fun, sprinklings of instruction, and a dollop of Locke's educational ideas into his books, Newbery became the first publisher of children's books on a large scale in Britain.[16]

Locke's ideas on the education of "a young Gentleman" indirectly appealed to middle-class parents and thereby contributed to the popularity of *Some Thoughts.* In contrast, Newbery directly courted the growing middle classes, and his books often seemed apologias for middle-class commercial activity. Linking commerce to the sweet benefits of education, the expression "*Trade and Plumb-Cake for-ever*" almost became the motto of his children's books. In *The Twelfth-Day Gift: Or, The Grand Exhibition* (1767), Mrs. Williams divided a plum cake among her scholars. The first piece went to Tom Hawes, her best student and the son of a tradesman. This angered Master Long, and he refused a piece of the cake because he believed that he should have been served first since his father was lord of the manor. To show Master Long that he was wrong, Mrs. Williams preached a short sermon on the necessity of trade to the well-being of Britons in general and to the good taste of plum cake in particular. "Is not the Tradesman and the Farmer as useful to the Public as the Gentleman?" she asked. "I think they are," she answered;

> Without the Farmer you would have no Corn, and without the Tradesman, that Corn could not be ground, and made into Bread. Nay, you are indebted to Trade for the very Cloaths you wear, and but for the Tradesman you would not have a Shoe to your Foot. Even this Cake before me, which you so long for, is the Product of Husbandry and Trade. Farmer *Wilson* sowed the Corn, *Giles Jenkins* reaped it, Neighbour *Jones* at the Mill ground it, the Milk came from Farmer *Curtis,* the Eggs from *John Thomas* the Higgler; that Plumb came from *Turkey,* and this from *Spain,* the Sugar we have from *Jamaica,* the candied Sweetmeats from *Barbadoes,* and the Spices from the *East-Indies.* And will you offer to set a Trade at naught, when you see even a Plumb-cake cannot be made without it?

"A Man of Fortune," she continued, "that does no Good, does Harm; for he leads an idle Life; lives, like the Drone in the Bee-hive, by the Labour of others; and is in this Respect greatly inferior to an honest, and industrious Tradesman."[17]

Newbery's first book for children, *A Little Pretty Pocket-Book,* appeared in 1744; before his death in 1767, this "professed friend of infancy and childhood" had published some twenty books for children and another twenty or so for young adults. Locke's ideas provided much of the particular content of and theory behind Newbery's books. *A Little Pretty Pocket-Book,* for example, began with a short essay on rearing children that had been "borrowed" from the first part of *Some Thoughts.* In writing about children's relationships to animals, Newbery was a thoroughgoing Lockean, and his books contained many vignettes teaching kindness to animals. *The Lilliputian Magazine: or, the Young Gentleman & Lady's Golden Library, being An Attempt to Amend the World, to render the Society of Man more Amiable* (1751), described the sad fate of "honest *Robin*," Mr. Littlewit's "Dunghill Cock." Selling three throws for two-pence, Littlewit tied Robin to a stake where young marksmen first bruised him, then broke a wing and both his legs. Because of this cruel behavior, six members were expelled from Newbery's "exclusive" Lilliputian Society. After learning that lobsters were roasted alive and young pigs were whipped to death to make them tender, the "ambassador of *Bantam*" declared in *The Newtonian System of Philosophy* (1761) that he would resign his post in England because it was not safe to live among people who practiced "such diabolical customs." In *The Valentine's Gift: Or, A Plan to enable Children of all Sizes and Denominations To behave with Honour, Integrity, and Humanity* (1765), "old ZIG-ZAG" was given a magic horn which enabled him to understand the conversation of animals. After having owned the horn for only a short time, Zig-Zag burned it, for he was unable to bear the complaints "which animals made of the cruelty of mankind." Newbery's longest sermon on the proper treatment of animals appeared in his most famous book, *The History of Little Goody Two-Shoes; Otherwise called, Mrs. Margery Two-Shoes* (1765). Mrs. Margery, Newbery told his young readers, was "very humane and compassionate; and her Tenderness extended not only to all Mankind, but even to all Animals that were not noxious; as your's ought to do, if you would be happy here and go to Heaven hereafter." Animals, Newbery stressed, were "God Almighty's Creatures," and he "placed them in this World to live among us" as "fellow Tenants of the Globe." How can you, Newbery asked, "who want to be made happy yourself, delight in making your fellow Creatures miserable?" Mrs. Margery herself often preached the virtues of kindness to animals and did not permit anyone to attend her school who was unkind to them. Resembling the unfallen Eve, she gathered stray animals about her and protected them from man's inhumanity. As childhood kindness to animals brought intangible moral benefits in the formation of character, so Margery's kindness emblematically brought beneficial returns. One morning Jumper, a dog which had been starving before she befriended it, forced her and a student out of the schoolhouse and then set about making all the other pupils leave, whereupon Margery, commonsensically trusting the dog's intuition, ordered everybody out. Shortly thereafter the roof collapsed. As Mrs. Margery's kindness to Jumper, Newbery showed, had indirectly saved her life and the lives of her pupils, so compassion woven into the character of a child would help determine the moral character of the future adult and thus contribute to his eternal salvation.[18]

Locke's belief that the child was the father of the man had long been current among educators, particularly among those with Calvinistic leanings. In his *Of the Childs Portion, viz: Good Education. Or, The Book of the Education of Youth* (1649), Hezekiah Woodward, for example, urged parents and teachers "to account *childehood* and *youth* our *seed-time.*" One should "not let slip our season" by sleeping or letting "our hands hang down," Woodward wrote, for the harvest depended upon "care and diligence in this ploughing and sowing *season.*" Like Locke, Woodward stressed the importance of benevolence to animals, warning that children should not be "suffered to bathe their recreations in bloud." Unlike Locke, however, he and educators with similar evangelical bents did not write broadly or profoundly about education. Believing that the end of all education was the perception of religious truth, Woodward and his fellow Calvinists appealed to a limited audience. In Arthur Dent's *The Plaine Mans Path-way to Heaven* (1601), honest Philagathus asked Theologus, a divine, what he thought about "learning, wit, and pollicie." Were "these things" not, he asked, "the essence of religion"? "No, no," Theologus quickly responded, they were "externall gifts, which may be in the most wicked men." The world in which Pamela's Billy would make his success was for Theologus "a sea of glasse: a pageant of fond delight, a Theatre of vanitie, a labyrinth of error, a gulfe of griefe, a stie of filthinesse, a vale of misery, a spectacle of woe, a river of teares, a stage of deceit, a cage full of Owles, a denne of Scorpions, a wilderness of Wolves, a cabbin of Beares, a whirlewind of passions, a fained Comedie, a delectable phrenzie: where is false delight, assured griefe: certaine sorrow, uncertain pleasure: lasting woe, fickle wealth: long heavinesse, short joy." In *The Young Mans Monitor* (1644), Samuel Crossman preached that right education directed the eyes of "Sweet Children" away from the worldly present and to their "resting place." "*You came hither,*" Crossman taught, "to settle the great case of your Souls heaven-ward on such solid terms, that neither the troubles of life, nor the very stroke of death should ever hereafter be able to amaze you."[19]

Only when Locke stripped such single-minded fervor from pedagogic theory did a work of educational apologetics have a broad and lasting appeal. Despite this, however, and the fears of some divines like William Sherlock, the dean of St. Paul's, who believed that Locke's theories would undermine religion, many of Locke's most influential followers were religious educators, often men like Philip Doddridge with strong evangelical predilections. To prove the necessity of a proper early education and to teach correct educational methods, Doddridge, for example, quoted Locke throughout his *Sermons on the Religious Education of Children.* It was "of great Importance," Doddridge wrote, "that Children early imbibe an Awe of God, and an humble Veneration for his Perfections and Glories." Those who were "trained up in the knowledge of GOD" from their childhood, he stated, gave "us an encouraging Hope that they will at length be set as Olive Plants around the LORD's table."[20]

In the history of children's books in the eighteenth century, the most influential religious educator writing under Locke's influence was Isaac Watts, the dissenting minister whose *Divine Songs* (1715) became the most popular book of poetry for children in Britain and the United States for one hundred and fifty years. Following Locke's suggestions, Watts stressed the importance of kindness to animals. In *A Treatise on the Education of Children and Youth* (second edition, 1769), he wrote that children should not be allowed to "set up *Cocks* to be banged with Cudgels" or thrown at "about *Shrovetide.*" Parents should be careful, he warned, that children did not "delight in giving a tedious lingering Death, to a young Litter of *Dogs* or *Cats,* that may be appointed to be destroyed and drowned," nor should "they take Pleasure in pricking, cutting, or mangling young *Birds* . . . lest their Hearts grow hard and unrelenting, and they learn in Time to practice these Cruelties on their own Kind, and to murder and torture their Fellow-Mortals; or at least be indifferent to their Pain and Distress, so as to occasion it without Remorse." Watts also enthusiastically accepted Locke's theories on the origin and the association of ideas. Adapting them to his religious didacticism, he stressed the crucial importance of natural theology in impressing proper ideas of God upon children. In *Some Thoughts,* Locke wrote that "there ought very early to be imprinted" on a child's "Mind a true Notion of *God*, as of the independent Supreme Being, Author and Maker of all Things, from whom we receive all our Good, who loves us, and gives us all Things." Although this statement could be taken as an apologia for rigorous early religious training, Locke counseled restraint in religious education, advising parents against "being unseasonably forward" to make their children "understand the incomprehensible Nature of that infinite Being." If they attempted to teach their children too much about religion too early, he warned, they would fill them with "false" or "unintelligible Notions of him." Locke's commonsensical approach to religious education influenced many of his evangelical followers. Doddridge, for example, advised that young children should only be taught "the plainest Things" of religion "by the plainest Words." "Just as in the World of Nature," he wrote, "those Kinds of Food which are most wholesome and nourishing are also the most common. We should shew our grateful Sense of the divine Goodness in this particular by our Care to imitate it, and should see to it that when the Necessities of our Children *require Bread, we don't give them a Stone.*" Although Locke's warning against premature religious education tempered the zeal of men like Watts and Doddridge, they were devoted to the ideal of religious education. They believed it was the most important instruction a child could receive. Locke taught them the science of education, and when they put it to what they considered its best use, they followed his counsel and avoided tangled doctrine. However, they placed more emphasis than Locke upon early religious training. In *A Treatise,* Watts used Locke's theories to show parents and teachers how they could form children's characters. From sense experience, Watts explained, children could be led to form complex ideas of God and to understand simple religious duties. The "thousand Objects," he wrote, which struck children's senses furnished matter for "their Curiosity" and a parent's "Instruction." Ordinary children aged three, he thought, could be led from this sense experience of the natural world to the reflection that there was "some Almighty Being" who made "the Heavens and the Earth, and the Birds, and the Beasts, and the Trees, and Men and Women." Once having reached this understanding, they could then "be instructed in a Way of easy reasoning in some of the most evident and most necessary Duties which they owe to the Great God, whom they see not."[21]

Although natural theology bore little literary fruit in his own writings, Watts was partially responsible for the natural theology that surfaced in children's books in the early 1780s. His works strongly affected Mrs. Sarah Trimmer, one of the most influential authors of children's books in the eighteenth century. This "Mother in Israel," as the *Monthly Review* called her, wrote her first children's book, *An Easy Introduction to The Knowledge of Nature, And Reading The Holy Scriptures, Adapted to the Capacities of Children* (1780), after reading Watts's *Treatise on Education.* The *Treatise,* she stated, convinced her that "a Book containing a kind of general survey of the Works of Providence, might be very useful; as a means to open the Mind by gradual steps to the knowledge of the SUPREME BEING." A parent should, she wrote, "seize the first opportunity of seasoning the Infant Mind with those spiritual graces which are calculated for Eternity." Consequently, the two young main characters of *An Easy Introduction* were taken for a long walk through the sense-awakening natural world. Since "every object in Nature, when carefully examined" would fill the observer with "Admiration" and afford "both Instruction and Amusement," the walk led through sense stimuli to God. The structure of the book itself was a metaphor for what became a Lockean religious education. For the first two hundred pages, the children were immersed in a rich natural world which appealed to sight and smell; then, for the final sixty pages, they were led to reflect on "God, who made you and all things in the World." In the preface to *The Rational Dame* (1790), Ellenor Fenn, like Mrs. Trimmer, stressed that a walk through nature could and should lead to God. "Under the inspection of a judicious mother," she wrote, "much knowledge may be acquired whilst little people are enjoying the recreation of a walk: queries arise spontaneously from the scene; affection seizes the occasion."[22]

An Easy Introduction was an apprentice work, preparing the way for Mrs. Trimmer's *Fabulous Histories. Designed For the Instruction Of Children, Respecting Their Treatment of Animals* (1786). *Fabulous Histories,* or *The Robins* as it was often called, soon became a nursery classic. Not an original thinker, Mrs. Trimmer was, however, a gifted assimilator, and as a result *Fabulous Histories* was a touchstone of late eighteenth-century attitudes toward the depiction of animals in books for children. No other children's book of the period encompassed such a range of attitudes toward animals and examined them so thoroughly and so successfully. *Fabulous Histories* was relentlessly didactic, a quality that instead of being considered a fault, made it all the more attractive as children's books came to be thought an important part of early education. "Nothing will be of more consequence toward the success of a young gentleman's endeavours," Locke's follower James Burgh wrote in *The Dignity of Human Nature* (1754), "than his getting early into a right track of reading and study." As publishers began to produce comparatively large numbers of children's books in the 1780s, critics were convinced that a minor literary and educational renaissance was occurring. Chapbook romances and "productions of old-wivery," the *Monthly Review* wrote, now gave "way to the realities of common life, and the dictates of common sense." There was "no circumstance," the journal thought, in which the "present age" had more indisputably the advantage over former periods than in "the provision" made for the education of children. Experience had proved "that the religious and moral character" was "more successfully formed by progressive impressions in its favour, made upon the fancy and the heart, by the aid of narration, real or fictitious, than by the most judicious and methodical system of truths addressed merely to the understanding and memory."[23]

Fabulous Histories was written for Henry and Charlotte, the main characters of *An Easy Introduction,* who Mrs. Trimmer stated, had "contracted a great fondness for Animals." Ostensibly the book was the biography of four young robins, each of whom had a readily identifiable personality. Mrs. Trimmer was uneasy, however, with the fabulous nature of her story. Believing that narration did make a greater impression upon the heart than methodical truth, she made use of it. Nevertheless, she stressed that before Henry and Charlotte read the *Histories,* they were taught not to consider them as "containing the real conversation of Birds" but as "FABLES, intended to convey moral instruction applicable to themselves at the same time that they excite compassion and tenderness for those interesting and delightful creatures, on which such wanton cruelties are frequently inflicted, and recommend *universal Benevo-*

lence." It came within "the compass of *Christian Benevolence,*" she wrote, "to shew compassion to the *Animal Creation*" and a "good mind" naturally inclined to do so. But through "erroneous education, or bad example" many children contracted "habits of *tormenting* inferior creatures" or fell into "the contrary fault of *immoderate tenderness* to them." In Mrs. Trimmer's desire "to point out the line of conduct, which ought to regulate the actions of *human* beings, toward those, over whom the SUPREME GOVERNOR hath given them dominion," she made the biographies of the robins relatively unimportant. Instead, she concentrated upon the "progressive impressions" right and wrong conduct toward animals made upon her young heroes, Harriet and Frederick Benson, aged eleven and six years, respectively.[24]

Fabulous Histories began with an instructive prologue. Frederick having asked her for a piece of bread in order to feed the birds, Mrs. Benson gave it to him and told him she was delighted with his "humane behaviour towards the animal creation." It was "a most commendable propensity" but one, she noted, that required "regulation," for it was not right to give bread to birds when there were many poor people who had "a superior claim" to benevolence. Shortly afterward, Mrs. Benson expanded her views on kindness to animals when Harriet criticized children who stole eggs from birds' nests. Children who committed such "barbarous actions," Mrs. Benson stated, were "insensible to the distresses" they occasioned. Certainly one should not "indulge so great a degree of pity and tenderness for such animals, as for those who are more properly our fellow-creatures," but, she preached, since every living being could feel, we "should have a constant regard to those feelings, and strive to give happiness, rather than inflict misery."[25]

The visit to the Bensons of Lucy Jenkins and her brother Edward, "a robust rude boy, turned of eleven," provided greater scope for instruction. Lacking a "kind mamma" to correct him and having a father who instead of reproving applauded him as a "lad of life and spirit," Edward had come "by degrees" to practice "horrid barbarities." To amuse himself, he plucked feathers off live chickens, tied cats and dogs together, stoned cocks, and threw cats off high roofs. On one occasion he told a crowd that little Jemmy's harmless pet dog was mad and urged them to beat it to death with cudgels and broomsticks. Another time he drowned puppies "whilst the bitch stood by" and "howled and cried, whilst they struggled on the surface of the water." Thwarted in his hopes of finding Frederick a suitable companion with whom to toss young birds about, he amused himself at the Bensons by pulling the wings and legs off flies and delighting in the "agonies they endured."[26]

Declaring that his son's actions showed that "he would be fit to go through the world," Mr. Jenkins did not listen to Mrs. Benson's warning that Edward's heart was growing "hard and unrelenting." Mrs. Benson was more successful, however, with the younger and more impressionable Lucy, who had thoughtlessly let captive birds starve and who numbered among her "curiosities" a necklace made from a hundred birds' eggs. How can "you expect that God will send his blessing upon you," she told Lucy, if "instead of endeavouring to imitate him in being merciful to the *utmost of your power,*" you are "wantonly cruel to innocent creatures." "Quite reformed" by Mrs. Benson's lecture, Lucy mended her ways; unfortunately, bad habits were woven into her brother's nature. When he attended school he became a bully, tormenting his schoolmates instead of animals. By the time he became a man, he "had so hardened his heart, that no kind of distress affected him." Not caring for anyone but himself, he "was despised by all with whom he had any intercourse." In this manner he lived for some years, Mrs. Trimmer wrote, until he was thrown and killed by a horse he was beating "because it did not go a faster pace than it was able."[27]

In a time when educators believe that the "great Thing to be minded in Education" was "what Habits" were settled, Frederick's sad history appeared in many children's books. In *Practical Education,* Maria Edgeworth wrote that it was "fortunate" that there were "butchers by profession in the world, and rat-catchers, and cats, otherwise our habits of benevolence and sympathy would be utterly destroyed." Although children had to learn the necessity of destroying "certain animals," she wrote, they "should not conquer the natural repugnance to the sight of the struggles of pain, and convulsions of death." In Dorothy Kilner's *The Life and Perambulation of a Mouse* (1783), Charles was severely beaten by his father, who caught him teasing a cat with a mouse on a string. "Every action that is cruel," his father explained, "and gives pain to *any* living creature, is wicked, and is a sure sign of a *bad* heart. I never knew a man, who was cruel to animals, kind and compassionate towards his fellow-creatures." The path from cruelty to animals more often than not led to the grave. In *The Adventures of a Silver Penny* (1787), "dear little readers" learned "the consequences of being a naughty child" from the fate of young George. "A great bird-nester," George "took great delight in destroying the eggs, and torturing the young ones in a most cruel manner." Since "one bad action naturally" led "to another," George was soon lying and stealing. Fearing that he would come to a bad end, George's father "sent him on board of a man of war, in which he had his head shot off in the first engagement." In the Cheap Repository Tracts, *The Two Cousins* (1797) described the contrasting fates of William, whose good habits were founded by rigorous early discipline, and poor Dick, whose mother liked her boy "with some spirit." First showing itself in barbarity to animals, this spirit ran its natural course and Dick became "addicted to gambling, cock fighting, bull baiting." Eventually he treated his doting mother like an animal, and after gambling away all the money she had saved for him, he was killed in a drunken brawl. In *The Apprentice* (second edition, 1815), one of the Scotch Cheap Repository Tracts, Charles Armstrong's moral deterioration began when he skipped church in order to rob birds' nests. Robbery of men followed soon after, and within a short time, Charles was dying as a transported convict in Australia, "lamenting, with his last breath, his first deviations from the paths of religion and virtue." In books for children, treatment of animals was an unfailing indicator of character. A girl in whose character cruelty to animals had become ingrained, Maria Edgeworth taught in *Mademoiselle Panache* (1801), would not make a good wife. Until he presented her a rosebud as a token of his love, young Montague's Lady Augusta seemed all that was fair. Lady Augusta received the flower gracefully and held it tenderly, much as a young mother would hold a newly born child. This idyllic scene was destroyed, however, when Lady Augusta saw a small green caterpillar crawling on a leaf of the flower. In a moment, "Lady Augusta's whole person seemed metamorphosed to the eyes of her lover," as she tore off the leaf, flung it to the ground, and crushed "the harmless caterpillar." All her "graces vanished," and where Montague had once seen gentle sweetness, he now saw "disgusting cruelty."[28]

The History Of Little King Pippin (1775) showed that cruelty to animals was closely tied to other evils. The boy who was cruel to animals was certain to be corrupt in other ways. Educators taught that a child's upbringing determined the character of the adult and greatly influenced his lot in life; the cruel child was doomed to unhappiness and failure. During the mid-day recess, Mr. Teachum's pupils gathered in the churchyard. Some read instructive books while others played games. Interrupted while shooting marbles with a group of bad boys including Ned Neverpray, George Graceless "took the Lord's name in vain." When Peter Pippin rebuked him, George scoffed. At two o'clock the schoolbell rang, and Peter along with the rest of the good boys, Billy Meanwell, Sammy Sober, Bobby Bright, and Tommy Telltruth, hurried back to class. As they had paid little attention to Peter's warning against cursing, so George's graceless crew of bad boys paid little attention to the bell and continued playing marbles. When they eventually grew bored with their game, they realized that class had long been under way and they decided to play truant and go bird-nesting. The first nest they found was that of a robin. Harry Harmless, who was not really bad but who tagged along with George because he was not strong enough to assert himself, urged them to spare the robin's nest. The robin red-breast, he said, was "a pretty innocent bird," and he reminded the boys that robins had covered the two children in the wood with leaves. Harry's plea did not touch Tom Tyger; if anything, it made him behave more inhumanely, and he destroyed the robin's nest and her eggs. Turning "a deaf ear" to the mother's cries, the hardened boys "left the pretty bird making such piteous moans as would have melted a heart of stone" and "went on, destroying every nest they could find, without paying any distinction to the most innocent of the feathered race."[29]

The destruction of the nests revealed the boys' corruption. Cruelty had destroyed their moral natures. A part of their beings, it would pull them down whenever they tried to climb toward success, either moral or worldly. His taking the Lord's name in vain was characteristic; George Graceless did not value anything religious. Without religion man was doomed, and when George climbed out on a high limb over a river to destroy a turtle dove's nest, the limb broke. Falling into the river as he had long since fallen into sin, he was swept to his death. The other boys felt guilty and frightened after George died, but like hardened sinners, they were unable to return to Mr. Teachum, their "master." Morally lost because cruelty had corrupted their characters, they decided to sleep in the woods. In the middle of the night, noises awakened them. Only Harry Harmless was able to pray, and he begged God to protect him. The others were too corrupt to pray; Sin being a relentless devourer, two lions appeared, killed them, and ate them. God, however, had heard Harry's prayer. Instead of eating him, the lions licked him and then lay down beside him to protect him from the other wild beasts who roamed the night. The next morning a white horse appeared, and Harry rode home to safety. For the Lockean, early education protected children from dangers in the forest of life and like a white horse carried them safely through the valley of the shadow to their eternal home.

The cruelties of Mrs. Trimmer's Tom Tyger, Edward Jenkins, greatly upset Harriet. So that she could put her feelings into proper perspective, Mrs. Benson consoled Harriet by pointing out to her that since animals were not "religious beings," their sufferings ended with their lives. Killing an animal, she stressed, was not like murdering a human creature who perhaps was "unprepared to give an account of himself at the tribunal of heaven." Possession of a soul distinguished man from animals, and writers of children's books in the last half of the eighteenth century usually emphasized this fact so that their young readers would not become immoderately tender. "Animals having no souls to survive in another world," Dorothy Kilner wrote in *Dialogues And Letters On Morality, Oeconomy, And Politeness For The Improvement and Entertainment of Young Female Minds* (1785), "may without any crime be put to death, whenever it is necessary either for the food or convenience of man." Although "Lambkins" skipped and played and "the Young of every species" were "filled with Life and Spirit" just like his "Young Readers," Newbery's *The Mosaic Creation* (1749) emphasized, animals did not have "a Fund of Knowledge to attain; and a Path marked out by the ALMIGHTY to lead them to Eternal Happiness." In Richard Johnson's *Letters Between Master Tommy and Miss Nancy Goodwill* (1770), Nancy's pet cat, "little Frisk," was stolen by cruel boys who "hunted it the next Day from one to the other, in the most barbarous Manner." Staggering home after being tortured for many hours, Frisk collapsed and died at Nancy's feet. Understandably, Nancy was upset, but after commending her benevolent sentiments, Nancy's mother criticized the child's grief. Such passions, she stated, interfered with Nancy's duty to humans. "If you do not keep Command enough of yourself to prevent being ruffled by every Accident," she warned, "you will be unfit for all the social Affairs of Life, and be despised by all those, whose Regard and Love are worth your seeking." For Nancy's mother, Frisk was only a cat. Even after the end of the century when animals began to have something akin to a soul, the author of *Biography of A Spaniel* (1816) begrudgingly admitted that a barrier separated the book's canine hero from his master. Having bitten a boy who tried to steal him, the spaniel refused to leave his blind master even though he knew the boy's influential father would have him killed. When two rough hirelings approached with guns, the spaniel crept near his master, who bent over him to protect him. Sadly, the sentiment of this touching picture did not affect the men. They fired and the bullet which passed through the dog's head carried on and penetrated his master's heart. "'Bury us together' was the last sound I heard with my mortal faculties," the spaniel recounted dolefully, "and likewise the first my aerial substance comprehended. Our shades met—we tried to embrace, but an invisible power tore us asunder."[30]

Because animals were placed below man "in the scale of beings" by "Providence," it was just as wrong, Mrs. Benson taught Harriet, to "suffer" animals "to occupy that share of attention and love" which was due to man as it was to treat them brutally. To enforce this lesson, Mrs. Benson took Harriet to visit a neighbor, Mrs. Addis. In the hall of Mrs. Addis's house, Harriet noticed "a very disâgreeable smell" and was "surprised" to see a parrot, a parakeet, and a macaw in "most elegant cages." In the next room were a squirrel and a monkey, each with "a little house neatly ornamented," a lapdog on a "splendid cushion," and "in a beautiful little cradle" a cat with a litter of kittens. Lavishing abnormal affection on her pets, Mrs. Addis banished her son to boarding school and neglected her daughter, who became "sickly, dirty, and ragged." Moreover, she refused to succor her poor neighbors, who starved while she fed delicacies to her cat and dog. Elevating animals "from their proper rank in life," Mrs. Addis in her seeming kindness was really cruel. The lapdog, Mrs. Benson pointed out to Harriet, was "full of diseases, the consequences of luxurious living," while the monkey would have enjoyed "himself more in his native wood" and the cat would have preferred "a basket of clean straw" to the cradle. By the end of *Fabulous Histories,* however, Mrs. Addis had reaped her well-deserved crop of chaff. Her "*dear darlings*" had all died when she was too old to fill their places with new ones. Wishing for "the comforts which other parents enjoyed," she ended her days in solitary "sorrow and regret." Having grown up scarcely knowing they "had a mamma," her children treated her with "utmost neglect." Even worse were the failings of the children themselves, who had not learned a proper attitude toward animals and consequently had not formed good habits when they were young. Deprived of his mother's love, Master Addis "conceived an inveterate hatred to animals," which he regarded as "his enemies," and whenever possible, he treated them barbarously, thinking he "was avenging his own cause." Although her brother was sadly warped, Miss Addis was the greater sufferer. Having been bitten by the monkey and terrified by the cat when it went mad, she came to fear all animals and could not walk in the fields or in the streets without being beset by irrational fears. Eventually her constitution gave way, and she became an invalid after having been frightened by a rat which darted across a path on which she was walking.[31]

Having exposed the abuses both of cruelty and of tenderness toward animals, Mrs. Benson now took Harriet to a farm conducted on right principles. Farmer Wilson, Mrs. Trimmer wrote, was "a very worthy man, possessed of a great share of natural good sense and benevolence of heart," while his wife, the daughter of a former curate of the parish, exercised "the Christian doctrine of UNIVERSAL CHARITY" toward not only "the human species" but also "every living creature which it was her providence to manage." Trying to conduct his farm, so far as was reasonable, "upon the principle of doing as I would be done by," Wilson rendered the lives of his animals as comfortable as was properly possible. When he fished for carp and tench, for example, he used nets, for he could not bear angling and prohibited his children from it on the grounds that "it hardens the heart, and leads to idleness." Mrs. Wilson had so endeared herself to the queen of her beehive that the bees came whenever she called and blanketed her "from head to foot" without ever stinging her. When she showed her guests the hen house, she opened a door which led to a meadow where the fowl were allowed "to ramble and refresh themselves." On seeing her approach the meadow, the "whole party" of birds collected and "like a troop of schoolboys" ran "into their play-ground." Even the pig sties were clean. The water they drank was "always sweet and wholesome," and the pigs themselves were frequently scoured. Like a sound education, the Wilsons' kindness to animals had both moral and economic returns. Treated well, their animals were fruitful, and the Wilsons prospered. In contrast, Wilson's brother, who treated his animals indifferently, failed and was kept off parish poor relief only by Wilson's charity.[32]

After they had admired "the whole party" of happy fowl, Mrs. Wilson explained to Harriet why it was necessary for some of them to die. They bred so fast, she pointed out, that there would soon be more than could be fed. To this Mrs. Benson added that she regretted that so many lives had to "be sacrificed to preserve ours." But "we must eat animals," she noted, "or they would at length eat us, at least all that would otherwise support us." When Harriet later said she thought it "a thousand pities" to slaughter lambs, Mrs. Benson warned her against indulging "feelings too far in respect to animals which are given us for food." The happiness of man, she repeated, was to be preferred to all creatures whatsoever. After this first responsibility to human beings, however, one had a duty to supply every dependent animal with "proper food, and keep it in its proper place." Once these immediate wants were supplied, Mrs. Benson continued, benevolence and compassion should be extended "as far as possible to the inferior ranks of beings."[33]

The lesson taught Harriet by her mother and Mrs. Wilson on the necessity of animals' dying for man's benefit appeared in many eighteenth-century children's books. In Dorothy Kilner's *The Life and Perambulation of a Mouse,* Charles learned from his father that people should not be condemned for killing vermin but for the ways in which they did it. Similarly, in Mrs. Trimmer's abridgment of Kilner in *Sunday School Dialogues* (1785), Mary asked her teacher if it were wrong to kill wasps and gnats. It was not wrong, she was told, if it were done "as quickly as possible, that they may not suffer for any time." In her *Original Stories*

(1788), Mary Wollstonecraft's Mrs. Mason, an educational kinswoman of Mrs. Benson, explained to her young charges that although it was necessary to kill insects to preserve her "garden from defoliation," she had it done "in the quickest way." Following her mother's teaching closely, Harriet Benson, not surprisingly, "grew up an *universal benefactress* to all people, and all creatures, with whom she was in any ways connected." Similarly, Frederick steered the middle path between cruelty and immoderate tenderness toward animals. As a result, right principles were woven into his nature, and he later displayed "the character of a GOOD MAN."[34]

In its depiction of eighteenth-century attitudes toward animals, Mrs. Trimmer's *Fabulous Histories* was the most representative children's book of the period. It was not perfectly typical, however, for about the time of its publication, descriptions of animals in children's books began to be sentimentalized, so much so that by the beginning of the nineteenth century Pooh Corner seemed but a short hop away. Although many fibers were woven together to form this new animal figure in the narrative carpet, three strands were prominent. The first and least significant of these had comic overtones and was derived from the sensibility of Sterne's Uncle Toby. In *The Life and Adventures of A Fly* (1789), for example, in a scene which parodied the famous fly incident in *Tristram Shandy,* Sterne himself appeared, albeit as eight-year old Master Laurence Sterne from the country. Quoting Uncle Toby, who had caught an "over-grown" fly that had "buzz'd about his nose" tormenting him during dinner and who had subsequently let him go, saying, "why should I hurt thee?—This world surely is wide enough to hold both thee and me," young Laurence urged his cousin Master Tommy Pearson to free a fly he had similarly caught in the dining room during dinner. Uncle Toby's kindness to the fly was the narrative stuff out of which warm tales were woven for children's books. In "What Animals Are Made For," a dialogue between Papa and Sophia, written by Anna Barbauld and her brother John Aikin, Papa told his daughter about Uncle Toby's kindness to the fly. Sophia was so impressed by Uncle Toby that she exclaimed, "I should have loved that man." Although *The Life and Adventures of a Fly* did teach kindness, it taught little else about the proper relationship between man and animals. Instead, animals seemed devices used by the author in hopes of imitating that mixture of the ludicrous and the sentimental which Sterne blended so successfully. Thus, for example, when the hero became stuck in a jar of honey, Jackie Lovebook rescued him, explaining to his father: "Perhaps, papa, this poor fly has a father, or a mother, or a brother, or a sister, who would have been grieved even to death, had he not returned to them. May we not venture to imagine that he was on his way to visit and comfort some uncle, or cousin, or friend in sickness or distress; and that he might dip into the honey only to carry with him a little load that might make a meal for some sick fly?" Later, when the fly tumbled into a milk jug, Sukey Jones refused to kill him, saying that she could not be so cruel "to a poor innocent fly." Instead, she stroked him "with a little feather" and placed him "upon her bosom" until "the kindly warmth of her little heart" restored his health. Then she kissed him "tenderly," put him "outside of a window upon which the sun fully shone," and bade him "a kind farewell."[35]

Although Shandy-like attitudes toward animals appeared in many children's books at the end of the century, it is usually impossible to determine if authors were consciously trying to capture Sterne's blend of the sentimental and the ludicrous or if they accidentally stumbled into it while attempting to write seriously. In his *Ballads* (1805), William Hayley solemnly celebrated the virtues of animals. Unfortunately, what Hayley described as the sublime often seems ridiculous. According to Hayley, the dog was given to man "by powers above" as "a guardian and a friend." Nowhere, Hayley thought, was this better illustrated than in the "inspirational" story of Lucy's Fido. When Edward, "the monarch of her breast," was stationed in India, Fido accompanied him, instructed by Lucy to make Edward's "life thy care." Lucy's wish was Fido's command. When Edward planned to swim in a river which he did not know was infested with reptiles, Fido tried to dissuade him. Unsuccessful in his attempts, Fido gallantly jumped into the water before Edward and with a farewell whimper disappeared down the gullet of a hungry crocodile. Fido's sacrifice saved Edward's life. And although Fido was gone, he was never forgotten. Lucy commissioned a statue of him and had it placed in her bedroom. On Edward's safe return, she and Edward were married, and, Hayley wrote, "The marble Fido in their sight, / Enhanc'd their nuptial bliss; / And Lucy every morn and night, / Gave him a grateful kiss."[36]

The second important strand shaping changing attitudes toward animals in children's books came from the warp of Rousseau. On the translation of *Emilius and Sophia* (1762–1763), Rousseau became a recognized, if not always approved, educational philosopher. In the first volume of *Emilius,* Rousseau argued that "all things are as good as their Creator made them, but every thing degenerates in the hands of man." Through human art, he said, the natural soil was compelled to nourish exotic plants and one tree forced to bear the fruits of another. "Improving man" made a general confusion of elements, climates, and seasons; he mutilated his dogs, horses, and slaves. He confounded everything, Rousseau declared, as if he delighted in nothing but monsters and deformity. Rousseau and his followers, rejecting such mutilation, tended to sentimentalize the natural world. The most famous English writer of books for children influenced by Rousseau was Thomas Day, best known for *Sandford and Merton* (1783–1789). The effect of Rousseau's views of nature are more clearly seen, however, in Day's shorter "The History of Little Jack" (1788). Unlike Mrs. Trimmer, Day did not believe man's harmonious relationship with animals depended upon a hierarchical structure in which man exercised "dominion" over and was careful not to indulge in immoderate pity and tenderness toward "inferior creatures." Day's world, however, was not so much an egalitarian natural world as it was a world without "Improving man." Since nature was not confounded by Mrs. Addis, Edward Jenkins, or even Farmer Wilson, man was able to lie down with the lion, or with the goat, as the case turned out.[37]

"Little Jack" told the history of a foundling who was abandoned on the steps of a tumbledown hut belonging to a decrepit soldier. The old soldier had no companions and only one "domestic," a goat named Little Nan. But whenever the old soldier beheld her, Day wrote, he thanked "the Deity" that "even in the midst of poverty" he had "one faithful friend." When he first found Jack, the poor man did not know how to feed him, for he had barely enough grain for himself. After praying he suddenly remembered, however, that Nan had just lost her kid. Seeing

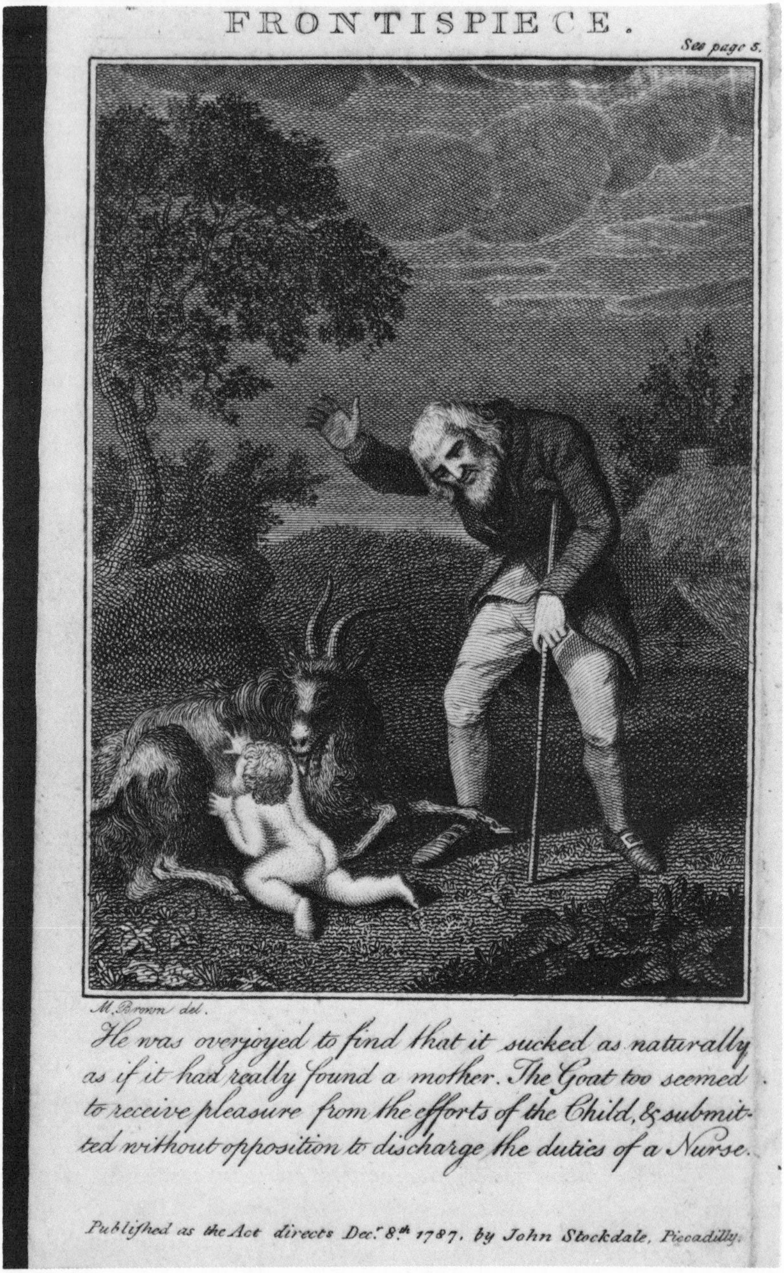
FRONTISPIECE.

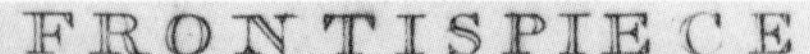

See page 5.

M. Brown del.

He was overjoyed to find that it sucked as naturally as if it had really found a mother. The Goat too seemed to receive pleasure from the efforts of the Child, & submitted without opposition to discharge the duties of a Nurse.

Published as the Act directs Decr. 8th. 1787, by John Stockdale, Piccadilly.

From Thomas Day, *The Children's Miscellany.* By permission of the British Library.

her "udder distended with milk," he called her to him, and "presenting the child to the teat" was "overjoyed to find that it sucked as naturally as if it had really found a mother." "Gentle Nanny" was also pleased, and "with equal tenderness," she adopted Jack as "her offspring." "She would stretch herself out upon the ground," Day wrote, while Jack "crawled upon his hands and knees towards her; and when he had satisfied his hunger by sucking, he would nestle between her legs and go to sleep in her bosom." After only a short time in this natural cradle, Jack grew robust; language followed soon after as he began "to imitate the sounds of his papa the man, and his mamma the goat." This unspoiled harmony lasted for several years until "mammy Nan" died and was "buried in the garden." Not long afterward, the old soldier turned his face to the wall, and Jack set out to seek his fortune. Treading lightly, free from the burden of an unnatural education, he survived being marooned on the desolate Comoro Islands, thrived as a prisoner of the Tartars on the incipient empire's eastern border, and eventually returned to England to become "one of the most respectable manufacturers in the country."[38]

According to Mrs. Trimmer, man was "*the Lord of the Creation,*" and since animals had "been made in some measure for our use," we were "able to apply them to our purposes." Although Rousseau certainly did not humanize animals, neither did he emphasize keeping them in their proper place. Overreacting, apparently, to attitudes typical of Mrs. Trimmer and her followers, who ultimately viewed animals as things, Rousseau's disciples who wrote children's books often made their animals extremely manlike. In grafting human characteristics on to animals and depicting them as friends and mothers, such writers were themselves nourishing exotic plants and forcing one tree to bear the fruits of another. In their books, animals often became important for their own sakes, and not merely as educational devices to help children form good habits. Thus, in his *Memoirs* (1800), "Dick, the Little Poney" criticized man's mutilation of the natural world and his creation of monsters and deformity more out of a sense of resentment than out of a desire to help children form habits of benevolence. Dick was particularly critical of an operation "the exquisite torture and fatal consequences" of which "delicacy" forbade him to explain but which deprived him of "all the privileges" of his sex. Of the docking of his tail, he was less circumspect, declaring, "Ye tasteless sons of men! is Nature such a bungling performer, that her works must submit to your improvements in almost every instance? Why do you not practise the same experiments on yourselves?"[39]

Closely related to that spun by Rousseau, the third and most important fiber coloring the changing picture of animals in children's books was the growth of English romanticism. As Wordsworth began to sentimentalize the peasantry and write poems in which meetings with Cumberland beggars and old leech gatherers led to epiphanic experiences, so writers of children's books began to sentimentalize animals. As the romantic poets often equated rough simplicity with truth, so the animals, even rougher and simpler, became appealing. With a Wordsworthian ability to see beyond deceptive surface reality to the deeper, inner reality, writers of children's books began to see a beauty within every beast. Rarely were these new animals described unfavorably; instead they resembled noble savages or noble peasants, from whom they were but one step removed. At the extreme, the plea for kindness to animals became, not a device for shaping a benevolent adult, but an argument for natural rights. Instead of ranging over a wide spectrum of man's relationships to animals and embodying Lockean educational theory, books concentrated on cruelty to animals. In a better book like *The Hare: Or, Hunting Incompatible With Humanity* (1799), this focus led to a narrative and didactic tediousness, which Mrs. Trimmer was able to avoid because her pedagogic intentions were more complex. In worse books, and these were unfortunately the majority, well-intentioned romanticism often led to the ludicrous.

In order to teach children "lessons of compassion," Mary Pilkington published *Pity's Gift* (1798), a miscellany of "interesting tales," most of which were written by Samuel Jackson Pratt. Typifying the changing attitude toward animals, the volume contained several "remarkable pieces." A "Superannuated Horse" sententiously begged his master not to kill his "old and poor" servant, but to let him "a little longer hobble round thy door." A "friend" from Holland described a harsh winter during which he generously shared his house with more than twenty "winged pensioners." While he wrote his account, he said, a sparrow rested a beak's length from the end of his paper, a robin trotted across

PITY'S GIFT. 69

THE ADDRESS OF

THE SUPERANNUATED HORSE

*TO HIS MASTER**.

AND haſt thou fix'd my doom, ſweet Maſter, ſay?
And wilt thou kill thy ſervant, old and poor?
A little longer let me live, I pray,
A little longer hobble round thy door.

For much it glads me to behold this place,
And houſe within this hoſpitable ſhed;
It glads me more to ſee my maſter's face,
And linger near the ſpot where I was bred.

* *Who, on account of his (the Horse) being unable, from extreme old age, to live through the winter, had sentenced him to be ſhot.*

From Mary Pilkington, ed. *Pity's Gift.* By permission of the British Library.

the carpet, and a chaffinch slept before the fire. The most striking piece in the collection, however, was entitled "The Robin." "A mighty odd character" who was a "keeper of sheep" had taught his children to be kind to animals. His lessons seem, however, to have fallen on rocky ground, for one day when he was away from home, his eldest son found a nest of young robins and gave the birds to his brothers and sisters to play with. He tied a string to the legs of the bird he kept for his toy and dragged it about the floor. The second son ran pins through the eyes of his bird and "took a delight in seeing it bleed to death," while the third son teased the cat with his nestling until she pounced on it and "carried off one of the legs." The eldest daughter wanted to care for hers, but one of her brothers grabbed it, and between them, they pulled it to pieces. Mercifully, the youngest girl, who had listened to her father more closely than her brothers and sisters, put her young robin in a cage and covered it with a protective layer of wool. When the father returned home, he was shocked by his children's cruelty and set about taking fearful revenge on these "Barbarous wretches." To the leg of his eldest son he tied a rope and "did to him as he did to the bird." He scratched the second boy with pins until "his hands were all over with blood," while he set his dog on his third son, which "caught him by the leg as he used to catch the sheep." He pitied the daughter who had lost her bird, but the youngest who protected hers he "*hugged to his very heart.*" Some six or seven months later, "it pleased God" that the oldest boy died. "And many people," the tale stated, "are now living who say, that as he was going to be put into the ground, the ravens, rooks, kites, and other vast birds, all flew over his coffin, screamed, and could by no means be got away, nor could he rest in his grave for them; because the animals were always digging up the earth under where he lay, as if they were resolved to eat him up—and some declare *he is actually gone.*" In contrast, the little girl who treated her bird kindly died from smallpox a year later, and "her grave is a perfect garden, for the Robins do not suffer a single weed to grow upon it, and God Almighty has adorned it with wild flowers, as innocent as the baby which they cover."[40]

The father's emotional reaction and the Hebraic revenge of the animals were far from Mrs. Trimmer's and Locke's more considered view that cruelty to animals, if not stemmed in youth, would lead to cruelty to man. In 1802 Mrs. Trimmer founded the *Guardian of Education* in order to remedy abuses both in education and children's books. In the journal she spent much energy attacking books which she thought taught improper behavior toward animals and which thereby settled wrong "habits of thinking in the understanding." In reviewing a later edition of *Pity's Gift,* which had been popular as a gift book for children, she agreed that it was important for children to be kind to animals. But she thought it wrong "to ascribe feelings to the lower creatures, any farther than the sense of present pain extends," for the want of reflection made "a material difference betwixt the suffering brute and the human sufferer." Moreover, she held, to talk of "the *virtues* of the lower animals" was not consistent "with the order of the creation." As for "The Robin," it was an "exceptionable" story. Practicing such cruelties upon nestlings, she thought, "certainly deserved punishment." But "'*an eye for an eye, a tooth for a tooth*'" was not, she wrote, "the doctrine of Christianity, even in respect to *animals*"; the father would have acted "with more propriety and justice, had he given each of the young rogues a *good whipping.*"[41]

In defending the proper "order of creation," Mrs. Trimmer stood like Horatio at the bridge. Unlike Horatio, however, she was unsuccessful, for the old order was breaking and yielding to the new. In 1798 Thomas Young, a fellow of Trinity College Cambridge, published *An Essay on Humanity to Animals.* Drawing from Hogarth's "Four Stages of Cruelty," Young argued conventionally that "many of those brought to the scaffold for capital crimes" began "their progress in wickedness" as children who mistreated animals. However, amid chapters on cruelties to bees and horses, particularly the gelding and docking which so angered Dick the little pony, Young included an exposition of "the Rights of Animals." According to Young, the rights of animals like the rights of man were "deduced from the Light on Nature." Since animals were "endued with a capability of perceiving pleasure and pain" and since "abundant provision" was made in the world for "the gratification of their several senses, we must conclude," Young wrote, "that the Creator wills the happiness of these his creatures, and consequently that humanity towards them is agreeable to him, and cruelty the contrary."[42]

E.A. Kendall's *Keeper's Travels In Search of His Master* appeared in the same year as Young's *Essay.* The most popular of Kendall's animal books, several of which were published at the turn of the century, *Keeper* described the sufferings of a dog who became separated from his master. Although the narrative conventionally described accounts of man's inhumanity to animals, the preface was a remarkable statement, indicating how rapidly attitudes toward animals were shifting. Many exertions were being made, Kendall wrote, "to obtain our compassion for the various animals for whom, in common with ourselves, the rain descends, and the sun shines." The time was not distant, he thought, when men would "acknowledge the RIGHTS; instead of bestowing their COMPASSION upon the creatures, whom, with themselves, GOD made, and made to be happy!" Although Keeper was a dog, the book, Kendall wrote, pled not for him alone, "nor for the race of DOGS only, but for the whole breathing world!" "I shall be fortunate," he continued, "if I contribute to the happiness of any one of those whom I am proud to call my fellow-creatures."[43]

As could be expected, the popularity of *Keeper* provoked a devastating, albeit ineffective, review from the *Guardian of Education.* "Humility," Mrs. Trimmer wrote, was "doubtless a great virtue" and indeed indispensable "in the character of a Christian." But she could not recollect, she said, "any injunction in Scripture for Mankind to put themselves upon a level with the brute creation," though there were many texts in which the wicked were "compared to *beasts that have no understanding,* and reproached for their resemblance to brutes, in their appetites and passions." Long, she continued, had Britons been used to hearing of the rights of man and the rights of women, but "the levelling system, which includes the RIGHTS OF ANIMALS, is here carried to the most ridiculous extreme." Happily, however, "the cattle of the field, and the fowls of the air, and all the animal tribes" were "secured, by their limited faculties, from the influence of their Advocate's sophistical arguments; and kept in their proper stations by the over-ruling power of the Almighty!" The power that kept animals in their proper stations did not, however, pay much attention to books written for children. And if Kendall's campaign for the rights of animals fell on uncomprehending ears, his depiction of animals which resembled human beings became widely popular. No longer would animals be used simply as devices to help children form habits of benevolence. The day was not far off when animals would amble through the pages of children's books with little fear of meeting either a teacher ready to point out a lesson or "*the Lord of the Creation*" swinging an ax in his hand.[44]

CHAPTER TWO

Notions of *Spirits* and *Goblings*: The Dangerous World of Fairy Tales

The literary fairy tale did not enter English literature until the eighteenth century, when many French tales were translated. In 1729 Robert Samber translated Charles Perrault's *Histoires ou Contes du temps passé.* Of the eight stories in the volume, seven have now become Mother Goose favorites: "Sleeping Beauty," "Little Red Riding Hood," "Bluebeard," "Puss in Boots," "Diamonds and Toads," "Cinderella," and "Hop o' my Thumb." In 1699 some of Madame d'Aulnoy's *Contes des fées*, including "Gracioca and Percinet" and "The Blue Bird," were translated. In 1721–22, a three-volume edition of her works was published, and for the first time "The White Cat," "The Royal Ram," "Finetta the Cinder-Girl," and the "Yellow Dwarf" appeared in English. In 1756 Madam de Beaumont's *Magasin des enfans* was printed in London. Translated as *The Young Misses Magazine* in 1761, it introduced English readers to "The Three Wishes" and "Beauty and the Beast."[1]

Although most of these stories are now celebrated as classic fairy tales, they were not highly thought of in the late eighteenth century. In reviewing a selection of tales in 1788, the *Monthly Review* wrote, "we have little to say in their praise. Fairy tales were formerly thought to be the proper and almost the only reading for children; it is with much satisfaction, however, that we find them gradually giving way to publications of a far more interesting kind, in which instruction and entertainment are judiciously blended, without the intermixture of the marvelous, the absurd, and things totally out of nature." In 1783 one of leading publishers of children's books assured suspicious parents that his publications were safely free from such unnatural things. *The Histories of More Children than One; or Goodness better than Beauty,* John Marshall advertised, had "no other merit to boast, than that of being calculated to engage the *attention* of children, at the same time that it" was "totally free from the prejudicial nonsense of *Witches, Fairies, Fortune-Tellers, Love* and *Marriage.*" Although she ranged broadly over the whole of children's education, Maria Edgeworth did not consider fairy tales in her *Practical Education* because, as she explained in 1798, they were "not now much read." In her *Poetry For Children* (1803), Lucy Aikin defended poetry as the proper matter of children's books, writing that it was preferable both to novels, which gave a "false picture of the real world," and to "the fairy fictions of the last generation, which only wandered over the region of shadows." Fairy tales did not now, she thought, constitute a danger to children, for, she stated, "the wand of reason" had banished "dragons and fairies, giants and witches" from the nursery.[2] Despite this seeming unanimity of critical opinion, the banishment was only temporary, and fairy fictions were on the verge of emerging from the darkness of the outer realms where critical disapproval had put them. By the middle of the nineteenth century, dragons and fairies, giants and witches were basking if not in the warm beam of widespread middle-class approval, at least comfortably in bright critical sunshine. Late eighteenth-century disapproval of fairy tales now seems wrong-headed, but we forget that the general repudiation of fairy tales rested soundly on Lockean educational theory.

Fairies had been suspect long before the eighteenth century. In the *Canterbury Tales,* the Wife of Bath lamented the fact that the friars had driven fairies from Britain. Praise from the Wife of Bath was practically prima facie evidence of the corruption of fairies. In *The Book of Nurture* (1558), Hugh Rhodes lectured parents on the dangers of children's reading "famed fables or vain fantasies, or of foolish love," stating that youth was the time to "learne pure and clene doctrine" so that one could "poure out plenty of good and pure waters" in his age. In *The discoverie of witchcraft* (1584), Reginald Scot classed fairies with a colorfully inclusive group of "bugs" which were "feared of sicke folke, children, women, and cowards." The basis for such fear was often laid in childhood. At that time, Scot wrote, "our mothers maids . . . so fraied us with bull beggers, spirits, witches, urchens, elves, hags, fairies, satyrs, pans, faunes, sylens, kit with the cansticke, tritons, centaurs, dwarfes, giants, imps, calcars, conjurors, nymphes, changlings, INCUBUS, Robin good-fellowe, the spoorne, the mare, the man in the oke, the hell waine, the fierdrake, the puckle, Tom thombe, hob gobblin, Tom tumbler, boneles, and other such bugs, that we are afraid of our owne shadowes." These bugs, however, were something more than devices used by servants to frighten children or by a "knave in a white sheet" to cozen and abuse the superstitious. Instead, they were a remnant of paganism which, Scot declared, was being eradicated by "the preaching of the gospell." Within a "short time (by Gods grace)," he stated, all the "illusions" would "be detected and vanish awaie." In *A Candle in the Dark: Or, A Treatise Concerning the Nature of Witches & Witchcraft* (1656), Thomas Ady listed fifteen "*Causes*" which upheld "*the damnable Doctrin of Witches Power.*" The fourteenth of these, Ady argued, was "Old Wives Fables, who sit talking, and chatting of many fake old Stories of Witches, and Fairies, and *Robin Good-fellow,* and walking Spirits, and the Dead walking again; all which lying fancies people are more naturally inclined to listen after than to the Scriptures."[3]

Reacting to seventeenth-century witchcraft trials, Ady maintained that "*ascribing power to Witches*" was the "*Grand Errour of these latter Ages*" and was responsible for the "*wrongfull killing of the innocent.*" By the end of the century, however, concern over the danger of fairies and old wives' tales had lessened considerably, with the result that criticism existed in a general theoretical vacuum. However, the *Essay Concerning Human Understanding* and *Some Thoughts Concerning Education* provided a theoretical structure that brought fairy and old wives' tales into critical focus and explained how they could be psychologically harmful. If those "insensible Impressions on our tender Infancies" did indeed furnish the cabinet of the mind with indelible objects, then parents could not be too careful in selecting their children's reading. Moreover, in emphasizing the dangers of an unhealthy association of ideas, Locke warned parents particularly against letting servants frighten children with "Notions of *Spirits* and *Goblings*" and "of *Raw-Head* and *Bloody Bones,*" the matter of old wives' and fairy tales. Once such "*Bug-bear* Thoughts . . . got into the tender Minds of Children," he stated, they sank deep and fastened "themselves so as not easily, if ever, to be got out again." Not only did they "haunt" children with "Strange Visions," but they made them "afraid of their Shadows and Darkness all their Lives after." Even worse was the effect such stories had on religion. "Coming abroad into the World," young adults whose "tender Minds" had received "early Impressions of *Goblins, Spectres,* and *Apparitions*" and who had suffered "fearful Apprehensions, Weakness, and Superstition" as a result, often grew "weary and asham'd." In order to make "a thorough Cure, and ease themselves of a load, which has sate so heavy on them," Locke wrote, they threw "away the thoughts of all *Spirits* together" and ran "into the other but worse extream."[4]

As he had done with Locke's educational theories and his attitude toward kindness to animals, Isaac Watts absorbed Locke's ideas on the danger of fairy and old wives' tales. "The Memory," Watts wrote, was "a noble Repository or Cabinet of the Soul," which "should not be filled with Rubbish and Lumber." "Silly tales and foolish Songs, the Conundrums of Nurses, and the dull Rhimes that are sung to lull Children asleep, or to sooth a froward Humour" should be forbidden as entertainment, he thought, to children for whom "a good Education" was intended. "Something more innocent, more solid and profitable" ought to be "invented" to replace "these Fooleries." When viewed in the searching light of Watts's criticism, even the gayest fairy tale tumbled among the fooleries or fell into the bin for rubbish and lumber. Worse still were the "dismal *Stories of Witless and Ghosts, of Devils and evil Spirits, of Fairies and Bugbears in the Dark,*" for these tales "made such a deep and frightful Impression" on children's "tender Fancies" that "their Souls" were enervated and "their Spirits" broken. Mingling "with their Religion," Watts wrote, they oftentimes "laid a wretched Foundation for Melancholy and distracting Sorrows."[5]

Although Locke's strictures on bugbears and the supernatural were initially more applicable to old wives' than fairy tales, they were rigorously applied to fairy tales in the latter half of the century. In 1803 Mrs. Trimmer based criticism of a collection of Mother Goose's stories on Locke's ideas. "Though we well remember," she wrote, "the interest with which, in our childish days, when books of amusement for children were scarce, we read, or listened to the history of '*Little Red Riding Hood,*' and '*Blue Beard,*' etc. we do not wish to have such sensations awakened in the hearts of our grandchildren, by the same means; for the terrific images, which tales of this nature present to the imagination, usually make deep impressions, and injure the tender minds of children, by exciting unreasonable and groundless fears."[6]

In *Some Thoughts,* Locke balanced his damning criticism of old wives' and fairy tales by suggesting several educational substitutes. "Learning," he thought, should "be made a Play and Recreation to Children." And he urged the invention of "*Play-things*" with which children could be "cozen'd into a Knowledge of the Letters." Once a child began to read, "some easy pleasant Book suited to his Capacity" should be given to him as a bait to "draw him on." It was essential, he stressed, however, that this book should not "fill his Head with perfectly useless trumpery, or lay the principles of Vice and Folly." To this end, he thought *Aesop's Fables* the best book in print. Not only were the "stories apt to delight and entertain a Child," but unlike fairy tales, they afforded "useful Reflections to a grown Man." If these were firmly impressed upon a child's memory, later the adult himself would "not repent to find them there, amongst his manly Thoughts, and serious Business."[7] Whether Locke's praise contributed to the general use of the *Fables* as a children's primer in the eighteenth century or was merely a reflection of the already widespread acceptance of Aesop is impossible to determine. However, judgments similar to those of Locke dominated eighteenth-century criticism. Throughout the period fables were favorably compared to fairy tales, and toward the end of the century, the contrast between the two became a commonplace of criticism of books for children.

Since he was the first successful publisher of children's books and since his books were widely imitated in Britain and America, Newbery's attitude toward fables and fairy tales can be taken as a touchstone of eighteenth-century opinion. Moreover, because his first children's book appeared in mid-century, before attitudes toward fairy tales hardened into the rigorous condemnation of the 1780s, his view of fairies and fairy tales serves as a literary signpost pointing ahead to what was to come and behind to what went before.[8] Newbery's *A Little Pretty Pocket-Book* included two important letters from Jack the Giant-Killer to Little Master Tommy and Pretty Miss Polly. Instead of the clever rascal of chapbook fame who lived by "Wit and Policy" and who pranced through the castles of evil giants in fabulous clothes—a coat which made him invisible, shoes of extraordinary swiftness, a cap of knowledge, and a sword which could cut anything "in sunder"—Newbery's Jack resembled a benevolent uncle with evangelical leanings. He was glad, Jack wrote Master Tommy and Miss Polly, that they were dutiful to their parents, said prayers in the morning and evening, were loving and kind to their playfellows and obliging to everybody. Such conduct would make everybody love them, and so long as they "continue so good," they could depend, he promised, on "my obliging you with every thing I can." Accordingly, he sent both children a copy of *A Little Pretty Pocket-Book* and a plaything modeled on Locke's suggestions. Instead of teaching the alphabet, however, these toys taught good conduct, for Newbery's Jack was a moral giant. To Tommy he sent a ball and to Polly a pincushion. Each toy was divided into red and black halves and was accompanied by ten pins. Every time the child was good, a pin was struck in the red side of the ball or pincushion; when the child was bad, a pin was stuck in the black side. When all ten pins were in the red side, Jack promised the child a penny. When all ten pins were on the black side, he said, he would send a rod, and Master Tommy or Miss Polly would be "whipt."[9]

In comparison to the two-headed beast Jack killed by running "his sword up to the hilt" in his "fundament," the poetical baker in "Tom Thumb" who ground bones to make his bread, and the ravenous ogre in "Hop o' My Thumb" who mistakenly slit the throats of his seven daughters, Newbery's most famous giant, Woglog the great, was relatively tame. Woglog had begun life like most giants, with a hankering for dastardly deeds. But before he had irrevocably hardened into improper habits, he had been thrashed and forcibly reformed by young Tommy Trip. While strolling through "a Meadow on a Moon-light Night," Tommy heard someone crying. Putting a bridle on his dog Jouler, young Trip cantered to the rescue and found Woglog preparing to throw "a little boy" into a pond. "Little Boys should never loiter about in the Fields, not even in the Streets, after it is Dark," Newbery warned; "however, as he had been a good Boy in other Respects, little Trip was determined the Giant should not hurt him." "Here, you great

Giant, you Woglog!" he shouted; "set down the little Boy, or I'll make you dance like a Pea on a Tobacco-pipe." Angered by Tommy's bold familiarity, Woglog tried to grab him and crack him "as one does a Walnut." When, however, the giant reached down for Tommy, Jouler nipped him on the thumb, and Tommy pulled out his whip and beat Woglog "till he lay down and roared like a Town Bull, and promised never to meddle with any little Boys or Girls again." Like all other giants, Woglog had, as Newbery put it, prodigious abilities, but these were not "so amazing as some would insinuate; for the story of his stamping on, and sinking the pier at *Westminster Bridge,* and some other things related of him, are false and invidious." After his reformation, Woglog became preternaturally moral. When greeted familiarly by a lady of fashion in Bath, he informed her that he had been to church and after wittily expressing his disapproval of her life, "stept into Mr. *Leake's* to read one of Mr. *Newbery's* little books."[10]

Woglog's reformer, young Tommy Trip, was Newbery's Tom Thumb. Unlike Thumb, who exotically owed his begetting to Merlin, Tommy Trip was simply "the only Son of Mr. William Trip of Spittle-Fields, London." Although he was "not much bigger than Tom Thumb," who had been known at school only for his tricks and dishonesty, young Tommy was "a great deal better" and was "a good Scholar." "Whenever you see him," Newbery declared, "you will always find him with a Book in his Hand." Instead of traveling luxuriously about the countryside in a walnut-shell coach drawn by "foure blew flesh-flyes," healthy young Trip galloped about on Jouler. Although he was "allowed to be one of the best Poets of the Age" and had tamed Woglog, Tommy's life was more mundane than that of Thumb, who had enjoyed many unique dietary experiences. As a youth he had been baked into a suet pudding, eaten by the Red Cow that "turned him out in a Cowturd," and swallowed by a giant who disgorged him "at least three miles into the Sea," where as soon as he splashed down he was gobbled up by a fish. Like that of Jonah in the whale, this experience proved the making of him, for his finny jailer was hooked and fortuitously brought to King Arthur's Round Table, where Thumb was rescued, to the amazement of all the boast of heraldry. Accepted for "his Highnesse Dwarfe," Thumb, unfortunately for the safety of his soul, became a great favorite of "Gentlewomen" who let him sleep upon their knees and "runne at tilt against their bosomes with a bul-rush." In contrast, Tommy Trip had better things to do than tilt fleshly windmills. Knowing the crucial importance of early education, he was forever riding through town and stopping at houses "to know how the little Children do within." If they were good and studied their books, he left "an Apple, an Orange, or a Plumb-Cake at the Door" as baits to draw them on farther.[11]

Although he was the most famous, Woglog was not the only good or reformed giant to appear in eighteenth-century children's books. In *The Prettiest Book for Children; Being The History of the Enchanted Castle; Situated in one of the Fortunate Isles, and governed by the Giant Instruction* (1770), Don Stephano Bunyano described his "renowned and virtuous" master and his home on an island called "the *Seat of Education.*" The undersecretary of Instruction and "a distant relation of the famous *John Bunyan,*" Don Stephano was more Calvinistic than Newbery's avuncular Jack the Giant-Killer. A large black dog called Shocky accompanied Don Stephano on his journeys. Unlike Jouler, who confined his aggression to larger villains, Shocky could "smell out a naughty boy, or a naughty girl even at the distance of twenty yards or more." When he discovered such a child, Shocky would first bark and then run after and seize the child by the lappet of his coat or the tail of her gown. Don Stephano himself resembled Merlin. He had a bushy blue beard, carried a white wand, and wore a long flowered gown and hairy cap. In contrast, Instruction resembled a genie. Over ten feet tall, he was very handsome and had curly golden hair. He wore a turban decorated with bright gold and sparkling diamonds and a purple vest which was bound about his middle by a golden girdle covered with pearls. Despite this oriental appearance, Instruction was a Christian, "remarkable for his piety and devotion." Every morning and evening he said his prayers. He even kept a chaplain in the castle to assist in public worship. Only those children who were good and knew their letters, a sure sign of goodness, were admitted to Instruction's castle by Mr. Alphabet, the porter. Once inside, children entered the picture gallery. About its walls hung paintings of instructive scenes from the Bible—for example, Absalom dangling by his hair from a tree, the murder of Abel, and "foaming bears" pursuing the wicked children who mocked Elisha. In the museum, children saw several curiosities. They could learn "the real value" of their money by placing it in the Moneycup and seeing it turn to dust. It they did not have guilty consciences, they could look into the mirror made by "Mr. *Flatter-none*" and see themselves as they really were. Finally, children could go into Instruction's library, over the door of which was "a fine inscription in the language of the country, which runs thus: THEF EAROF THELOR DIS THEBE GINING OFWIS DOM, and means in English, *The Fear of the Lord is the Begining of Wisdom.*"[12]

In giving a moral spine to Scot's "boneles" and changing the frightening and lascivious characters of fairy and old wives' tales into friendly domestic companions and teachers, Newbery and his imitators were often delightfully creative. Although didactic, Newbery was not oppressively so, and he was a master at turning instruction into play. In the midst of his playfulness, however, Newbery did not lose sight of the older, more dangerous aspect of fairies and fairy tales. In *The History of Little Goody Two-Shoes,* the young heroine was accidentally locked in the parish church with Lady Ducklington's coffin. Forced to stay all night, Goody was frightened by noises. However, when she began to pray, the source of the noise was revealed to her, not as a "bug" but as Mr. Saunderson's dog Snip. "After this, my dear Children," Newbery wrote reflectively, "I hope you will not believe any foolish Stories that ignorant, weak, or designing People may tell you about *Ghosts;* for the Tales of *Ghosts, Witches,* and *Fairies,* are the Frolicks of a distempered Brain. No wise Man ever saw either of them. Little *Margery* you see was not afraid: no, she had *good Sense,* and a *good Conscience* which is a Cure for these imaginary Evils."

To emphasize the dangers of superstition, Newbery repeated his criticism in a slightly different form in the second part of the book. Goody Two-Shoes had now grown up and become a successful schoolmistress. Kind not only to people but also to animals, she had collected a diverse group of strays who accompanied her wherever she went. Unfortunately, superstitious individuals who had been suckled on fairy and old wives' tales thought she had cast a spell over the animals and said she was a witch. When Gaffer Goosecap saw her "walking about" with a raven on one shoulder, a pigeon on the other, a lark on her hand, and a lamb and a dog beside her, he immediately shrieked, "a Witch, a Witch."

Because Goody Two-Shoes had studied her lessons when she was a child, she was able to construct a barometer, which enabled her to help her neighbors by advising them when to mow their crops. Ignorant people like Gaffer Goosecap interpreted her skills as confirmation of demonism and charged her with witchcraft. According to Newbery, such ridiculous things occurred because "People stuff Children's Heads with Stories of Ghosts, Fairies, Witches, and such Nonsense when they are young, and so they continue Fools all their Days." Little Goody was, of course, proved innocent of witchcraft and her true merits were recognized, so much so that the local squire, Sir Charles Jones, proposed to her. Just before the wedding, Goody's long-lost brother appeared. Having made a fortune overseas, he made a proper settlement on her, and at the altar, Sir Charles's poor girl turned into a wealthy middle-class princess. This moral girl was not, however, destined to waste her days dancing in glass slippers. To encourage the poor to attend church, Lady Jones presented each poor person the price of a loaf of bread when he appeared at church. To encourage matrimony, she gave courting couples "something towards House-keeping." On Sunday evenings she lectured the parish children on religion and morality and taught the catechism, after which she gave them supper and then books to read. Unlike the heroine of a fairy tale, recognition of her true worth did not elevate her to an untouching and untouchable world of glitter and diamonds. Instead, it rooted her in the practical soil of benevolence, and she spent her days as "a Mother to the Poor, a Physician to the Sick, and a Friend to all who were in Distress."[13]

Goody Two-Shoes was a popular character. Through the evil machinations of Sir Timothy Gripe and Farmer Graspall, her father Farmer Meanwell lost first his land, then his life. After her mother died from a broken heart, Goody was turned out into the world as a poor orphan. Like Cinderella, though, she rose from rags to riches. Her story was not, however, so much an eighteenth-century fairy tale as it was an educational fable for the times. Virtue and learning were Goody's fairy godparents. They enabled her to endure and to triumph over hardship. As commerce increased the national wealth and as society became less rigid, opportunities for crawling out from under the hay, where little Goody had spent many chilly nights, and settling down in a comfortable bed in a manor house greatly increased. Although Goody's rise was meteoric, parents from the middle classes could legitimately see in her story justification of their great expectations for their children. Locke's educational ideas taught the malleability of children. The "gifts of nature," Priscilla Wakefield stressed in *Leisure Hours* (1796), were "more equally bestowed than pride and ignorance" were willing to allow. Education made the difference. "The son of the peasant, born in a cottage, and allotted to the menial occupations of poverty," she wrote, "may possess abilities, were they nourished by the fostering hand of cultivation, suited to the noblest pursuits."[14]

Education had made the difference between poverty and wealth for Goody Two-Shoes. Virtue and discipline had been so woven into her character that her marriage to Sir Charles Jones was almost inevitable. It was also practically inevitable that Goody Two-Shoes would become the mother of several literary offspring. As second-generation aristocrats, however, these were often more proper and consequently duller than their mother. Near the end of the century John Marshall published two of the best of Goody's children. *The Entertaining History of Little Goody Goosecap* (1780) told the instructive story of Frances Fairchild. When she was four years old, Frances's parents died, and she, like the children in the wood, was left to the care of an evil uncle. Instead of hiring ruffians to kill her as the wicked uncle had done in *The Children in the Wood,* Goody Goosecap's relative merely sold her inheritance, pocketed the money, and absconded to the West Indies, leaving his niece as a burden on the parish. Sent to charity school, Frances soon distinguished herself. She learned the alphabet so well that she tutored younger children. Impressed by Frances's virtue and learning, Lady Bountiful took her off the parish and treated her like a daughter. Sixteen years and numerous instructive adventures later, Frances suddenly received ten thousand pounds from her uncle. Repenting on his deathbed, he sent his savings to her as partial atonement for his misdeeds. Shortly after she received the money, Frances married Lady Bountiful's son.

The Renowned History of Primrose Prettyface, who By her Sweetness of Temper, & Love of Learning, was raised from being the Daughter of a poor Cottager, to great Riches, and the Dignity of Lady of the Manor (1785) described how munificently the virtue and learning of Goodman Thompson's daughter was rewarded. Although Primrose was not born in genteel society and did not inherit a fortune, she so impressed her benefactor that Lady Worthy encouraged her son Sir William to marry her. Financially poor but spiritually rich, Primrose resembled a simple flower. Like a trellis, her love of learning and virtue directed her growth and enabled her to bloom naturally and diffuse sweetness about her. Since she did not unexpectedly become an heiress, Primrose's happy history resembled a fairy tale more than did the accounts of Goody Two-Shoes and Goody Goosecap. Because of this and Primrose's comparatively low birth, Mrs. Trimmer found the book wanting and in 1802 criticized the conclusion. It was "very wrong," she wrote, to teach "girls of the lower order to aspire to marriages with persons in stations so far superior to their own, or to put into the heads of young gentlemen, at an early age, an idea, that when they grow up they may, without impropriety, marry servant-maids."[15]

Despite Mrs. Trimmer's protest, books like *Goody Two-Shoes* and *Primrose Prettyface* implied that learning not only made the woman but influenced her station in life. Sir Charles Jones proposed to Goody before she was wealthy. Taking advantage of the general view of Goody as the Cinderella whose rags learning turned to riches, J. Harris published *The Alphabet Of Goody two Shoes* in 1808. As many of Newbery's nostrums were cure-alls for the body, so Harris's *Alphabet* was a cure-all for the pocketbook. To follow Goody's footsteps to success was not easy, but the *Alphabet* pointed children in the right direction. Goody Two-Shoes influenced not only her literary "children" but also more distant literary relatives. In 1806, Harris discovered Dame Partlet. She was said "to have been," her biographer declared, "a very near relation of that renowned person GOODY TWO SHOES, so well known to every good child who hath read those pretty books sold at the corner of St. Paul's Church-yard, London." Dame Partlet lived in the village of Innocence. Her husband, Simon Partlet, died when he was only thirty, leaving her six children to raise, two of whom later died from smallpox. Not only was the life of Goody Two-Shoes an inspiration to Dame Partlet, but Goody had been Dame Partlet's teacher. Dame Partlet "brought up her children to be industrious, and always kept them clean and neat, and taught them to read, without applying to the parish for relief," her biographer recounted, "for Goody Two Shoes having taught her to read, and having early instructed her in the necessity and the usefulness of being industrious, she was not only very clever, but was also so good a woman, that almost every body in the parish was willing to do something for her."

Goody Two-Shoes taught well, for Dame Partlet read better than anyone in the parish except the parish clerk. She had read the Bible "three times quite through from Genesis to Revelations, and could say many of the Psalms of David by heart." Although she had only a garden, an orchard, and "a few books on a shelf just over the salt-box" and Squire Takeall owned much land, kept dogs and horses, employed servants, and possessed a fine library, she did more good in the village than the squire. Mr. Lovetruth, the rector, believed that her ceaseless industry taught young people the value of work and shamed old people out of idleness. When Farmer Tipple fell into his horsepond and drowned on a dark night while returning from a public house, Farmer Pleasant took over his farm. Because she was so industrious and charitable, Dame Partlet received the lease of Farmer Pleasant's old farm. She worked hard and within a few years became wealthy. When she died, the whole parish mourned.[16]

In domesticating giants, making Tom Thumb an educational familiar, and warning children against nonsensical fairy tales, Newbery did not neglect Aesop. In 1758 he published an edition of the *Fables*, but here too he reduced the exotic, if the classical can be called exotic, to the familiar. The *Fables* were written, not simply by Aesop but by Abraham Aesop, Esq.; moreover, "Woglog the great Giant" was a contributing author. Drawing on Locke's advice on "Baits," the preface defended fables and mixing amusement with instruction. People who read the book would discover, Newbery wrote, that "under agreeable allegories" children had been given "such lessons in prudence and morality, as may be of service to them in their riper years, and help to conduct them through the world with peace and tranquillity." Like exercise, he argued, reading became tedious and painful if used only for "improvement in virtue." In contrast, "the virtue and instruction" got from a fable was like health got by hunting. Engaged in an agreeable pursuit, children became "insensible of the fatigues with which it" was "attended."[17]

By the end of the century most authors and publishers of books for children no longer felt compelled to defend fables. Even if they were not entirely comfortable with them, they clearly preferred fables to fairy tales. Moreover, the Lockean observation that the "blending of *instruction* with *amusement*" made the former "the more easily retained" had become a commonplace. The "want of proper books of instruction," once so justly complained of, the *Monthly Review* stated in 1784, was now supplied as "much laudable pains" had been taken to "furnish children with lessons of instruction in the agreeable forms of tales, fables, and historical anecdotes." In contrast to other stories for children, fables were occasionally identified with Christ's parables. When Constant attacked all fiction in Fordyce's *Dialogues,* Hiero responded "that the *Parabolical* or *Allegorical* Way of instructing Mankind is vindicated by good Authority." If not fables, what, he asked, were "our Saviour's Parables"? For Ellenor Fenn, the author of a series of primers adapted from Aesop, there was but "one accusation against Fables, namely, Falsehood." This, she wrote, should be explained away by telling children that fables partook of "their own usual favorite sport of *making believe.*" Since fables were "generally pleasing to children" and could be used to "convey simple Morals adapted to the duties of childhood," "debating whether or no Fable-writing" was "the most desirable mode of instruction" was, she thought, a waste of time.[18]

Other writers agreed, and instead of stressing the merits of fables, they emphasized the close resemblances between their books and fables and implicitly or explicitly stressed the distance between their commonsensical worlds and the imaginary world of the marvelous. Mrs. Trimmer, it will be remembered, had stressed that before Henry and Charlotte read *Fabulous Histories,* they were taught "to consider them, not as containing the real conversation of Birds" but "as a series of FABLES, intended to convey moral instruction." In *The Canary Bird* (1799), E.A. Kendall apologized to Melanthe, his young reader, for making his birds talk "philosophically." In defense he cited Aesop, noting that he was "by no means the first fabulist that has assisted animals to speak of their own condition." Since a fabulist tried "to amuse and instruct," he was allowed "to make use of a few imaginary circumstances." The imaginary circumstances permitted to the fabulist were not, however, permitted to the teller of fairy tales. In Dorothy Kilner's *A Father's Advice to His Son*

(1784), Mr. Goodwin considered books "about *giants* and *fairies*" as "nonsense" and told James, his young son, that he did not want him "to spend a moment's time in looking at them." In contrast, James was permitted to read Marshall's fanciful and instructive biographies of animals and inanimate objects, particularly *The Life and Perambulation of a Mouse, Memoirs of a Peg-Top,* and *The Adventures of a Pincushion.* These gave "good advice" and even if "the events they are *made believe* to tell did not really happen; or if they have not exactly, yet things so like them have, that we may very well fancy them true."[19]

Even after making allowance for a massive infusion of didacticism in a story peopled by talking mice or benevolent pincushions, it is not now readily apparent why its effect upon young readers would differ greatly from that of a tale filled with crafty cats or good fairies. Certainly the willing suspension of disbelief necessary to enjoy the make-believe adventures of a peg-top is little different from that required to enjoy Jack the Giant-Killer, Puss in Boots, or the Yellow Dwarf. Fairy tales, however, were criticized in the eighteenth century for many reasons, not all of which could be traced to Locke. By the middle of the eighteenth century, the fairy tale had become a staple of chapbooks. Indeed, most young readers made their first acquaintance with Perrault's classic fairy tales through chapbooks. Unfortunately, this introduction was fraught with critical consequences for the fairy tale. During the century chapbooks had come in for mounting criticism and fairy tales suffered from guilt by association. In some instances, though, the association was amorously close.

As Perrault's tales had become known as "Mother Goose's Tales," so Madame d'Aulnoy's were often printed as "The Celebrated Fairy Tales of Mother Bunch." Unfortunately for the reputation of the fairy tale, Mother Bunch was the most famous Miss Lonelyhearts in eighteenth-century chapbooks. Like the Wife of Bath, she was eminently qualified to give advice on matrimonial matters, for she had enjoyed three husbands. The first had been a "Straw Joiner"; the second, "a Mouse Trap-maker"; while the third, as she recounted, had been in "the Gentle Craft" and had approached her with his "Awle in his Hands" and had pricked her, but amazingly had not hurt her. Addressing those who had languished "in single Sheets till fifteen," she promised to show them the person who would "ease" them of "the simple Thing so much talk'd of, call'd a Maiden head." Although she urged each maiden "to hold thy Legs together, till thou has authority to lay them wide open," her advice often seemed conducive to more generous behavior. Mother Bunch's methods for discovering the identity of a future husband ranged from the safe and simple—looking between the "great Toes" of one's right foot for a hair which would match those on the head of one's future spouse—to the complicated and the "dangerous." One maiden was advised to sweep out her bedroom, put on a clean smock, pare a St. Thomas's onion, and after placing it on a clean handkerchief, put it firmly under her head when she lay down to sleep. Once in bed, the girl was to lie on her back, spread her arms, and say: "*Good* St. Thomas *do me Right, / And Bring my Love to me this Night; / That I may look him on the Face, / And in my Arms may him embrace.*" While she was asleep, Mother Bunch assured the young girl, she would dream "of him who is to be thy Husband." "He will come," she continued, "and offer to kiss thee; do not hinder him, but strive to catch him in thy Arms; and if thou dost get hold of him, hold him fast, for that is he."[20]

This advice must have contributed to contentment below stairs, and any maiden who followed it closely would most certainly have lost that simple thing so much talked about. Getting a husband, however, was a different matter, for many an ardent swain disappeared between the "dream" and the altar. Chapbooks like those in which Mother Bunch occasionally appeared offered hope for the unlucky maidens whom St. Thomas betrayed. *Dreams and Moles with their Interpretation and Signification* contained a recipe which described "*How to restore a lost Maidenhead, or solder a Crackt one.*" First, the sufferer was to beat myrtle berries into a powder. Next, the powder was mixed with the "beaten flour of cotton." If the girl drank this compound in the morning in a glass of white wine, she would, the chapbook assured readers, "find the effects wonderful."[21]

In her *Cobwebs to Catch Flies: Dialogues in Short Sentences, Adapted to Children from the Age of Three to Eight Years,* Ellenor Fenn addressed parents who paid little attention to what their children read, warning them that "If the human mind be a *rasa tabula,*—you to whom it is entrusted, should be cautious what is written upon it." By the publication of the

Cobwebs in 1783, many educators were extremely cautious and proscribed not merely fairy tales but all stories whose appeal seemed aimed primarily at a child's imagination rather than his understanding. Despite warning parents against the dangers of "dismal *Stories*" of the supernatural, neither Locke nor Watts went this far. On the contrary, Locke stressed that curiosity "should be as carefully *cherished* in Children, as other Appetites surpressed." Watts was more suspicious of the imagination than Locke. But after stating that children's "*Thoughts and Fancies should be brought under Early Government,*" he added that parents and teachers should be careful not to "overwhelm an active and sprightly Genius, and destroy all those Seeds of Curiosity which promise well for maturer Years."[22]

What neither Locke nor Watts foresaw was the epidemic popularity of the romance and the novel in the latter half of the eighteenth century. "Of all the multifarious productions which the efforts of superiour genius, or the labours of scholastic industry, have crowded upon the world," Anna (later Barbauld) and John Aikin wrote in 1773, "none are perused with more insatiable avidity, or disseminated with more universal applause, than the narrations of feigned events, descriptions of imaginary scenes, and delineations of ideal characters." "The gloom of solitude, the languor of inaction, the corrosions of disappointment, and the toil of thought," the Aikins argued, "induce men to step aside from the rugged road of life, and wander in the fairy land of fiction; where every bank is sprinkled with flowers, and every gale loaded with perfume; where every event introduces a hero, and every cottage is inhabited by a Grace." Clearly the Aikins' fairy land of purple fiction was not Perrault's land of fairy tales which, although it did have maidens who wasted their sweetness on the cottage air, was a rather more gruesome place "peopled" by ogres, giants, and dwarfs. However, this inaccurate identification of the world of the novel with the world of fairy tale was significant. Since both forms appealed to the imagination rather than to the understanding, often little distinction was made between them, particularly by critics of children's books. Consequently, when educational critics treated the novel harshly, some of the criticism rubbed off on fairy tales. Richardson's Pamela, for example, explained why she had read "few Novels and Romances" and analyzed the dangers of the genre in a critique which could almost be applied to fairy and old wives' tales. "They dealt so much in the *Marvelous* and *Improbable*," she wrote, "or were so unnaturally *inflaming* to the *Passions*, and so full of *Love* and *Intrigue*, that hardly any of them but seem'd calculated to *fire* the *Imagination*, rather than to *inform* the *Judgment*." "Tilts and Tournaments," she continued, "breaking of Spears in Honour of a Mistress, swimming of Rivers, engaging with Monsters, rambling in Search of Adventures, making unnatural Difficulties, in order to shew the Knight-Errant's Prowess in overcoming them, is all that is requir'd to constitute the *Hero* in such Pieces." Moreover, what distinguished the heroine was when she learned "to consider her Father's House as an inchanted Castle, and her Lover as the Hero who is to dissolve the Charm, and to set her at Liberty." Such books, Pamela concluded, provided no instruction "for the Conduct of common Life" and drowned "the Voice of Reason" in "that of indiscreet Love."[23]

Seeing the novel's appeal to the imagination not as a spur to curiosity or sprightly genius but as a threat to morality, educators like Pamela led the attack on the genre in the late eighteenth century. Maria Edgeworth warned parents that novels lowered the tone of the mind and induced indifference to "common pleasures and occupations." "By delineating human life in false colours," Mrs. West wrote in *The Advantages of Education* (1803), novels formed romantic expectations which could never be realized. In Hannah More's tract *The Two Wealthy Farmers* (1795), the daughters of Farmer Bragwell were "contaminated" by novels which they read at boarding school. Stories which described the transformation of "Beggars to-day" into "Lords to-morrow" and "Waiting maids in the morning" into "Duchesses at night" made them contemptuous of "humble and domestic duties." According to Mrs. Trimmer, novels filled with "nonsense about lords, and ladies, and squires, falling in love with one another, and running away from their parents, and shooting themselves" made it difficult for servants to see life as it really was and "to *resist evil* and *hold fast that which is good*."[24]

With both the novel and the fairy tale appealing to the imagination rather than the understanding and often depicting loves and marriages, if not in the world of the supernatural, at least so far out of the ordinary that they seemed supernatural, the failure of educators to distinguish fairy tales from the fairy land of fiction was understandable. As understandable as this was, however, criticism of the novel contributed to the bad reputation of the fairy tale at the end of the eighteenth century. In the preface to her *Dialogues and Letters on Morality* (1785), Dorothy Kilner wrote that it was "much to be lamented . . . that almost the whole catalogue of entertaining books for children, turn chiefly upon subjects of *gallantry, love,* and *marriage.* Subjects, with which no prudent parents would wish to engross the attention of their children, of six, seven, eight, or even a dozen years of age." Although these remarks were directed primarily at novels, they were also applicable to fairy tales. When measuring by this standard, prudent parents would keep their children from such famous stories as "Sleeping Beauty," "Cinderella," and "Beauty and the Beast."[25]

Suspicion of fiction was so pervasive that even relentlessly moral tales were not free from criticism. "*The love of truth,*" Priscilla Wakefield explained in the preface to *Juvenile Anecdotes* (1795), "*seems inherent in the human mind, even at a very early period.*" However, fear of punishment or the wish to obtain a point, she continued, sometimes caused "*a deviation from it.*" She was thus induced, she explained, by the objections she had "*frequently heard Children raise against the influence of moral tales on their own conduct, that they were not true, but merely fictions to entertain*" to "*believe, that real anecdotes of characters of their own ages, and dispositions, judiciously selected, so as to interest their lively imaginations, and at the same time, place their virtues and faults . . . in a perspicuous point of view, would probably reach their hearts with peculiar force.*"[26]

Rousseau also contributed to the poor reputation of the fairy tale at the end of the eighteenth century. Eschewing Locke's baits for seducing children into a love of reading and knowledge, Rousseau posited a new educational world. "I hate books," he wrote in *Emilius and Sophia*; "they only teach people to talk about what they don't understand." Declaring that children would learn better by themselves, he thought knowledge ought to be conveyed by experience and practical trial-and-error experiment. Emilius discovered what private property was, not from precept, but from experience. After digging up a gardener's Maltese melons in order to plant beans, he was rebuked. The correction prompted him to inquire about the concept of property, which his tutor accordingly explained. After they had completed "the first term of childhood," Rousseau urged giving children a taste for practical science rather than impractical books. Children, he thought, should be taken into the shops of artisans, encouraged to observe and question, and to deduce "the laws of nature." At "twelve years of age," Emilius, wrote Rousseau, would "hardly know what a book is." Even fables were banished from his education. Appealing to the imagination, they were inadequate "moral lectures." "Seduced by the charms of falsehood," children, Rousseau argued, did not notice the truth "crouched underneath" the fable and as a result were led more "to vice than virtue."[27]

Although Rousseau carried his "mortal aversion to books" to an extreme, the seemingly logical basis of his method of education had a strong appeal.[28] To educators who had begrudgingly acquiesced in Newbery's reformed giants because Locke taught that children had to be cozened into knowledge, Rousseau offered an alternative. No longer would it be necessary to convey knowledge into the "noble Repository or Cabinet of the Soul" on a cart hammered out of the "Rubbish and Lumber" of silly narratives. Accordingly, some educators pragmatically ignored Rousseau's criticism of books for children and wrote children's books which emphasized his educational methods. The most literate of these writers was Maria Edgeworth. Published in 1801, the first series of her *Early Lessons* read like instructive dialogues written by Rousseau. Resembling Emilius, young Frank asked innumerable questions and learned from experience. He learned the importance of close observation, for example, when he noticed the road taken by a runaway horse and, as a result, was able to give proper directions to its owner. Later, when Frank became tired walking home, the horse's grateful owner gave him a ride and Frank's father remarked, "now you have found one of the uses of observing what you see, and of relating facts exactly." In response to Frank's asking what the other uses were, his father replied, "I would rather that you should find them out for yourself." On an occasion that was cut from the same educational vine as Emilius's experience with the Maltese melons, young Harry visited a brickyard with his father. While there, he unthinkingly ruined many soft bricks by poking his fingers into them. After being corrected, he not only learned about the sanctity of private property but successfully set about constructing his own kiln so that he could replace the bricks he ruined.[29]

Maria Edgeworth did not discuss fairy tales in the *Early Lessons.* She had already done so in the preface to *The Parent's Assistant* (second edition, 1796), in which she criticized Dr. Johnson's objection to instructive books for young children. "Endeavouring to make children prematurely wise," Johnson had said, was "useless labour." At an early age, he thought it better "to gratify curiosity with wonders than to attempt planting truth" and suggested that children could do no better than to read "Jack the Giant-Killer," "Parismus and Parismenus," and "The Seven Champions of Christendom." Too much, he told Fanny Burney's father, was "expected from precocity, and too little performed." As an example of the failure of what was in effect Lockean educational practice, he cited Anna Barbauld and ridiculed her *Lessons for Children,* books which Maria Edgeworth greatly admired. Anna Barbauld's "early cultivation," Johnson said, ended in marriage to "a little Presbyterian parson" who kept an infant boarding school and in writing books which taught, "this is a cat, and that is a dog, with four legs and a tail."

Maria Edgeworth criticized the tales "of giants and fairies, and castles and inchantments" that Johnson recommended. Predictably, she warned that they were dangerous for children's imaginations. Even if children enjoyed them, she asked, was this "a reason why they should be indulged in reading them?" Instead of losing "so much valuable time," vitiating their "taste," spoiling "their appetite, by suffering them to feed upon sweetmeats," and filling their minds with "fantastic visions," parents should teach children "useful knowledge." The "reign of fairies" was over, she wrote, and she hoped "that the magic of Dr. Johnson's name" would not be able to restore it.[30]

In 1802 Charles Lamb wrote to Coleridge lamenting that "all the old classics" had been banished from the nursery. At Newbery's bookstore his sister Mary had had trouble finding them. "Science," Lamb wrote, had "succeeded to Poetry no less in the little walks of children than with men." "Is there no possibility of averting this sore evil?" he asked. "Think," he told Coleridge, "what you would have been now, if you had been crammed with geography and natural history." [31] Although

Lamb thought that instructive children's books of the sort written by Mrs. Trimmer and Maria Edgeworth had banished fairy-tale and chapbook heroes from the book store, he was mistaken. If Mary Lamb had looked carefully, she would have discovered that many of the characters of old wives' and fairy tales were alive.

Moral and educational books dominated *Newbery's Catalogue Of Instructive And Amusing Publications For Young Minds, Sold At The Corner Of St. Paul's Church-Yard,* which Elizabeth Newbery published in 1800. Newbery's bookstore stocked more titles by Mrs. Trimmer than any other author. Thirty of her books, including a French translation of *An Easy Introduction,* were for sale. A heavy load of instructive books then weighed fairy tales down and some of their heroes were tamed. But if a child examined the fourteen twopenny books on Newbery's shelves, he would have found accounts of Tom Thumb and Robin Goodfellow. For sixpence he could have bought an account of Sindbad the Sailor or a description of the adventures which Sindbad's cousin Captain Gulliver had on Lilliput and Brobdingnag. Among the thirty sixpenny books for sale were Solomon Winlove's *Collection* of entertaining stories including "Jack Horner," "Cinderella," "Little Red Riding Hood," and "Fortunatus." An entire sixpenny book was devoted to the *History of the White Cat. Mother Goose's Tales* and *Mother Bunch's Tales* cost nine pence each, while seven shillings purchased two volumes of fairy tales and fourteen shillings, four volumes of either *Arabian Nights* or *Arabian Tales.*[32]

Having grown older, the heroes of some of the books sold in Newbery's bookshop had become more moral. Even Tom Thumb had reformed. Having retired from his travels and put his coach into storage, he had become interested in education and had mounted an exhibition of "valuable curiosities for the instruction and amusement of all the pretty masters and misses of Great Britain, who are little and good like myself." Tom did not exhibit his famous bulrush, and his show was composed entirely of moral toys. He did, however, exhibit the "wonderful optic glass" which he had purchased from its maker, Mr. Longthought, and which made all objects viewed through it "appear in such a form as is most suitable" to their "natural qualities or probably effects." Mr. Soberman had used it, Tom related, to great advantage in curing his son Jacky "of a most bewitching, and indeed a dangerous relish, for sweet tarts and fulsome custards." Thinking these "luscious geegaws" would ruin Jacky's health and "lay a foundation for some violent destructive disorder," Mr. Soberman borrowed the glass. "After setting out a table in the best parlour with the richest pies and tarts, and with the greatest dainties which could be procured in the pastry way," he told Master Jacky that he could eat all he wanted after he looked through the optic glass. Jacky eagerly took the glass from his father, Tom recounted, "but when he looked through it, and instead of pies, tarts, and custards, saw the table covered with ugly toads, newts, and scorpions (for that is the appearance it will always produce in such cases) he screamed out with great violence and ran out of the room immediately." "From that hour to this," Tom summed up, Jacky "has never been remarkably fond of tarts, custards, etc."[33]

Like many famous men, Tom Thumb was the subject of several biographies. Not surprisingly, these mirrored the concerns of the times in which they were written. If the accounts of Tom's life did not teach children that they could make their lives sublime and leave behind footprints in the sands of time, they did depict Tom as growing progressively moral. By 1770 Tom closely resembled Tommy Trip. Merlin no longer had anything to do with Tom's birth, and he was simply the minute son of Mr. Theophilus Thumb of Thumb-Hall in Northumberland. Instead of being known for his mischievous tricks, Tom, like Tommy Trip, became a scholar praised for his "Wisdom and Virtue." As the central event in Trip's life was the taming of Woglog, so the major event in Tom's life was his reforming Grumbo, the giant who ruled the Kingdom of the Cuckows. Tom rode a cuckoo to Grumbo's realm. When the bird reached home, he collapsed and Tom fell from his back into a "Mess of Milk-Porridge" intended for Grumbo. Growling so loudly that the valleys rang, Grumbo scooped Tom out of the porridge without examining him. Tom then crept into Grumbo's coat pocket, where the giant kept his bread. Whenever Grumbo reached for a piece of bread, Tom hid behind the giant's snuff box. After a few days, Tom became quite bold. Whenever he discovered the giant "about a bad action," he would stick his head out of the pocket, jab him with his sword, and cry "*Sirrah! what are you at there, Sirrah?*" after which he would duck behind the snuff box. Living in the pocket was inconvenient, but Grumbo seemed to have suf-

12 Tom Thumb's Exhibition.

Learn, then, to hearken to each worthy friend;
And to his good advice with care attend.

II. The next curiosity you will see is the INTELLECTUAL PERSPECTIVE GLASS, which I purchased of the ma-

ker, one Mr. Longthought, who is a man of great understanding, and a very ingenious

From *Tom Thumb's Exhibition.* By permission of the British Library.

20

He had comforted and fed the cuckoo, as well as he could, with a powder which his mother put into his
pocket to serve him as food; but the
poor bird grew so weak, at the time
they arrived in his own country, that
he fell down; and our hero, by endeavouring to save himself, plunged
into a large mess of milk porridge,
which was intended for the Giant

From *Tom Thumb's Folio.* By permission of the British Library.

fered more than Tom. "The Giant," Tom's biographer explained, "not only missed his Bread, but found something instead thereof which he did not like; for *Tom,* who had conveyed all the Food among the Linings of the Folds, where he had Room to range, made use of the Pocket for another Purpose, which was not altogether fair, but he could not help it."

While in the giant's pocket, Tom learned the language of the kingdom. Since Grumbo was "proud, selfish, surly, and so tyrannical and cruel, that his Subjects were afraid to come near him," Tom, like young Trip facing Woglog, determined to reduce "him to better Manners." Whenever Grumbo began to fall asleep, Tom pricked him with his "little Sword." After "some Time," Grumbo was "so weak for want of Rest, that he could not walk." Judging that the time was ripe, Tom climbed on to the exhausted giant's chest and addressed him saying, "Are you inclined, oh *Grumbo,* to live or to die? If you would live, you must take my Advice, and behave with Humanity and Kindness to all your Subjects and to me; but if you would rather die than be good, do so, for nobody will be sorry for you." Thinking that Tom had fallen from the moon to punish him for his evil deeds, Grumbo "begged that he might live to make amends for his bad Behaviour." On Grumbo's recovery Tom became his favorite, and he traveled about the country in a coach drawn by ten squirrels, dispensing justice. Grumbo married Tom to his daughter, despite the fact that she was a giantess; she loved her husband dearly and "carried him about in her Bosom." Eventually Tom became the father of two bouncing boys, each of whom was nine hundred times as big as his father. When Tom died, he was "greatly lamented" both by the king and his subjects.

Grumbo's minister of justice was more respectable than the individual who traveled through the Red Cow. However, the details of Tom's necessary but untoward behavior in the giant's pocket and the intimate perch he assumed whenever he traveled with his wife were too strong for children's books sold in 1800. Although Carnan and Newbery had first published this account of Tom in *Tom Thumb's Folio* and it contained an alphabet, fables, and religious and moral lessons, Elizabeth Newbery did not list the book in her catalogue. Children had to be satisfied with the moral side show of *Tom Thumb's Exhibition* (1775).[34]

Tom Thumb's exhibition was one of several collections of instructive curiosities which children were able to view at the end of the eighteenth century. Left sole executor of the will of "his Uncle *Timothy Curious,* Esq., a celebrated Lilliputian Virtuoso," Master Charly Chatter invited all little masters and misses to *The Lilliputian Auction* (1773). Among the possessions of Mr. Curious was a looking glass which revealed the "disagreeable figure" a child made when he was angry or put on "unnecessary Airs." A packet contained a slip of paper on which was written a never-failing recipe for making young ladies beautiful. "*If beautiful you would appear,*" it instructed, "*Always be good-humour'd Dear.*" The pride of the late Mr. Curious's collection of moral objects was, however, the "Learned Bottle." If dull people sniffed the bottle, Charly claimed, they would become sprightly; ignorant people, learned; foolish people, witty; and dunces, scholars. The remarkable liquid in the bottle was, Charly explained, distilled "from half a pound of *Reflection,* six ounces of *Memory,* a pound of *Reason,* eight ounces of *Thought,* nine ounces of *Attention,* and eleven ounces of *Care* and *Assiduity* mixed together."[35]

In her essay "Children's Literature Of The Last Century," Charlotte Yonge wrote that "fairyland had been under a ban" at the beginning of the nineteenth century. If "the poor things" appeared at all, she wrote, it was in the most arbitrary manner. Sometimes they were "the rewarders of the good"; other times they were "poor little sprites, loaded with priggishness." At the end of the eighteenth century, Robin Goodfellow was not a prig. Neither, however, was he a madcap, amoral prankster. In *Robin Goodfellow; A Fairy Tale. Written by a Fairy* (1770), a book for sale in Newbery's shop in 1800, Robin took Jacky Goodchild to fairyland for a visit. Robin made Jacky invisible so the little boy could observe a banquet at Fancy's Court. Over a mushroom a "spider's web, bleached with evening dew" was spread. The first course consisted of Head of a Blue-bottle "Turtleized"; the second, of Brains of Worms and Snails' Horns Stewed; the third, of Marrow of Mice, Haunch of a Gnat, and Beetle's Sweet-breads, while the final course was Slime of Slugs, Fricassee of Fleas, and Froth of Frog. During the meal King Fancy sensed Jacky's presence and made him visible. The king was glad to see him, for Jacky was "a good boy" and learned his book. Everybody loved him, and Dr. Birch never "had occasion to exercise his authority" over him. Because he was good, Jacky was given the privilege of being a fairy. After the ceremony, he and Robin traveled to the "bookseller's shop, at the corner of St. Paul's Church-Yard." Since they were invisible, Robin played instructive pranks on the children who were looking at books and talking to Mr. Alphabet, the bookseller. Into the pocket of Billy, for example, who was not quite three years old but who already wanted to learn his book, he slipped an orange, whereas he put a halter around the necks of Jacky Juggle and Billy Bilk, who misbehaved. After leaving the shop, Robin took Jacky to Bartholomew Fair, where he played more instructive tricks.[36]

Fairies sometimes flourished in highly instructive children's books, albeit, as the *Monthly Review* put it, they were "much improved in their manners." At the height of criticism of fairy tales, Ellenor Fenn wrote *The Fairy Spectator* (1789). One of Mrs. Teachwell's students, Miss Sprightly, became upset because she had been awakened from a dream just as a fairy was handing her two mysterious looking-glasses. After making certain that Miss Sprightly and young readers understood that fairies were "fabulous" and that only God knew children's "every action, word, and thought," Mrs. Teachwell promised to write dialogues to complete Miss Sprightly's dream. In doing so she stripped fairies of their miraculous appearance, making her fairy simply "a very beautiful female" instead of the exotic being who appeared to Miss Sprightly as a dragonfly accompanied by delicate perfume and beautiful music. According to Mrs. Teachwell's story, mysterious mirrors were given to a spoiled little girl named Miss Child. One of the "ENCHANTED GLASSES" showed Miss Child what she was, while the other showed her what she could be. After the mirrors had helped Miss Child reform her manners, the fairy gave her a locket decorated with pale rubies. If she became envious, one would turn dirty yellow; if angry, another would glow like fire; if foolishly timid, one would become white; and if she were niggardly the points would turn dull black, while jealousy would turn "the whole locket to a colour like that of a common pebble in a gravel pit."[37]

Ellenor Fenn's book was actually an anti-fairy tale with an anti-fairy heroine, who turned down the usual miraculous paraphernalia for solid moral reasons and in the process exposed the pedagogic dangers of traditional fairy tales. When offered a ring like Tom Thumb's, which would make her invisible, or a purse and a bonnet like those of Fortunatus, which would always be filled with money or would convey her to any place in the world, Miss Child rose above mortal infancy and, refusing them, became the ideal Miss Everychild. The ring, she explained, might tempt her to pry into other people's business, while the bonnet, although it would enable her to fly to the assistance of her friends, might be misused for selfish purposes. Finally, by making it impossible to have "*less*," the purse would render charity and generosity meaningless.[38]

If King Allgood had read *The Fairy Spectator* when he was young, he might have had a happier life. "The History of King Allgood" was among a group of *Instructive Lessons* collected by Lilliputius Gulliver and published by Elizabeth Newbery in 1800. Loved by his subjects and feared by his neighbors, the king was "wise, just, good, valiant." One day, however, a fairy visited him. She warned him that he would experience difficulties if he did not "make use of a ring" which she was about to give him. In the center of the ring was a diamond. When the diamond was turned downward, the king was invisible; when it faced outward, he was visible. Like Miss Child's enchanted mirrors, the ring was a boon, for it enabled the king to frustrate "several conspiracies formed against his person" and disconcert "all the measures of his enemies for his overthrow." In contrast to Miss Child, however, who refused several gifts because she realized they could be put to bad use and might undermine her character, King Allgood coveted other magical powers. Not satisfied with the ring, he asked for "the power of conveying himself in an instant from one country to another." Realizing that the ring was corrupting the king and that he was becoming less good, the fairy entreated him to be satisfied. "Let me conjure you," she pleaded, "not to covet a power which, I foresee, will one day or other be the cause of your misery." The king was adamant, however, so the fairy poured a "fragrant liquor" over him. Little wings immediately grew on his back. These were not visible beneath his clothes, and he "needed only to touch them with his hand, and they would spread so as to bear him through the air, swifter than an eagle." Now able to study his neighbors at will, he "entered into very extraordinary wars, and never failed to triumph."[39]

All did not go well with the king, however. His abilities enabled him to discover so much dissimulation and wickedness that he no longer placed confidence in others. The more powerful he grew, the less beloved he became. His powers revealed that those to whom he had been most generous had no affection for him. To remedy the isolation in which he now found himself, he decided to marry. For a long time he searched for a wife in vain; able to see "all without being seen, he discovered the most hidden wiles and failings of the sex." Eventually, though, he met Clarinda, the daughter of a poor laborer. A thing of beauty and a virtuous joy, she became his wife. At the court she "preserved her simplicity, her modesty, her virtue, and forgot not the place of her birth." After the marriage, the fairy redoubled her efforts and warned the king against misusing his powers. Happier than he had ever been, the king paid no attention, and finding the fairy's warnings tiresome, he ordered that she be refused admittance to the palace. "Desirous to instruct the Queen in futurity," the fairy disguised herself as a young officer and entered the queen's apartment. When she whispered who she was to the queen, the queen embraced her. Unfortunately, the king was lurking invisibly about the room outside earshot. When he saw the queen embrace the officer, he was instantly "fired with jealousy." Drawing his sword, he stabbed his wife, and she died in his arms. The fairy then assumed her accustomed shape. Upon seeing the true identity of the officer, the king wanted to kill himself. The fairy would not let him do so, however, and he spent the rest of his life mourning his wife. "Too late now Allgood cursed his folly, that put him upon wresting a boon from the fairy which proved his misery," Lilliputius Gulliver concluded; "he returned the ring, and desired his wings might be taken from him. The remaining days of his life he past in bitterness and grief, knowing no other consolation but to weep perpetually over Clarinda's tomb."[40]

In 1802, J. Harris, Elizabeth Newbery's successor, published *The Ruby Heart, Or, Constantio And Selima; And The Enchanted Mirror.* The book was dedicated to Isabella, to whom the author wrote a letter, saying, "Some wise men and learned ladies are of opinion, that Fables and Fairy Tales are improper for children, because they pervert their early minds, by deceiving them into a notion that Animals and Birds talk, and that wonderful events are occasioned by magic art." "You and I, my dear Isabella," the author continued, "are of opinion, that children should be induced to love reading; that Fables and Fairy Tales will produce that effect; that much good advice and information can be conveyed in a Fable and a Fairy Tale; and that the History of the White Cat, the Hare, and many Friends, and the Perambulations of a Mouse, will amuse and improve children as much as an account of Sir Isaac Newton's Philosophy, or an Abridgement of Locke on the Human Understanding." The beliefs held by the wise men and learned ladies whom the author of *The Ruby Heart* criticized dominated children's books at the end of the eighteenth century. In contrast to Lamb's opinion, however, the characters of old wives' and fairy tales had not been driven completely out of the nursery. Many had indeed reformed and like Tom Thumb had been powdered by the chalk of didacticism. But if one were willing to explore Newbery's bookshop, he could find several of the classics which Lamb mourned. Lamb's dirge was premature. The end of the eighteenth century was not fairies' finest hour, but neither was it solemn midnight. In 1823 *Grimms' German Popular Stories* would be translated. By 1850 fairy tales would be welcomed with a more open imagination. In *Hard Times* (1854), Dickens would preach that the "dictates of common life," not fairy and old wives' tales, were rubbish and lumber. Children shut out from the world of the marvelous, he taught, would grow up stunted not only mentally but often morally and physically. Unable to sympathize with the plights of others and understanding little about life, they would become, as Dickens described them, Gradgrinds and Smallweeds.[41]

CHAPTER THREE

Play and Recreation: Biographies of Animals and the Inanimate

In surveying the cultural accomplishments of her century, Priscilla Wakefield wrote in 1794 that "the spirit of improvement" which distinguished "this enlightened age" shined "in nothing more conspicuous than education." "Persons of genius," she stated, had "not thought it unworthy of their talents to compose books purposely for the instruction of the infant mind" and to invent "various ingenious methods of facilitating the acquisition of knowledge." One of the most ingenious and entertaining forms invented to instruct young children was the fictional biography of animals and inanimate objects. First written for children in the 1780s, it was the only kind of novel generally thought acceptable for children late in the eighteenth century.[1]

In *Some Thoughts,* Locke suggested several ways by which the education of young children could be improved. Instead of "the ordinary Method of Education; and that is, The Charging of Children's Memories, upon all Occasions, with *Rules,* and Precepts," which they did not understand and which they soon forgot, Locke urged that education should become "a Play and Recreation." Children, he thought, could be "cozen'd into a Knowledge of the Letters." To this end he suggested "*Play-things*" which would make learning more fun and lamented the scarcity of books "fit to *engage* the liking of Children." Engaging children's liking, however, required skill, for their minds, Locke said, were naturally disposed to wander. Although they were attracted by novelty, they were "as soon satiated with it" and had "almost their whole Delight in Change and Variety." "A lasting continued Attention," Locke thought, was "one of the hardest Tasks" which could be imposed upon them, and he urged teachers and by implication publishers to unite amusement with instruction and make their lessons or books as "agreeable as possible."[2]

Locke's suggestions on how to make learning more appealing to children determined the structure of John Newbery's "engaging books." Although he did teach, as the *Guardian of Education* emphasized, "religion, loyalty, and good morals," Newbery often seemed more concerned with the manner in which he cozened children into knowledge than with the particular lesson taught. With bubbles rising from that effervescent cheerfulness which Dr. Johnson said ranked him "among those whose presence never gives pain, and whom all receive with fondness," Newbery happily followed Locke's hints for uniting instruction with amusement. Bound by boards covered with Dutch floral paper, Newbery's books were visually appealing. Just as a proper early religious education became associated with a sense-awakening walk through nature that led to nature's God, so Newbery packaged learning as a healthy walk through books blossoming with many curiosities. Filled with games, rhymes, fables, moral tales, humorous stories, precepts, alphabets, and woodcuts, most of his books were amusing miscellanies built on Locke's belief that children's "Natural Temper" disposed "their Minds to wander." Instead of trying to "fix" children's attention by "Rebukes and Corrections," he appealed to their delight in change and led their "fleeting Thoughts" on a merry chase, making their lessons as agreeably sugared as possible. *The Twelfth-Day Gift* (1767), more accurately subtitled *the Grand Exhibition,* was a typical Newbery miscellany, consisting of short amusing and instructive stories and anecdotes selected from other books. Read by the members of "the *Bettering* Society," a select group of "young Gentlemen and Ladies" who met at "the most noble Marquis of SETSTAR'S," these excerpts were "registered at their Request, by their old Friend Mr. NEWBERY." As the society's ex officio secretary, the old friend seems to have influenced its members' reading. Tom Trinculo, for example, "an Urchin just breeched," read an account of Mrs. Williams and her plum cake from "Mr. *Newbery's* New Year's Gift," while Patty Summers read a piece from his "*Lilliputian Magazine,*"

Miss Sprightly, verse from "Poems published by Mr. *Newbery* for Children of Six Feet high," and Miss Jobson, a fable from "Mr. *Newbery's Valentine Gift.*" "YOU KNOW WHO" gaily explained away the narrative confusion of *The Fairing* (1765), writing: "A Metaphor is a Kind of Simile, and a Simile a Kind of Description, and a Description a Kind of Picture; and as all of them are intended to convey to the Mind an Image of the Things they represent, what they represent must be like themselves; and as this Book is a Metaphor, or Simile, or Description, or Picture of a Fair, it must be like a Fair, and like nothing else; that is, it must be one entire Whole, but a whole Heap of Confusion."[3]

In *A Little Pretty Pocket-Book,* Newbery carefully followed Locke's suggestions. The book was, the title page stated, "Intended for the Instruction and Amusement of Little Master TOMMY, and Pretty Miss POLLY." Headed "Delectando monemus" and translated as "*Instruction with Delight,*" the frontispiece showed a mother sitting in a chair before a fireplace and reading to a small boy and girl. The text itself began with an eight-page essay addressed to parents, explaining how to make children "*Strong, Hardy, Healthy, Virtuous, Wise,* and *Happy.*" The ideas in the essay were taken for the most part from the first portion of *Some Thoughts.* Instead of hiding his borrowings, however, Newbery called attention to them, referring on the second page of the essay to "the great Mr. *Locke.*" Not only did he accept Locke's ideas on education, but he also realized that *A Little Pretty Pocket-Book* would stand a better chance of success if it were clearly identified with Locke. The essay was followed by the two letters from Jack the Giant-Killer in which Jack explained to Tommy and Polly how to use the ball and pincushion which he had sent them. "Fit to *engage* the liking of Children," these "*Play-Things*" attempted to make good behavior habitual by associating it with amusement. Aware that his audience included the adults who paid sixpence for *A Little Pretty Pocket-Book* or eight pence for the book and a ball or pincushion and who eventually read the book to children, Newbery appealed to them, as he did throughout his books. In an "Advertisement" attached to Jack's letter to Polly, for example, he noted playfully, "A worthy and learned Gentleman, whose Presence I am at this time honoured with, intimates, that it would not be amiss for some Gentlemen to keep a *Ball* contrived in this Manner, and some Ladies a *Pincushion,* by way of Diary, especially if they are often apt to forget themselves."[4]

The next section of the *Pocket-Book,* entitled "A Little Song-Book," was the longest and most important, as Newbery linked learning to "Play and Recreation" and tried to cozen children "into a Knowledge of the Letters." In the "Song-Book," Newbery explained, "a *New Attempt*" was made "to teach Children the Use of the English *Alphabet,* by Way of Diversion." A separate page of the song book was devoted to each capital letter and to each small letter. Each letter was associated with a game, and typically at the top of each page was written "*The great* D *Play,*" "*The little* d *Play,*" "*The great* O *Play,*" and "*The little* o *Play.*" Below the inscriptions were woodcuts showing children playing games. Underneath the woodcuts were the titles of the games and songs, usually quatrains rhyming *a b a b,* which described how the games were played. Under the songs was either an instructive rhyming couplet called "Rule of Life" or another *a b a b* quatrain entitled "MORAL." The rules of life and the morals were not integrally related to the games or the letters with which they appeared. For example, the woodcut under "*The little* p *Play*" showed three boys playing hopscotch. Below the woodcut was the rhyme: "First make with Chalk an oblong Square, / With wide Partitions here and there; / Then to the first a *Tile* convey; / Hop in—then kick the *Tile* away." The rule of life which followed this verse had nothing to do with hopscotch or little *p.* "Strive with good Sense to stock your Mind," it taught, "And to that Sense be Virtue join'd." Thus, as children learned the alphabet, they learned games, and instruction became not a task but play. Moreover, they were painlessly introduced to instructive maxims. At "*The great* R *Play,*" however, Newbery, perhaps appealing to children's "delight in Change and Variety," discontinued both the games and the morals or rules of life. He continued the woodcuts, but from "*great* R" to "*little* w" he printed the alphabetical verses of the nursery rhyme which began, "Great A, B, C, / And tumble down D, / The Cat's a blind Buff, / And she cannot see." At the bottom of the page, in the place of morals, he printed the lower-case letters that corresponded with the "great" letters mentioned in the rhyme. At "*great* X" the nursery rhyme ended, and a rhymed version of Aesop's fable "The Wolf and the Kid" appeared. At "*little* x" Jack the Giant-Killer returned and wrote Master Tommy and Miss Polly a letter explaining the meaning of the fable. At "*great* Y" and "*great* Z" were two more fables, which Jack dutifully explained at "*little* y" and "*little* z." A fourth and last fable, "Mercury and the Woodman," was printed after the alphabet was complete. On the following page, Jack appeared for the last time and explained its significance.[5]

After the completion of the alphabet, Newbery changed pace and printed two instructive letters accompanied by woodcuts, the first showing a little boy riding in a coach and six and the other depicting a little girl with a watch in her hand. The letters themselves described the good fortune which accrued to well-behaved children. The little boy, it seems, had "learned his Book" to such a "surprising Degree" and had been so "dutiful to his Parents and obliging to his Playmates" that "every Body loved him." "His learning and Behaviour" had become habitual and were appropriately rewarded. He was soon esteemed by "the greatest People" and raised "from a mean State of Life to a Coach and Six, in which he rides to this Day." Likewise, the "little Lady," who was "no bigger than your pretty Miss," behaved so well that everybody loved her. She was dutiful to her parents and governess and kind to her school friends. She learned "her Book to Admiration," worked "well with her Needle," and was so modest and "engaging in Company" that "my Lady *Meanwell*" gave her a "fine Gold Watch."[6]

The remainder of the *Pocket-Book* appealed to children's "Delight in Change and Variety." Following the letters was a unit of four pages. On these were depicted a little boy and girl "*at Prayers,*" "*asking a Blessing of their Parents,*" "*reading,*" and "*bestowing their Charity.*" On each of the four pages was a simple instructive commentary. "All good Boys and Girls," Newbery wrote under the woodcut showing children giving alms, "when they see a poor Man, or Woman, or Child, in Want, will give them either Money, or such Meat and Drink as they have to spare; which makes the whole World love them." Next followed eight pages of "A Poetical Description of The Four Seasons." The descriptions were in rhyming couplets, and each season was accompanied by an appropriate woodcut. A twelve-line poem, "Time's Address to Plutus and Cupid," came next. In the poem, Time pointed out that he measured "vital space" and dealt "out Years to human Race." Yet, he warned, mortals had grown heedless and had forgotten the value of time. Last,

Newbery included a list of forty-five "Select Proverbs For the Use of Children." Despite the title, the proverbs were not particularly select, or at least not necessarily selected for children, and included such maxims as "After Supper walk a Mile," "Faint Heart never won fair Lady," "Good Wine needs no Bush," "It's a good Wife that never grumbles," "Set a Knave to catch a Knave," and "The Weakest goes to the Wall."[7]

Jack the Giant-Killer's ball and pincushion were not the only Lockean "*Play-Things*" Newbery stocked in 1744. In *Some Thoughts,* Locke suggested several "Contrivances" which could be used "*to teach Children to read,* whilst they thought they were only Playing." Dibstones, dice, and a polygon with twenty-four or thirty-two sides, he thought, could be adapted to make "*Learning a Sport.*" To this end, Newbery sold "A Sett of Fifty Six Squares, with CUTS, and DIRECTIONS for playing with them." Advertised in *The Penny London Morning Advertiser* on 21 March 1744 and for weeks thereafter, the device, which cost but a shilling, Newbery stated, had been "newly invented for the Use of CHILDREN." With little or no assistance, it taught, he claimed, preschool children to spell, read, write, add, and "make Figures" and was "so contrived as to yield as much Entertainment as any of their Play Games usually do." The "whole," he explained, was created "upon the plan of the Learned Mr. LOCKE, who in his excellent Treatise of Education hath the following Words on this Method of teaching Children. 'Thus Children may be cozen'd into a Knowledge of the Letters, be taught to read, without perceiving it to be any thing but a Sport, and play themselves into that which others are whipp'd for.'"[8]

In 1773, Thomas Carnan, Newbery's stepson, published Master Michel Angelo's *Juvenile Sports*, written, in fact, by Richard Johnson. In the introduction, young Michel described how his father had played him into a knowledge of his letters, using a set of squares which probably closely resembled those Newbery advertised in 1744. One evening, Michel recounted, his father "brought home with him a set of square cards." He had purchased these at a bookseller's for only a shilling, although they were obviously "worth their weight in gold." Michel's father removed twenty-four cards from the set. Each card was devoted to a separate letter of the alphabet, and on it were printed a capital letter and a corresponding small letter. Michel's father promised him some plums if he would learn the vowels. The boy accomplished the task in a day and rapidly progressed through the consonants to words of one syllable. Shrewdly Michel's father made learning a game rather than a chore. "I was the more eager in the pursuit of this infant knowledge," Michel explained, "as I was made to believe it was rather an indulgence than a compulsion." After Michel had mastered the initial twenty-four cards, he proceeded to the other thirty-two on which were printed the numbers, the italic alphabet, "besides a great number of moral sentiments."

One day, after he had become thoroughly familiar with the squares, Michel found "*the Royal Primer*" lying on the table. He picked it up and tried to read it. The primer had, of course, been left on the table by his father. "My father," he explained, "seeing I catched at the bait, told me, with a great deal of good humour, that he would now no longer amuse me with baubles, such as those little squares, but that for the future I should learn to read like a man, and study books proper for the purpose; that, if I made haste, and got through that book, he would then furnish me with others, all beautifully bound in gilt paper." Before the end of the year, Michel said, he could read all the lessons in the *Royal Primer*, adding, "I hope I shall not appear vain, when I say, that my memory was remarkably strong; and I was the darling of all the good old ladies in the parish, for the elegant manner in which I read the common service of the church."[9]

In 1756 Newbery published *A Little Lottery-Book For Children: Containing A 'new' Method of 'playing' them into a Knowledge of the Letters, Figures, Etc.* More a plaything than a volume, the *Lottery-Book* was cheaper than the squares and cost only threepence. Like the squares, however, it was inspired by Locke. In the introduction, Newbery repeated Locke's view that children's natural temper disposed their minds to wander. "It would be much easier to teach Children to read," Newbery wrote, "were it possible to fix their Attention on the Letters, 'til they were become familiar; but the Infant Mind, ever charmed with new Objects, roves so precipitately from One Thing to another, that no adequate Idea can be formed, for the Impression fleets with the Object, and the Remembrance of it is no more." "The Business of this little Book," he stressed, was "to prevent in some Measure that Precipitancy, and to fix the Minds of Children 'till they have acquired a proper Knowledge of the Letters and Figures." In the book a child was directed to stick a pin through one side of a page at a letter printed on the reverse side. When he turned the page, the child saw not only the letter but also on the opposite leaf a picture of two objects whose names were printed and which began with the letter the pin had stuck. Thus by sticking a pin through a page on which a monkey and a magpie appeared, the child pierced the letter *N*. When the page was turned, the child saw *N* and on the opposite page pictures of a nightingale and a negro. The process of looking at the letter and at the pictures and reading the latter's names aloud would, Newbery thought, eventually fix the letter in the child's mind.

Besides inspiring the general plan of mixing amusement with instruction in *A Little Lottery-Book,* Locke may have inspired the title and the principles of the games to which the book gave rise. The polygon with the twenty-four or thirty-two sides which he recommended as a plaything was, Locke wrote, modeled after that used in the Royal-Oak Lottery. Letters, he suggested, could be pasted on the sides of the polygon, and adults could play with it in the presence of a child, laying small wagers on "who shall first throw an A or B." This would attract the child, make him eager to play, and encourage him to learn his letters. Although his lottery game differed greatly from Locke's Royal-Oak polygon, Newbery seems to have envisioned, as Locke had, that small bets could be made, for example, on whether one was able to stick an *A* or *B* or who could identify a particular letter. As Locke had warned parents against cards and dice, "those dangerous Temptations and incroaching Wasters of useful Time," so Newbery was slightly uneasy with the gambling aspect of his new method of playing children into knowledge. Consequently, he prefaced his book with a letter from Peter Prudence, Secretary to the Court of Common Sense. In the letter, Peter stressed the dangers of serious gaming and the benefits of Newbery's play. "Whereas Gaming has been represented to us as one of the greatest Evils that ever crept into Society," Peter wrote,

> and stands indicted in this Court for being the principal Source and Cause of Lying, Cursing, Swearing, Sabbath-breaking, Stealing, picking of Pockets, and cutting of Throats, to the Ruin of Families in Multitudes too great to be mentioned; we have for many Years past made it a stand-

> ing Rule and Order, that no Man should be suspected of having the least Share of common Sense or common Honesty that followed any such Practice. But a Scheme and Petition having been presented to us in Favour of a certain Game, by which the Old and the Young, the Rich and the Poor, the Gentle and the Simple, may learn to read or otherwise divert themselves, so as to make Time sit easy upon their Hands, we have taken the same into our Consideration, and do hereby revoke our former Order, so far as that this said Scheme of a Game for the Benefit of Mankind may be carried into Execution. And we do order and strictly command the *Blacks* at *White's* and all Gamesters and Gamblers whatever, to play at this Game and no other, and that the Stakes they play for be either Apples, Oranges, Almonds, Raisins, or Gingerbread Nuts.[10]

In playing children into a knowledge of their letters, books like *A Little Lottery-Book* often imitated the games adults played. As Newbery was uncomfortable with the gaming aspect of the *Lottery-Book,* so authors of children's books were usually sensitive to the possibility of weaving bad habits into children's natures. Even as a parlor game, fortune-telling was thought bad for children because it taught them to put their trust in superstition or chance rather than in God. In *Anecdotes of A Boarding-School* (1784), when a gypsy found several young ladies unaccompanied by Mrs. Steward, their teacher, and offered to tell fortunes for sixpence, Miss Creedless, significantly, was the first to have her fortune told. Because her fortune turned out to be a "black catalogue of evils," Miss Brownlow was upset. In contrast, good little Martha Beauchamp refused to have anything to do with the gypsy. Trying to restore Miss Brownlow's perspective, Martha asked rhetorically how she could "make herself uneasy for what this wicked woman" told her. When Mrs. Steward discovered that some of her charges had listened to a fortune-teller, she was more critical than Martha. She was sorry, she said, "to find any of you pay so little regard to what is right, as to think of consulting a GIPSY to know what shall befal you in futurity; as if any body could possibly tell that but God above."[11]

Despite criticism like that of Mrs. Steward, fortune-telling was fun, and the renowned Doctor Hurlothrumbo, "chief Magician and Astrologer to the King of the Cuckows," used it to cozen children into knowledge of their letters. Doctor Hurlothrumbo was not an ordinary seer, and his *Fortune Teller. By Which Young Gentlemen and Ladies may easily fortel a Variety of important Events that will happen both to Themselves and their Acquaintance* (1769) was a book of which Peter Prudence and the Court of Common Sense would have approved. Although he was "an astrologer by title," Doctor Hurlothrumbo explained, he had "as little veneration for the irrevocable decrees of the planets as for the humble predictions of the scattered and inoffensive grounds at the bottom of a coffee-cup." Instead, he was a "plain philosopher" and his magic was "purely natural." He was able to foretell events, he said, from the knowledge he had of "their disposition and behaviour." In the *Fortune-Teller,* Doctor Hurlothrumbo invented a game like that in the *Lottery-Book* in which children were encouraged to learn the letters by sticking pins through them. A page of the *Fortune-Teller* was divided into squares. All the capital and small letters of the alphabet were printed within the squares. When a child stuck a pin through this page from the opposite side of the leaf, he pierced a square. When he turned the page, he saw the square and the letter he had stuck. For each letter there was a page of "prophetic Verses," and the child who wanted "to peep into the Regions of Futurity" could turn to the page appropriate to the letter and "study the Mysteries of Fortune." Unlike the bleak and often immoral mysteries which gypsies revealed, these mysteries were highly instructive, for Doctor Hurlothrumbo was a moral fortune-teller, expert in higher truths as well as in the alphabet. Each fortune which the doctor revealed was in verse. The rhymes associated with capital letters were admonitory, while those associated with small letters were celebratory. Thus, the child who stuck "great K" learned not to be a knave. "*Knave,* play your part, and pilfer while you may," the child read, "Nor let a fear your nimble hands delay; / But know, at last, stern judgment will pursue / Thy lawless theft, and justice have its due." The fortune of the child who pierced "little p" was happier. "*Pious* without deceit," it read, "your righteous mind, / Esteem and love from God and man shall find." The child who stuck "little c" learned that if he were "*Courteous* to all, and yet to all sincere," his virtue would to all his "name endear."[12]

Pierre Coste said that John Locke "was born for the good of mankind." In the world of children's books in mid-eighteenth century, Locke seems to have been born not simply for the general good of mankind but for the particular good of John Newbery. In *Some Thoughts,* Locke suggested that children be given "some Notions of this our planetary World." Sometime after 1698, Locke, who was then living with Sir Francis and Lady Masham, composed *The Elements of Natural Philosophy* for twelve-year-old Frank Masham. Divided into twelve chapters, two of which focused on Locke's own view of the senses and theory of understanding, the essay explained Newton's cosmology in simple language for children. First published in 1720, the essay was buried in *A Collection Of Several Pieces Of Mr. John Locke, Never before printed, or not extant in his Works.* In 1750 it was duly reprinted as a small pamphlet. Then in 1761, like a butterfly flying free from its cocoon after a long sleep, it sprang forth brightly as *The Newtonian System Of Philosophy Adapted to the Capacities of young GENTLEMEN and LADIES, and familiarized and made entertaining by Objects with which they are intimately acquainted: Being The Substance of Six Lectures read to the Lilliputian Society, By Tom Telescope, A.M. And collected and methodized for the Benefit of the Youth of these Kingdoms, By their old Friend, Mr. NEWBERY, in St. Paul's Church Yard.*[13]

Locke provided the matter and the method of *The Newtonian System.* Although Tom Telescope turned the twelve chapters of *The Elements of Natural Philosophy* into six lectures, he did not neglect any of the topics covered by the essay. Tom's second lecture, for example, "*Of The* Universe, *and particularly of the* Solar System," combined Locke's second and third chapters "Of The Universe" and "Of the Solar System," while his fifth lecture, "*Of* Minerals, Vegetables, *and* Animals," was taken from Locke's eighth, ninth, and tenth chapters: "Of several Sorts of Earth, Stone, Metals, Minerals, and other Fossils," "Of Vegetables or Plants," and "Of Animals." In contrast to *The Elements,* which was written concisely to provide information but not amusement, Tom's lectures were "fit to *engage* the liking of Children." To insure that learning was not boring, Newbery added play to Locke's explanation of Newton's cosmology. Locke's statement that "Motion is so well known by the sight and touch, that to use words to give a clearer idea of it would be in vain" became Tom's more familiar "As to Motion, I may save myself and you the trouble of explaining that; for every boy who can whip his top knows what motion is as well as his master." Newbery often advertised

Frontispeice .—

Lecture on Matter & Motion.

THE
NEWTONIAN SYSTEM
OF
PHILOSOPHY

Adapted to the Capacities of young GENTLEMEN and LADIES, and familiarized and made entertaining by Objects with which they are intimately acquainted:

BEING

The Subſtance of SIX LECTURES read to the LILLIPUTIAN SOCIETY,

By TOM TELESCOPE, A.M.

And collected and methodized for the Benefit of the Youth of theſe Kingdoms,

By their old Friend Mr. NEWBERY, in *St. Paul's Church Yard*;

Who has alſo added Variety of Copper-Plate Cuts, to illuſtrate and confirm the Doctrines advanced.

O Lord, how manifold are thy Works! In Wiſdom haſt thou made them all, the Earth is full of thy Riches.

Young Men and Maidens, Old Men and Children, praiſe the Lord. PSALMS.

LONDON,

Printed for J. NEWBERY, at the BIBLE and SUN, in *St. Paul's Church Yard.* 1761.

From Tom Telescope, *The Newtonian System of Philosophy.* By permission of the British Library.

The Newtonian System as *The Philosophy of Tops and Balls,* a title which linked learning with toys; if the book itself were not one of the playthings which Locke said should be used to make learning fun, and it may well have been a plaything, the explanations it provided for Newton's ideas and the experiments it described to test them often used children's toys. Children, or children and their parents and teachers, could move easily from the book to the playroom. To explain a lunar eclipse, Tom, for example, set up an experiment children could duplicate. He used an orange as the sun, a cricket ball as the earth, and a top as the moon.[14]

If children's minds were naturally disposed to wander, they must have found Tom's lectures appealing, for he constantly digressed. When his explanation of the nature of the earth flagged slightly, he gave a short account of the world's most famous volcanoes. Newbery's favorite device for providing "Change and Variety," however, was the interruption. Itself a kind of wandering, the interruption allowed him to vary and enliven the lectures. Sometimes he introduced members of Tom's audience and topics which he thought beneficial but which often had little to do with natural philosophy. On other occasions he supplemented and expanded the information found in *The Elements.* In describing motion, Locke wrote, "No parcel of matter can give itself either motion or rest; and therefore a body at rest will remain so eternally, except some external cause puts it in motion; and a body in motion will move eternally, unless some external cause stops it." In his lecture, Tom quoted Locke's statement almost word for word. However, an interruption by Tom Wilson provided the occasion for explaining the principle in greater and homier detail suitable for children. "*No body or part of matter can give itself either motion or rest,*" Tom declared, "and therefore a body at rest will remain so for ever, unless it be put in motion by some external cause; and a body in motion will move for ever, unless some external cause stops it."

> This seemed so absurd to Master *Wilson,* that he burst into a loud laugh. What, says he, shall any body tell me that my hoop or my top will run for ever, when I know by daily experience that they drop of themselves without being touched by any body? At which our little Philosopher was angry, and having commanded silence, Don't expose your ignorance, *Tom Wilson,* for the sake of a laugh, says he: if you intend to go

through my course of Philosophy, and to make yourself acquainted with the nature of things, you must prepare to hear what is more extraordinary than this. When you say that nothing touched the top or the hoop, you forget their friction or rubbing against the ground they run upon, and the resistance they meet with from the air in their course, which is very considerable though it has escaped your notice. Somewhat too might be said on the gravity and attraction between the top or the hoop, and the earth; but *that* you are not yet able to comprehend, and therefore we shall proceed in our Lecture.[15]

By the sixth lecture on the senses and the understanding, in which Tom as a thoroughgoing Lockean taught his audience that "all our ideas . . . were obtained either by *sensation* or *reflection,*" he had made a believer of and silenced doubting Thomas Wilson. His discussions, however, of "*Boys Philosophy*" had become celebrated, and this final lecture at the Marquis of Setstar's drew a mixed audience of adults and children, commoners and nobility. One of the hardest tasks to be imposed on children, Locke wrote, was a "lasting and continued Attention." Although Tom Wilson now listened carefully to the lectures, Sir Harry, a young baronet attending his first lecture, was unaccustomed to devoting continued attention to anybody or any instruction. Consequently, when Tom began to speak on the sense of smell, Sir Harry interrupted him. Typically, Newbery used the interruption to change the tone and add variety to his course in natural philosophy. Playfully he criticized the manners of the fashionable world and, by implication, the manners of those members of the middle class who aped their betters. In the process he taught children simple lessons on politeness and paying attention. Tom "had scarcely spoke three words," Newbery wrote,

before he was interrupted by Sir *Harry;* he therefore stopt for some time, and then began again; but the tongue of the young Baronet silenced him, and he stood, without speaking, a considerable time. On this, the company looked at each other, and the Marquis bade him go on. My Dear, says the Marchioness, how can you expect this young Gentleman to read a long Lecture, when you know that Sir *Harry,* who loves to hear himself talk of all things, has not the patience to support so much taciturnity! Why, Madame, says the Ambassador of *Bantam* (Who came in with the Marquis) I thought we had all been assembled to hear the Lecture. That was indeed the intention of our Meeting says the Marchioness; but I hope your Excellency knows the polite world better, than to expect people should be so old fashioned as to behave, on these occasions, with any sort of good manners or decorum. In my country, says the Ambassador, all the company keep a profound silence at these meetings. It may be so, replied the Marchioness; but, I assure your Excellency, it is not the custom here. Why, Sir, I have been often interrupted in the middle of a fine air, at an Oratorio, by a Gentleman's whistling an Hornpipe; and at the Rehearsal at St. *Paul's,* it is no uncommon thing to hear both Gentlemen and Ladies laugh louder than the organ. Hush, Madame, says the Marquis, if your friends and neighbours are fools, you ought not to expose them, and especially to foreigners. Take care, while you condemn this unpolite behaviour in others, that you don't run into it yourself. *Politeness* is the art of being always agreeable in company; it can therefore seldom deal in *sarcasm* or *irony;* because it should never do any thing to abridge the happiness of others; and you see, my Dear, you have made Sir *Harry* uneasy, for he blushes. The company laughed at Sir *Harry,* who joined them, and being determined to hold his tongue, our Philosopher thus proceeded."[16]

While Newbery the practical publisher adapted Locke's suggestions for making learning a recreation as the basis of his books, other writers were influenced more by Locke's theory of the association of ideas. This theory played an important part in fictional biography for children and its influence reached the form from two sources: one direct from educational writings and children's books and the other roundabout from prose fiction. Fictional biography of animals and inanimate objects first became popular in the 1750s. In 1749 someone, perhaps Tobias Smollett, published *The History and Adventures of an Atom.* After the beginning, however, the biographical ingredient of the book was neglected as the author concentrated on political satire. And the first "pure" fictional biography seems to have been Francis Coventry's *The History of Pompey the Little: Or, The Life and Adventures of A Lap-Dog* (third edition, 1752). Dedicated to Henry Fielding, *Pompey the Little* was the offspring both of Fielding's play *The Life and Death of Tom Thumb the Great* and his sprawling novels *Tom Jones* and *Joseph Andrews,* which it resembled structurally. Although he did not formulate a theory of the ridiculous like Fielding, Coventry similarly believed in the medicinal effects of light satire. "To convey instruction in a pleasant manner," he wrote, "and mix entertainment with it, is certainly a commendable undertaking, perhaps more likely to be attended with success than graver precepts." In the 1780s, when fictional biographies for children began appearing, more emphasis was put on conveying instruction than entertaining, and animals' lives invariably illustrated graver precepts.

Pompey's life provided the narrative frame on which Coventry hung observations on English society. The son of Phyllis, the "favourite little bitch" of a "*fille de joye*" in Bologna, Pompey was carried to England by a traveling nobleman and presented to Lady Tempest. Although Pompey's own experiences were not uninteresting, for he "had seldom less than two or three amours at a time with *bitches of the highest fashion*" (during his stay with Lady Tempest), Coventry focused primarily on the adventures of Pompey's owners. At various times, Pompey belonged to an ale-house keeper's daughter, a half-pay captain, Mrs. Pincushion a milliner, Mr. Rhymer a poet, a Cambridge student, and a blind beggar who took him to Bath. When he was "gathered to the lap-dogs of antiquity," a monument was raised over his remains. Taking an apologetic biographical view, Coventry wrote: "Far be it from us to deny, that in the first part of his life he gave himself an unlimited freedom in his amours, and was extravagantly licentious, not to say debauched, in his morals; but whoever considers that he was born in the house of an *Italian* courtesan, that he made the grand tour with a young gentleman of fortune, and afterwards lived near two years with a lady of quality, will have more reason to wonder that his morals were not entirely corrupted, than that they were a little tainted." "As to religion," Coventry continued, "we must ingenuously confess that he had none; in which respect he had the honour to bear an exact resemblance to all the well-bred people of the present age, who have long since discarded religion, as a needless and troublesome invention, calculated only to make people wise, virtuous, and unfashionable."[17]

From Newbery, writers of children's books learned the importance of novelty, and his followers came to think amusement an essential ingredient in their books. With rare exception, *Goody Two-Shoes,* for example, Newbery's books resembled the "heap of Confusion" of *The Fairing.* Although Coventry did not directly influence writers of children's

From Tommy Trapwit, *Be Merry and Wise.*
Copyright Bodleian Library Oxford.

books, *Pompey the Little* helped make the fictional biography of animals a popular form. Providing a flexible narrative structure, it was ideally suited to children's books. While ordering confusion, it gave writers freedom to move swiftly from one topic or scene to another. Moreover, the form appealed to readers' delight in novelty at the same time it provided books with structure enough so that they did not, as Newbery's works often did, resemble tenuously connected fragments.

Part of the attraction of fictional biography to writers of children's books was its apparent foundation in Lockean psychological truth. Despite the overarching unity which the biographical structure provided, the novels were often wildly episodic. Moving rapidly from one subject or level of society to another, they appeared related, if not by ideas, at least by ways of life "not at all of kin." As a result, the "extravagant" motion of their narratives could be seen as a metaphoric depiction of the eccentric workings of the association of ideas within the mind. "Wrong Combinations of Ideas," Chambers's *Cyclopaedia* stated in explaining association of ideas, was "the Foundation of the greatest" and almost "all the Errors in the World." Inserting a ridiculous debate on the immortality of the soul into *Pompey,* Coventry explained his narrative *non sequitur* by asserting that "nothing is more common on the stage, than to suspend the curiosity of an audience in the most interesting scenes of a play, and *relieve* them (as it is called) with a dance of ghosts, or furies, or other out-landish beings."[18] Although Coventry broke the narrative flow of his book only to invigorate readers' attentions, his dance of ghosts could be interpreted as an unconscious illustration of Locke's theory of the association of ideas. And despite Coventry's not paying lip service to Lockean psychology, the book should be seen as anticipating Sterne's conscious use of the association of ideas as the theoretical basis for the eccentric ramblings of *Tristram Shandy* and the bitter-sweet jaunting of *A Sentimental Journey.* With the publication of *Tristram Shandy,* episodic novels whose narratives were based on the association of ideas immediately became fashionable.

Prose fiction describing the lives of inanimate objects was more popular and more successful than that describing the lives of animals. The best of these was Charles Johnson's *Chrysal; or, the Adventures of a Guinea. Wherein are exhibited Views of several striking Scenes, with Curious and inter-*

esting Anecdotes of the most Noted Persons in every Rank of Life, whose Hands it passed through in America, England, Holland, Germany, and Portugal. First published in 1760, the year after *Tristram Shandy* began to appear, *Chrysal* was a Shandyesque work, purporting to be the records of an eccentric alchemist. Like *Tristram, Chrysal* grew haphazardly throughout the 1760s as more and more of the alchemist's papers turned up in accordance with public demand. By the sixth edition in 1768, the book had doubled its original size. The "spirit" of an "incorruptible mass" refined by the alchemist, Chrysal had begun its history in order to prepare the alchemist "for the reception and proper use of that *grand secret.*" Filled with historical, moral, sentimental, and bawdy episodes and a circus-like cast of characters, the novel was a remarkable miscellany, not unworthy of Sterne himself. Unfortunately for posterity, just before "*the mystick birth*" when the "*philosophick king*" would arise "*in all the glory of the morning*" and reveal "the consummation of human knowledge," Chrysal praised the alchemist for having listened to his long history without eating, even though, Chrysal said, he must have smelled the hot ox-cheek cooking in a nearby shop. "O doleful and deplorable event," the alchemist moaned, "never to be told without wailing; never to be read without tears. Just as the spirit had arrived at this most interesting point, human weakness, unable to surpress the impulse of internal vapour, which the mention of the fatal ox-cheek set in motion, in my empty bowels, by the longing it raised in my stomach, emitted an explosion that filled the room with a fetid steam.–The spirit started at the unpardonable offence to his purity; and looking at me with ineffable contempt, indignation, and abhorrence, vanished from my sight, without deigning a word more."[19]

Chrysal was the most original of the biographies of inanimate objects, all of which were more or less Shandyesque. In the second rank was Thomas Bridges's *The Adventures of a Bank-Note* (1770–1771). This book was more clearly derived from Sterne, and the Bank-Note even declared that he was "very glad" he had not gone to France, for, he stated, he would "have given a very poor account" after "Tristram Shandy." By the 1780s Sterne had come to be recognized as the creator of fiction based on Locke's theory of association. "Chance," the author of *The Adventures of a Hackney Coach* wrote, "put into my hand an old worn-out pen of Yorick's." "'This Pen,' whispered my Genius," he continued, "'may do wonders yet;—whip out your knife,—put it in repair;—if this world presents a blank of ingenuity, take a trip to that of invention! You are certain of the Prize of Fame, while you brandish this renowned Talisman!'" Unfortunately, reviewers did not agree with the author's Genius. "Prithee come hither honest grave-digger, and cover up *Yorick's skull,*" the *Monthly Review* exclaimed, "the flies have blown on it.—Cover it up!—*Maggots* and all!"[20]

By the 1780s fictional biography had become commonplace. For a form whose appeal relied heavily on wit and originality, this was fatal. In a critique of *The Adventures of a Rupee,* the *Critical Review* observed, "this mode of making up a book, and styling it the Adventures of a Cat, a Dog, a Monkey, a Hackney-coach, a Louse, a Shilling, a Rupee, or—any thing else is grown so fashionable, that few months pass which do not bring one of them under our inspection." Although the form was "almost exhausted," it did provide, the journal wearily wrote, "a better entertainment than cards and dice, during the long evenings of the Christmas holydays."[21]

By the end of the century, the deterioration of fictional biography into scandalous and nonsensical memoirs threatened the reputation of biography itself. According to William Roberts in 1792, "a greater rage for biography" had never existed "than at the present moment." However, the form was being "discredited," he thought, because it was "rendered a vehicle for profligate examples, or the purposes of scandal and abuse." In exasperation, Roberts outlined the narrative of a biography which he thought captured the spirit of contemporary fictional biography. "The heads and particulars of the life of an ass might run as follows," he wrote:

> How he was born in an obscure village in Yorkshire, and was christened Jack. How his youth was spent in play, etc. How he became very wild as he came to years of discretion. How he formed some bad connexions, and saw many troubles. How he ran away with a young gipsy wench. How he came up to London, and found many rich relations. How he forsook the gipsy wench, and carried about a market-girl to all the public places. How he made a great noise, and kicked up a great dust. How he took part in many dirty occupations. How he changed sides like the

Vicar of Bray. How he became callous to all correction. How successful he was in haranguing the populace, and commanding attention. How he was loaded with more employment than he could bear. How he raised his hopes to the Woolsack. How he was promised a Stall for his brother, and the Order of Thistle for himself; and how he was turned out of place without any provision. How he was bribed to hold his tongue by a lady in the straw. How he lay in clover for three years. How he grew very amorous, and how the Queen's Zebra was talked of. How he was bought and sold by people in power. How he put on a lion's skin, and grew very formidable. How he turned tail on being pulled by the ears. How he sat upon thorns. How he was turned out of place, fell again into obscurity, died, and left all he possessed among his natural children.[22]

If, however, fictional biography seemed imaginatively played out, at best offering adults only dry intellectual provender, it was not found unsuitable for children's books. Besides unifying Newbery's episodic narratives while appealing to children's love of novelty, the form seemed safer than the novel. Novels, as has been pointed out, were condemned by educators because they taught "false views of human life" and were addressed more to the imagination than to the understanding. Since fictional biography was founded upon or seemed to reflect the association of ideas, it appeared psychologically truer than the novel. Moreover, since the form was masked as biography, educators seem to have thought that it appealed more to the understanding than the ordinary novel. Finally, fictional biography offered educators an attractive alternative, not only to the novel but to the fairy tale. Consequently, when Mary Ann Kilner's *The Adventures of a Pincushion* (1784) was published, the *Critical Review* hailed the event as "a favourable prospect for the succeeding age." Similarly, the *Monthly Review* celebrated the appearance of the *Pincushion* as the harbinger of glad tidings for the world of children's books, noting that in "this age of universal improvement in all operations both of the head and hand," the "manufacture of *first* books for children" came "in for its share of the general advantage." Happily, the journal stated, "the little volumes of the nursery" were "no longer filled with the nonsensical fables of witches, hobgoblins, and Jack the Giantkiller, which formerly disgraced even the *Children's* libraries." "Experience hath convinced us," the *Monthly Review* concluded, "that truth and nature are not only more intelligible to the infant mind, but may be rendered more interesting and entertaining, than the absurd fictions with which our grandmothers used to burthen the heads, and distort the imaginations of the little pupils whom they undertook to instruct."[23]

After Newbery's death in 1767, his relatives opened separate publishing houses. By the 1780s many publishers paid special attention to children's books, but no single publisher was able to dominate the trade as Newbery had done. The man who published the most original books was John Marshall at 4 Aldermary Churchyard. Not only was his list large, but it was he who popularized fictional biography for children. According to Marshall, such books were not "absurd fictions" which distorted "imaginations" but were, if not in fact at least in spirit, true. In an advertisement inserted in the first part of *A Father's Advice to His Son* (1784), Marshall defended and publicized his fictional biographies. In response to his son's asking if "reading all those little books we buy of Mr. *Marshall,* can be of any use to us," Mr. Goodwin answered that although some were "foolish enough," many were "very instructive" and "well worthy your most serious attention." If James followed "all the good advice" found in them, he would, Mr. Goodwin assured him, like a good Lockean, be "one of the best boys in the world, and consequently, in time, one of the best men." Pressing further, James asked how the books could "be of any service, or teach us any thing," since they were "only *make-believe* stories." Although they were "very entertaining," the boy continued, he thought they would teach "a great deal better if they were true." "Do you think that *peg-tops,* and *pincushions,* and *mice,* can talk," he asked, "or that there ever were such things as *giants* and *fairies*?" Besides calling attention to the publisher's best fictional biographies, these questions enabled Marshall to separate fictional biography from fairy tales and to explain that the appeal of fictional biography to the imagination did not undermine but strengthened the understanding.

After saying that he would not have James "fancy" that "those things" were "true," Mr. Goodwin declared emphatically that "the little books about *giants* and *fairies*" were "generally such nonsense, that I would not wish you to spend a moment's time in looking at them." Still, he stated, even they sometimes gave good advice; not all children, he reminded James, were fond of reading and "many would never be persuaded to read at all, if it were not for the sake of learning pretty stories." The best of the pretty stories, however, were fictional biographies, which unlike fairy tales were true in all but name. In fairy tales, all laws of probability were often suspended, but fictional biographies for the most part violated only one law. Once the anthropomorphism of a mouse or pincushion was established, the story followed simply and logically. The mouse or pincushion was usually more a reporter than an actor. Ogres and fairy godmothers neither threatened nor protected fictional biography's human characters. Instead, such characters lived conventional lives, never dancing until midnight in glass slippers or climbing bean stalks to regain the family fortune. "If, therefore for the sake of entertaining their little readers," Mr. Goodwin told James, "they *make believe* that a *mouse,* a *peg-top,* or any other inanimate thing, or dumb creature, can speak and tell what they have seen and heard; though the *mouse,* or *top,* could *not* in earnest speak; that is no reason that the events they are *made believe* to tell did not really happen; or if they have not exactly, yet things so like them have, that we may very well fancy them true."[24]

"One of the prettiest and most instructive books that can be found for very young readers," Mrs. Trimmer wrote in 1802, was *The Life and Perambulation of a Mouse* (1783). There could be "but few infant readers," she thought, who were unacquainted with "the Adventures of *Little Nimble,*" for it was a book which "Mothers and even Grandmothers" could "read with interest and pleasure." In her *Thoughts On The Education of Daughters* (1787), Mary Wollstonecraft singled it out in suggesting that books about animals were particularly suitable for young children. "Animals," she wrote, "are the first objects which catch their attention; and I think little stories about them would not only amuse but instruct at the same time, and have the best effect in forming the temper and cultivating the good dispositions of the heart. There are many little books which have this tendency. One in particular I recollect: The Perambulations of a Mouse."[25]

Written by Dorothy Kilner, *Perambulation of a Mouse* was one of the best fictional biographies for children published in the eighteenth century. It was "the only impossible autobiography," Charlotte Yonge recalled, that "we ever really relished." The story began with the narrator's

From Dorothy Kilner, *The Life and Perambulation of a Mouse.*
By permission of the British Library.

genially explaining that she had been a member of a party which had been snowbound at Meadow Hall. To pass the time, each individual present agreed to tell the history of her life. Having retired to her room, the narrator sighed aloud that her life would "be insipid and unentertaining to others." "'Then write mine, which may be more diverting,' said a little squeaking voice." After an initial surprise, Dorothy Kilner agreed. However, before she wrote the mouse's life, she carefully assured her young readers "that, *in earnest,* I never heard a mouse speak in all my life; and only wrote the following narrative as being far more entertaining, and not less instructive, than my own life would have been."[26]

Like earlier fictional biographies, the *Perambulation* resembled a miscellany. Ranging broadly across society like *Pompey the Little,* its bent was not bawdy but didactic, as each episode drove home a moral and educational truth. Locke stressed, for example, the importance of instilling "noble and manly Steadiness" in children. As "a good preparation to meet more real Dangers," he thought children should be taught to overcome "vain Terrors," particularly irrational fears of harmless animals. To the accompaniment of shrieks from a little girl who cried "out as if violently hurt" when she saw them, Nimble and his three siblings, Longtail, Softdown, and Brighteyes, scurried into the narrative to provide the occasion for a short lesson on irrational fears of animals. "It is certainly foolish to be afraid of *any* thing," the girl's mother sternly lectured her, "unless it threatens us with immediate danger; but to pretend to be so at a *Mouse,* and such like inoffensive things, is a degree of weakness that I can by no means suffer any of my children to indulge." Such irrational fears, she warned, if not corrected in childhood often led to "very disagreeable accidents."[27]

The events witnessed by Nimble served as lessons, and Nimble's life itself was written to "instruct and improve." In teaching him and his brothers how to find food, their mother had told them "upon no account, for no temptation whatever, to return frequently to the same place." Paying little attention to their mother's good advice, they stole sugar from the same closet for over a week until Softdown was caught in a trap and then crushed on the hearth by John the footman. Later, Brighteyes and Nimble themselves were trapped by two boys, who tied a string to Brighteyes' tail and teased the cat with him. Although the cat eventually ate Brighteyes, Nimble escaped when the boys' father interrupted their fun, whipped them for torturing animals, and lectured them on "the Custom of Tormenting and Killing of Beasts."[28]

After Brighteyes' death, Nimble and Longtail pushed onto the open road. Among the rustic inhabitants of a humble cottage, they and young readers learned the importance of being "well contented" with one's station in life and that true happiness depended not upon wealth but upon temper. Unfortunately, the lesson was not deeply impressed upon them, for after having lived comfortably in a barn for seven months, they grew vaguely discontented and, setting out again, immediately plunged into trouble and were separated by a cat. "We ought to have been contented when we were at peace," Nimble said, "and should have considered that if we had not every thing we could wish for, we had every thing that was *necessary;* and the life of a mouse was never designed for *perfect* happiness." Missing Longtail's companionship, Nimble asked Dorothy Kilner to help him find his brother. "At this moment" though, a servant entered the room and, Dorothy Kilner wrote, Nimble jumped from her table, ran into a hole, and was not heard from again. Should he or any other mouse, she promised, "ever again favour me so far with their confidence, as to instruct me with their history, I will certainly communicate it with all possible speed to my little readers."[29]

Happily for little readers and luckily for Nimble, Dorothy Kilner later rescued him from a jar of Turkish figs into which he had fallen while looking for a meal. Once resuscitated, he filled a second volume with his adventures. After having been frightened by the servant, he had left Meadow Hall and had been caught in a snowstorm. In danger of freezing to death, he had been scooped up in a handful of snow by a boy making snowballs. Luckily the snowball in which he suddenly found himself was thrown into a warm barn and, after melting free, he climbed into the pocket of a coat. Later John the coachman put the coat on and wore it into the servants' quarters of a gentleman's house. Here Nimble was once more privy to edifying discussions of topics like contentment, honesty, behavior at public school, and the loss of character. Although he searched the house thoroughly, he was unable to find Longtail and, giving up his efforts, he contrived his return to Meadow Hall "concealed in the middle of a floor-cloth." After almost dying amid the Turkish figs, Nimble decided to end his roving, and he passed the rest of his life in a "large green-flowered tin cannister" which Dorothy Kilner furnished him. Like a good teacher, Dorothy Kilner concluded her book by urging "little readers . . . to follow all the good advice the *Mouse*" gave them and warned them "to shun all those vices and follies, the practice of which renders children so *contemptible* and *wicked.*"[30]

Perambulation of a Mouse was better than the other children's biographies of animals published during the late eighteenth and early nineteenth centuries. Some, like *Memoirs of Dick, the Little Poney* (1800) and *The Dog of Knowledge; or, Memoirs of Bob, the Spotted Terrier* (1803), appear to have been written for both children and adults. As a result, their narratives were too sophisticated for children and too silly for adults. Others, like Kendall's *The Sparrow* (1798) focused on a single topic and lacked the breadth of the *Perambulation.* Much of Dorothy Kilner's success stemmed from her design "to instruct and improve."[31] Ranging far beyond the limitations of a single issue like cruelty to animals, the various episodes in Nimble's life each contributed to a large educational whole.

In a review of *The Life and Adventures of a Fly* (1789), the *Guardian of Education* stated in 1803 that "Every thing, animate or inanimate, may, by means of reflection and ingenuity, be made subservient to moral instruction." Unfortunately, "in this book, as in many others of modern date," the *Guardian* judged, "humanity towards animals is carried to an extreme." Toward the very end of the eighteenth century, the concerns discussed in biographies of animals became increasingly limited. Instead of ranging over a wide moral and educational spectrum, such books concentrated on cruelty to animals. In great part, this narrowness reflected the spirit of the age, as animals were being sentimentalized throughout English literature. In former times, Mrs. Trimmer wrote disparagingly, "Animals were made use of in an *emblematical way*"; now they were "elevated to the rank of *human beings,* they are our *fellow creatures,* our *equals* if not *superiors in virtue.*" Although sentimentalization of the kind found in *Keeper's Travels* was fine for living animals, it was not good for fictional biography. Activities such as floating kittens on wood chips in tubs and making waves until they were swept overboard and drowned, slitting puppies' ears, spinning cockchafers on pins, and putting a cat on an iron plate over a chafing dish of hot charcoal in order to watch it "dance" did not evoke a great variety of reactions, least of all the gentle humor which contributed to the success of the *Perambulation.* Consequently, like all narrow propaganda, the form became artistically moribund.[32]

Unlike animals, inanimate objects do not readily lend themselves to the sentimental. Rarely are campaigns launched for the rights of pincushions or didactic treatises written on man's inhumanity to peg-tops. As a result, children's fictional biographies of inanimate things did not deteriorate so rapidly as biographies of animals. Since the publication of *Adventures of an Atom,* satire had been an important ingredient in such biographies for adults. Writers of children's books, however, thought satire undermined proper behavior, and as the sentimental became the unacknowledged enemy of the biography of animals, so satire became the acknowledged enemy of biographies of inanimate objects. "To exhibit their superiors in a ridiculous view," Mary Ann Kilner wrote in the preface to *The Adventures of a Pincushion,* "is not the proper method to engage the youthful mind to respect. To represent their equals as the objects of contemptuous mirth, is by no means favourable to the interest of good-nature. And to treat the characters of their inferiors with levity, the Author thought was inconsistent with the sacred rights of humanity. Circumscribed therefore to the narrow boundaries of simple narrative, it has been the design of the following pages, carefully to avoid exciting any wrong impression, and, by sometimes blending *instruction* with *amusement,* to make it the more easily retained."[33]

Despite these restrictions, *The Adventures of a Pincushion* was among the best of the children's biographies of inanimate objects. Mary Ann Kilner began this book with the conventional disclaimer that the *Adventures* were only "*making believe.*" Little readers, she explained were to understand the tale "in the same manner" as when they were "at play" and called themselves "gentlemen, and ladies" although they knew they were "only little boys or girls." Containing adventures which were witnessed or experienced by the pincushion and from which appropriate lessons were drawn, the book was, like all other children's fictional biographies, a miscellany of instructive stories. The pincushion itself was stitched together by ten-year-old Martha Airy, in whose home it learned the virtues of orderliness, paying attention to trifles, governing one's tongue, and heeding constructive criticism. After being given to Eliza Meekly, the pincushion traveled to a small boarding school where Eliza was a pupil and which was run by Mrs. Stanley, a clergyman's widow, who took in six girls in order to support herself and her two sisters. After overhearing several instructive moral tales, the pincushion was accidentally dropped on the floor, where it was wedged under the foot of a bookcase and soon forgotten. This, however, was actually a fortunate fall, for here the pincushion began its history. "Long have I remained in this dull state of obscurity and confinement," the pincushion recounted, "unable to make known my distress, as I want the power of articulation: at least my language can be only understood to things inanimate as myself. A pen, however, which fell down near me, engaged to present these memoirs to the world." The unhappy period which the "heroine" spent under the bookcase not only provided young readers with the memoirs themselves but also with a subject for instructive reflection. "And here," the pincushion declared, "let me take this opportunity to suggest a useful hint to my young readers, which, as my inactive situation allowed me sufficient time for reflection, I had frequently to reason the force of: namely, that although I fretted and fumed every day at my unfortunate condition, I never found it was at all improved by it, or that my ill-humour in the least degree made me happier, or assisted my escape . . . though *children* are not *Pincushions,* yet they will find, that whenever they are fretful and dissatisfied, they will be unhappy, and never succeed in any thing they undertake."[34]

Mrs. Stanley having moved her school to another house, the pincushion was later found by Jacob, a workman who presented it to his friend Mother Trusty, a charwoman. In turn, she gave it to Jenny, her grandchild. Now living on a radically different level of society, the pincushion discovered the virtues of frugality and a good disposition and the dangers of petulance, pride, and selfishness. From Jenny the pincushion was stolen by Polly Chaunt, a cobbler's daughter, who gave it to Hannah Mindful, the daughter of a small farmer. Taken by Hannah's vain cousin Sally Flaunt to the annual party for the local peasantry at nearby Oakly Hall, the pincushion was left behind. After a short stay in the servants' quarters, it ended up in the poultry yard where, as it declared, "I was pecked at alternately by almost all the fouls, till at last I was tossed by a bantam hen, under a little water tub, where I have lain ever since." Even this final indignity was instructive, and sadly wise the pincushion explained, "the catastrophe which has thus reduced me, was entirely unexpected: and should teach them, that no seeming security can guard from those accidents, which may in a moment reduce the prospect of affluence to a state of poverty and distress; and therefore it is a mark of *folly,* as well as *meanness,* to be proud of those distinctions, which are at all times precarious in enjoyment, and uncertain in possession."[35]

Since the *Pincushion* was "designed chiefly for the use of young Ladies," Mary Ann Kilner wrote a companion piece for boys, *Memoirs of a Peg-Top* (1783). Although "the laws of justice, probity, and truth" were "of *general* obligation," by consulting the "*different amusements* . . . in which each sex were more particularly concerned," her books, she hoped, would be more interesting to children and would have "in consequence, a better chance for approbation." Like the pincushion, the peg-top recounted experiences pregnant with instruction. Sold by a shop in Piccadilly, the peg-top was bought by Henry, who lived in a "handsome building in *St. James's—square.*" Carried by Henry to boarding school, the top soon had the raw material for his memoirs, which were written when he was left on a writing desk. Although structurally and thematically similar to the *Pincushion,* the tone of the *Memoirs* was less polite, as Mary Ann Kilner tried to suit it to the rougher world of boys. On one occasion, for example, when the schoolboys decided to go to a nearby village to buy sweets, Frank Powel bet Tom Swallowell sixpence that he would be unable to walk blindfolded to the turnpike. Having already spent his allowance, Tom accepted the bet so that he would have money for cheesecakes. On the way Will Grinmore said he would give Tom some custard if he would eat it blindfolded. An incorrigible glutton, Tom agreed, but instead of custard, he swallowed a spicier blend of custard and cow dung. Tearing off his blindfold, which lost him the bet, Tom mistakenly struck Frank. Frank paid him back in kind and "left battered *Tom* rolling in the middle of the road, to taste a second time, the cow-dung." The incident was not without its moral, however, for Frank received a lecture from his father "on the warmth of your temper." "To forgive an injury, and overlook an affront," Mr. Powel said, "is a much higher instance of *true* magnanimity, than to obtain the most complete conquest."[36]

The success of these two children's biographies led Marshall to bring out a third, *The Adventures of a Whipping-Top. Illustrated with Stories of many Bad Boys, who themselves deserve Whipping, and of some Good Boys, who deserve Plum-Cakes* (1784), probably written by Dorothy Kilner. Bearing a closer resemblance to Newbery's books, the *Whipping-Top* was more playful, albeit still as instructive as the *Pincushion* and the *Peg-Top*.[37] Deprecating "the custom of writers in general . . . to give a minute detail of all the little circumstances of the birth of their heroes and heroines, when and where, at what o'clock, whether it was on a cloudy or sunshiny day, or a moonlight night, what particular planet they were born under, and many other such nonsensical things," the whipping-top humbly said he would pass over these vanities, although, he assured readers, he could boast of his birth "being the heart of a fine piece of oak." On a trip from Yorkshire, Farmer Clodd bought the top in London as a present for his son Roger. On the way north, like small boys anticipating the pleasures of manhood, the top reflected "on the joy of coming into life: and like them, not dreaming of the crosses and troubles" he would "be exposed to." After a whip had been made for him from the skin of the largest eel in the orchard pond, the top spun in and out of the lives and hands of many owners. From his aristocratic birth, he eventually descended to a lowly and instructive end as a plaything for a dog named Keeper. Thrown into the river one day when Keeper was "surly" and refused to fetch, the top was carried "a great way" until he stopped in the shallows behind a large stone not far from a town in Yorkshire. Here the top wrote his history and pitched it into the current, addressed to "Mr. *Marshall,* Printer to the King of *Lilliput,* at No. 4, *Aldermary Church-Yard.*" Here beside the stream, the top lamented, "I shall lay and rot" unless rescued by a kind boy or washed downstream by a flood. If he were "saved," he wrote, he promised to describe more of his adventures and make a "six-penny book, as big as the Memoirs of a Peg-Top; which is sold at the *Lilliputian* Warehouse, *Aldermary Church-Yard.*" [38]

The top's autobiography reached Mr. Marshall and was published, al-

WHIPPING-TOP. 23

ſoon able to ſtand alone; till *Roger* being called by his father, left me to reel, till the force of gravity took me off my toe, and pinned me by the ſide to the floor.

This puts me in mind, that when naughty boys have been correcled for ſome time they continue very good,

B 4 till

From Dorothy Kilner, *The Adventures of a Whipping-Top.*
By permission of the British Library.

though the printer to the king of Lilliput suspected that there might be a teaspoon or two of the tall tale in the account. Accordingly, he addressed young readers at the conclusion of the book. How, he wondered, was the top able to find pen, paper, and ink near a stream in the wilds of Yorkshire? Even if the top did find these writing instruments, how was it able to make use of them without hands? Even more suspiciously, the top never mentioned being taught to read and write. And if it could write, Mr. Marshall asked, why didn't the top write "some good little boy" and ask him to rescue him? As a result of such unanswerable questions, Mr. Marshall said he was forced to conclude "that some one who wishes well to all little boys and girls in *Great-Britain*" had written the story in the character of a whipping top. Still, Mr. Marshall added, there was much "to be gathered from this little history," for "it pictures out the characteristics of good and bad boys and girls, shewing how amiable is carefulness even in play-things; and how those who mind neither their books or marbles are to be despised."[39]

There were many more successful children's biographies of inanimate objects than there were successful biographies of animals. Where the latter got stuck in the seriously sentimental, the former was able to smile with humorous seriousness. Among the best of these was *The Adventures of a Silver Penny* (1790). Stamped from the same metal as *Chrysal*, the penny was born in a mine in Peru. After having lived through many exotic experiences in all quarters of the globe over a period of three hundred years, the penny was presented to the British Museum by the noted numismatist Dr. Solander, who, among other things, had accompanied Captain Cook around the world. "Farewell, my dear pretty readers," the aging penny concluded from his comfortable exhibition case, "may you so live in this life as to merit an abode in that MUSEUM, where no cares can reach us, no infirmities torment us,no revolutions of states or empires disturb our tranquillity, but where every thing will be changed into endless love, harmony, and joy!" Smiles cracked across the pages of these biographies. Unlike comparable accounts of animals, even the second-rate tale of an inanimate object tickled the funny bone several times during its course of adventures. Thus, the spare hero of *The History of a Pin* (1798) stated that he started life with advantages over his contemporaries, for, as he recounted, he had "a good head." Moreover, he had benefited from a good education, having been "prepared by various hands with *sharp* qualities."[40]

Fictional biography of animals and inanimate objects did not die at the beginning of the nineteenth century. Throughout the century memoirs or adventures of old wigs, rings, cotton bales, velvet cushions, Bibles, arm chairs, and ostrich feathers were published. Most of these, however, could be dismissed as the *Monthly Review* dismissed *The Adventures of a Watch* in 1789. "Finding it impossible," the journal wrote, "to convey to our Readers any idea of this very clumsy piece of workmanship, we take the liberty of presenting them with the repetition of a well-known anecdote:—A scribbling French Abbé being asked by Count d'Argenson, why he had published a certain book which had given offence, attempted to justify himself by the following answer,—*Monsieur, il faut que je vive.* On which the Count immediately observed, —*Je n'en vois pas la necessité.*" The golden age of fictional biography had ended, and the products of the nineteenth century now lie, like the silver penny, covered with dust, albeit not in the British Museum but the British Library. For a short period, however, the form, heated in the educational kiln of Locke and Newbery, had "in great measure supplied . . . children with lessons of instruction in the agreeable forms of tales" and, as Mrs. Trimmer put it, had "a decided claim" to "a conspicious place in the *Infant Libraries.*"[41]

CHAPTER FOUR

Peddling books and Insensible Impressions: Chapbooks and Religious Tracts

According to Harvey Darton, the chapbook "as a common vendible piece of reading-matter" came into existence in the seventeenth century. Printed unbound on rough rag paper, chapbooks cost from a penny to a shilling. Those which children were probably most familiar with in the mid-eighteenth century measured four by six inches and were twelve or twenty-four pages long and cost a penny or two each. Illustrated by crude woodcuts, they were distributed throughout Britain by hawkers who bought them in bulk. Through chapbooks, most young readers were introduced to fairy tales. But like that odd crew which sailed with the Bellman in search of the Snark, the matter of chapbooks was diverse. They were written not only for children but also for the lower classes, and some of the credit for the rapid spread of literacy in Britain in the eighteenth century can be attributed to their wide distribution and broad popularity. In the first years of the eighteenth century the chapbook was the most easily obtainable kind of children's book in Britain. After visiting his eight-year-old godson, Richard Steele wrote in *The Tatler* in 1709 that the boy had once been "a very great Historian in *Aesop's* Fables." However deciding that they were not true, he had "turned his Studies" to chapbooks, and for the past year had studied the "Lives and Adventures of *Don Bellianis* of *Greece, Guy* of *Warwick,* the *Seven Champions,* and other Historians of that Age." The young scholar, Steele recounted, could "tell you the Mismanagements of *John Hickathrift,* find Fault with the passionate Temper in *Bevis* of *Southampton,* and

THE

HISTORY

OF

GUY, Earl of Warwick.

Printed and Sold in Aldermary Church-Yard, London

From *The History of Guy, Earl of Warwick.*
By permission of the British Library.

loved *St. George* for being the Champion of *England;* and by this Means, had his Thoughts insensibly moulded into the Notions of Discretion, Virtue, and Honour." About the same time that Steele's godson was blossoming as a medievalist, Uncle Toby was spending his "pocket money" on Guy, Earl of Warwick, Parismus and Parismenus, Valentine and Orson, and the Seven Champions of England. If Locke's contention that childhood reading made the man is correct, then Uncle Toby also had his thoughts insensibly molded into virtuous notions. Subsequently, Widow Wadman's vigorous seige failed, not because Toby had a disabling wound, but because, like the Earl of Warwick, he was a true "Knight of Chivalry" pledged to an ideal Phillis, alongside whom even "Helen the pride of all Greece, might seem as a Black-a-Moor."[1]

The golden day of Guy and the fair Phillis occurred at the winter solstice. Although the sun has not completely set on the chapbook empire today, the popularity of traditional chapbooks had waned considerably by the end of the eighteenth century—so much so that in the 1805 version of *The Prelude,* Wordsworth wrote: "Oh! give us once again the Wishing-Cap / Of Fortunatus, and the invisible Coat / Of Jack the Giant-killer, Robin Hood, / And Sabra in the Forest with St. George!" In his nostalgia, Wordsworth was almost alone. Those "mighty workmen" who had "the art / To manage books, and things, and make them work / Gently on infant minds"—Lockean educators—had forbidden traditional chapbooks.[2] In lamenting children's books past, however, Wordsworth ignored the present. If he had looked carefully, he would have discovered that although the contents of chapbooks had changed, the form itself had remained popular. Moreover, large numbers of chapbooks were being written each year for the same public for whom they had been published early in the eighteenth century: children and members of the lower classes.

The subjects of traditional chapbooks were varied. Many like *Guy of Warwick* were romances and typically described the fantastic adventures of such mighty warriors as Bevis of Southampton "in slaying Giants, Monsters, Wild Beasts." Among the most widely circulated romances were *Valentine and Orson; Hector, Prince of Troy; The Life and Death of St. George; the Noble Champion of England;* and *The Seven Champions of Christendom.* Akin to romances were the accounts of "The Merry Life and Mad Exploits" of highwaymen and adventurers like the heroes of *Johnny Armstrong of Westmoreland, Captain James Hind,* and *George Barnwell.* Other chapbooks celebrated the more domesticatable virtues of the protagonists of *Sir Richard Whittington* and *The Blind Beggar of Bethnal Green* while some, like *The History of Moll Flanders* and *The Surprising Life, And Most Strange Adventures of Robinson Crusoe,* outlined the sensational parts of popular early eighteenth-century novels.[3]

Old wives' tales and tall English legends about Tom Thumb, Thomas Hickathrift, and Jack Horner filled many other chapbooks. Generally these tales were a great deal more lively than the nineteenth-century versions with which we are now familiar. Little Jack Horner, for example, was not the shy lad presently associated with corners and Christmas pie. Only thirteen inches high, he was a rambunctious scalawag who delighted in upsetting his master's cookmaid "lusty Joan." Having started a fight by pulling bread and throwing it into a pan for a sop, he darted under Joan's skirts after she crowned him with a basting ladle. There he "strait way" seized "by both his hands her beauty spot." When he gnawed her by the knees until she bled, Joan, somewhat understandably, "pist upon his head, and put out both his eyes." Not daunted by rough treatment, this little David tripped Joan over and bit her "by the arse" until the female Goliath promised never to correct him again.[4]

In the early eighteenth century, all chapmen sold "adult" chapbooks. Doe-eyed Margy Meanwell demurely reading before the grate was just as likely to be studying the amorous adventures of "Wanton Tom," who got sixteen maids with child in as many weeks, as she was the inspirational swashbuckling of Guy of Warwick or the Seven Champions of Christendom. Although he did not discuss it with his godfather, Steele's young expert on chapbooks had probably seen a copy of *The Friar and the Boy.* In this tale, a young shepherd who suffered cruelly from the malicious persecution of his stepmother was given his choice of three fabulous gifts by an "aged man" with whom he generously shared his meager lunch. First the boy asked for "a cunning bow" with which to shoot birds. Second he requested a "pipe" whose "sweet and pleasant sound" would make people unable to "forbear" from dancing when they heard it. Last, he asked that whenever his stepmother glared at him scornfully "her bum might then let go, and crack like roaring thunder." The old

And when he in the Kitchen came,
She him would overlook.
She oftentimes would play her part,
And call him creeping cur ;
This vex'd Jack Horner to the heart,
He could not bear with her.
Upon a certain day young Jack
A ſlice of bread did take,
And threw it in the dripping pan,
That he a ſop might make.
So ſoon as ſhe ſame did ſee,
It put her in a rage,
And with the baſting ladle ſhe
Jack Horner did engage.

She gave him knocks upon the crown,
So hard and ſtuck ſo faſt,
That he at length did tumble down,
And gaſping lay at laſt.
If tho' he did at firſt retreat,
He ſoon return'd again.

From *The History of Jack Horner.* By permission of the British Library.

man agreed to these playful requests, and for the rest of the chapbook, the stepmother's "tail" cacophonously resembled "a horn."[5]

Many of the chapbooks which found their way into children's hands at the beginning of the century were anecdotal miscellanies. Written before Freud, when laughter rather than meaningful silence accompanied the shattering of maidenheads and chamberpots, the stories contained in these chapbooks were often broad. In *Poets Jest, or Mirth in Abundance* appeared the typical story of a man who called "his wife Warming Pan." Forcing her to "go to-bed first in the winter, to warm his place," he selfishly "turned her into the cold" when he came to bed. "At which," the poet recounted, "she was vexed, and vowed revenge. So to-bed she went one night, and very orderly beshit it. -By-and-by he comes, bidding her turn out, which she did. Then he jumped into bed, and lying down was so besmeared, that you might have smelt him down stairs. On which he cried out You have beshit the bed; but she answered, It was only a cinder dropped from the Warming Pan."[6]

The simple countryman was the butt of many chapbook stories. In *The History of Four Kings,* for example, Tom Hodge and his schoolfellows agreed after a long day of pranks that "every one should tell a Tale, let a Fart, or call his Father a Cuckold." Since he was the oldest, Tom began with a merry tale. A famous town in Lancashire being "strangely pestered" with witches, the queen, he said, "sent some judges down to arraign and try them." The news of this court spread throughout the shire and reached the ears of "a husbandman living near forty miles from the place." Believing the judges had come "to tell the folks whether they were Witches or no," the countryman "resolved to go to be satisfied in himself, for he was possessed with a fear that he was a witch, because he had a whart grew on his neck, which he imagined to be a dug." His wife "who had a friend in a corner" encouraged him and, dressing him in "his best leathren suit and broad brim'd hat," sent him on his way. When he arrived in the town where the court sat, the husbandman pushed his way into the court itself. The urgency on his face drew the attention of the crier. Thinking that the man had evidence to present, the crier bade him come forward, whereupon the countryman asked for a diagnosis of his "whart." "Seeing the simplicity of the man," the crier, Tom recounted, "said, No, no, my friend, I can assure thee

(3)

TALE I.

ONce upon a time when geeſe were ſwine, and birds built neſts in old men's beards, as hereafter they may do in mine, there was a queen in this realm, whoſe name was Elizabeth, and by reaſon that the famous town of Lancaſhire was ſtrangely peſtered with witches the queen ſent ſome judges down to arraign and try

them in order to bring them to Juſtice Now the news of this court being kept

From *The History of Four Kings.* By permission of the British Library.

thou art no witch; thou lookest more like a cuckold than a witch or a conjuror." Reassured, the countryman happily started for home. The next day he was met by his wife "at the town's end." "Well husband," she asked, "what do the gentlemen say? are you a Witch or no? A witch, sweet wife, no," he replied, "they tells a body one looks more like a cuckold than a witch or a conjuror. Why say you so, replied she, I prithee go back and have them taken up for witches; for except they had been so, they would not have known you was a cuckold."[7]

The sensational and the supernatural were stock ingredients of the traditional chapbook. Often they were blended with the bawdy to make a narrative appetizingly salable. From *The Foreign Travels of Sir John Mandeville. Containing, An Account of remote Kingdoms, Countries, Rivers, Castles, etc. Together with a Description of Giants, Pigmies, and various other People of odd Deformities,* readers would most certainly have been intrigued by the descriptions of men with lips so large that they covered their faces when they slept and of the people who had no heads but whose eyes were in their shoulders and mouths in their backs. Even more astounding was the effect heat had on the inhabitants of an island near India. It is "so warm," Mandeville wrote, "that the men's members hang down to their shins." Lest modest travelers avoid the island, Mandeville reassuringly noted that natives "of better breeding" concealed their endowments "by tying them up." Among the more popular chapbooks which leaned heavily on the sensational were *The History of Dr. John Faustus, The History of The Learned Friar Bacon,* and *Bateman's Tragedy.* In this last chapbook, hardhearted Isabella forsook poor Bateman and married a wealthy German. Overcome by despondency, Bateman hid himself in a closet near the bridal chamber; when all in the house had fallen asleep, he crept out and hanged himself before the bedroom door. After the birth of Isabella's child, however, the broken-necked lover was revenged, for a spirit stole Isabella away. On the night she disappeared, the stench of sulphur filled her room, the casement burst, and the townspeople testified that they heard "great cries and shrieks," "a great clap of thunder," and saw "violent flashes of lightning."[8]

Witches and demons were common characters in chapbooks. Often, however, they did not make "frightful" impressions on "the tender Minds of Children" but instead employed their supernatural powers to punish sinners and drive them, if not back on, at least close to the path of virtue. Unfortunately for the late eighteenth-century reputation of chapbooks, many of the sinners reformed by demonic intervention had wallowed in eminently describable sins of the flesh. Moreover, the reformation was not so important as the sensational process by which it was accomplished. Thus, in *The Witch of the Woodlands; Or The Cobler's New Translation,* the focus was not upon the cobbler's translation to a state of grace but upon his unique penance. Before his sufferings this "very merry disposed cobler" used "to swagger, swear, and domineer" and say "He cared not a fart for all the Witches alive; for if he said his prayers in the morning, they had no power over him." This, alas, was shortsighted special pleading, for though the cobbler "served God in the morning, he served the Devil at night; and would seduce the girls by his dissembling tongue." By promising to "marry them on the morrow," he "got three maids with-child" on a single night. Forced by Mother Webb to marry her daughter and then presented with three children on the same day, the cobbler stole away. Sin will out, however, and as this rustic Lothario delectated in thoughts of future conquests, he fell into the clutches of four witches and their three familiars: a wolf, a bear, and a cat. The witches stripped him and, so that he would not escape, set their familiars on him as warders. "The wolf bit him by the throat, the bear by the bum, and the cat by the members." To atone for his past misdeeds, the cobbler was forced to undergo three days of punishments. On the first day the witches changed themselves into dogs and the cobbler into a fox that they chased across the countryside. On the second day the cobbler became a horse that all the witches rode at the same time. On the third day he was an owl. Forced to hoot at noon, he was attacked by scores of birds who plucked out his feathers, broke one of his wings, and pecked his eyes out. Finally, he was transformed into a swan, whose torments the publisher of the chapbook chose to omit. "For his wenching tricks" this seemed "pennance enough." And after making "him kneel down and kiss every one of their fleshly parts," the witches gave him leave to depart. Broken in body and spirit and looking "like one of Pharaoh's lean kine," the poor cobbler became the sport of idle boys and village ruffians. After enduring his misfortunes like Job, the cobbler was

THE

WITCH of the Woodlands;

OR THE

COBLER's New Tranſlation.

Here Robin the Cobler for his former Evils,
Is puniſh'd bad as Fauſtus with his Devils.

Printed and Sold in Aldermary Church
Yard, Bow Lane, London.

From *The Witch of the Woodlands.* By permission of the British Library.

fortuitously befriended by a blind beggar who made him his heir. After serving his master faithfully, the cobbler eventually inherited a fortune of two hundred and fifty pounds. Instead of wasting this treasure on idle pleasure, the cobbler returned to Mother Webb's daughter. After giving ten pounds each to the mothers of his two bastards "for the injury he had done them," he turned the rest over to his wife.[9]

The devil himself was rumored to be the father of Mother Shipton. If there were any doubt on the matter, the baby's appearance swept it away, for the child's body was "long, and very big boned." Its "great goggling sharp, and fiery eyes" burned above an "unproportionable nose, full of crooks, turnings, and red pimples" which gave out "such a light" that her maid did not need "a candle to dress her by." The grotesque appearance of suckling Shipton augured well for her supernatural abilities, for chapbooks were filled with inspired fools. Although he was "an ideot, and followed the plow," Robert Nixon "was in an amazing manner endowed with the spirit of Prophecy." Despite his formidable appearance—he was "a short squab fellow" with "a great head and goggle eyes"—people listened to whatever Nixon said, for he had predicted James II's fleeing the country. Unfortunately, Nixon-following was not particularly rewarding, for he seldom spoke and was "extremely surly." Children in particular were warned to avoid him, for he had "a spite" against them and "would run after and beat 'em" especially "if they made sport of him." Readers of chapbooks coveted Nixon's prophetic gifts, and chapbooks purporting to give keys to "every lawful Question whatsoever" were popular. Usually these books provided insights into fleshly matters. If her lover had a mole on his right arm, a wavering maiden could be sure that he was given to gaming. If, however, he had a mole on the center of his breast with a single black hair curling out of it, he was poetically inclined. Sadly though, if he had a mole on the ankle, he was not marriage material, for he was certain "to act the part of a woman, like Sardanapalus at the spinning wheel."[10]

For haying time or below-stairs harmonizing, there were numerous chapbook miscellanies of songs and poetry, many containing bawdy songs. "The Jolly Tar" from *The Lover's Magazine; or Cupid's Decoy* was typical. Once when he was "Brim full of grogg, this rowling dog" was

(4)

hope will be much delighted with it as myſelf. — By the way, this is not a prophecy of to-day, it is as old as the powder plot: and the ſtory will make it appear, that there is as little impoſture in it as the Jacobites pretend there is in the perſon it ſeems to have an eye to; but whether or no they are both impoſtures or not, I leave it to the Reader to determine.

ROBERT NIXON.

NIXON's

From *Nixon's Cheshire Prophecy.* By permission of the British Library.

suddenly surrounded by "six flashing whores." Not daunted by what mortal male flesh would have considered overwhelming odds, this salty son of Mars and Venus sailed up to one well-rigged galleon and touched off his vocal cannon. "If you will stoop," he crooned, "I'll lash your poop, / Unto my yardarm tackle, / Into your hull I'll shoot my gull, / And all your charms I'll shatter: / There's nought to fear, when gun-rooms clear / Then clear your decks from lumber, / Come open wide for a broadside, / And I'll throw it in like thunder."[11]

During the seventeenth century and early years of the eighteenth century when chapbooks flourished, there had been an undercurrent of criticism. For the most part this came from Calvinists. In *A Little Book For Little Children* (1702), Thomas White advised children to "read no Ballads and foolish Books, but the *Bible,* and the *Plain-mans path way to Heaven.*" After reading "the Court of *Venus,* the *Pallace of Pleasure, Guy of Warwicke, Libbius* and *Arthur, Bevis* of *Hampton,* the wise men of *Goatam, Scroggins* Jeasts, *Fortunatus,*" Henry Crosse concluded in 1603 "that the floudgates of all impietie" were "drawne up, to bring a universall deluge over all holy and godly conversation." There was "no greater meanes," Crosse wrote, "to affright the mind from honestie, than these pedling bookes." The authors of "these idle pernicious bookes" dived "into the bottome of their braine" for "imbossed words, to varnish theyr lyes and fables" so that they would "goe downe without chewing." "One such wanton toye," he warned, "dooth more breed Vice, then twentie godly treatises can induce to *Vertue.*" According to Arthur Dent, books like *Bevis of Southampton, The Court of Venus,* and "The mery Jest of the Friar and the Boy" were "devised by the divel: seene, and allowed by the Pope: Printed in hel: bound up by Hobgoblin" and first published so that "men might be kept from the reading of the scriptures." In *The History of Genesis* (1708), the author preached:

> *Indeed it is a great Blessing of God, That Children in* England *have liberty to read the holy Scriptures, when others abroad are denied it. And yet alas! how often do we see Parents prefer* Tom Thumb, Guy *of* Warwick, Valentine *and* Orson, *or some such foolish Book, before the Book of Life! Let not your Children read these vain Books, profane Ballads, and filthy Songs; for these fill them with wanton Thoughts, and nasty and obscene Discourse. Throw away all fond and amorous Romances, and fabulous Histories of Giants, the bombast Atchieve-*

> *ments of Knight Errantry, and the like; for these imprint false Notions, and irregular Conceits, and fill the Heads of Children with vain, silly and idle Imaginations. Do not think of curing the Diseases of Ignorance with such dangerous Remedies.*[12]

In London in 1673 Francis Kirkman published *The Unlucky Citizen,* supposedly an autobiographical account of the "Misfortunes" he suffered during his first twenty years. The son of a well-to-do merchant who owned property in London, Kirkman was apprenticed to a harsh master. Having broken his indentures, Kirkman rambled about the country like Pompey the Little, meeting many odd characters and having many strange experiences. In the book Kirkman described his childhood reading. Chapbooks, he implied, had influenced his character and were greatly responsible for his leaving his master and the misfortunes he later suffered. When he was young, Kirkman recounted, he could only remember one time when he was the "Master of any money." "Having lately read that famous Book, of the *Fryar and the Boy,* and being hugely pleased with that, as also the excellent History of the *Seven wise Masters of Room,* and having heard great Commendation of *Fortunatus,* I laid out all my money," Kirkman recalled, "for that, and thought I had a great bargain, conceiting that the Lady *Fortune* would one time or other bestow such a Purse upon me as she did on *Fortunatus.*" Kirkman continued,

> Now having read this Book, and being desirous of reading more of that nature, one of my School-fellows lent me *Doctor Faustus,* which also pleased me, especially when he travelled in the Air, saw all the World, and did what he listed; but I was as much troubled when the *Devil* came to fetch him; and the Consideration of that horrible end did so much terrifie me, that I often dreamed of it. The next Book I met with was *Fryar Bacon*, whose pleasant Stories much delighted me: But when I came to Knight Errantry, and reading *Montelion Knight of the Oracle,* and *Ornatus* and *Artesia,* and the Famous *Parismus*; I was contented beyond measure, and (believing all I read to be true) wished my self Squire to one of these Knights: I proceeded on to *Palmerin of England,* and *Amadis de Gaul;* and borrowing one Book of one person, when I had read it my self, I lent it to another, who lent me one of their Books; and thus *robbing* Peter *to pay* Paul, borrowing and lending from one to another, I in time had read

> most of these Histories. All the time I had from School, as *Thursdays* in the Afternoon, and *Saturdays,* I spent in reading these Books; so that I being wholly affected to them, and reading how that *Amadis* and other Knights not knowing their Parents, did in time prove to be Sons of Kings and great Personages; I had such a fond and idle Opinion, that I might in time prove to be some great Person, or at leastwise be Squire to some Knight: And therefore I being asked, What Trade I would be of? first scorned to be of any, hoping that I was not born to so mean a Quality; but upon second thoughts, I resolved to be a Chirurgion, and that for several Reasons; as first, because I often found them mentioned in the Books of Knight Errantry; and secondly, that I might travel, and thereby see all these several Countries of *Constantinople, Trebizond,* and I know not what Places; and then I did judge that if I were a Chirurgion and did travel, and meet with Knights Errant who were wounded; I should be very necessary and useful in dressing and healing their Wounds.

Aware of the reasons why he wanted to be a surgeon, Kirkman's mother, who had little use for chapbooks, scotched the idea. Next he suggested that he become a bookseller. As a bookseller, he thought that he would have much time for reading. His father, however, refused this choice, saying that such a business was unprofitable. His choices having been summarily rejected, Kirkman was apprenticed to the scrivener whose service he later left for an errant wandering life (see note 13).

Despite accounts like those of Kirkman and criticism like that of White, chapbooks were not generally held responsible for the misfortunes of youth or thought a dangerous remedy for the diseases of ignorance before Locke's ideas on education dyed the fabric of society. In *A Catalogue Of The most vendible Books in England* (1657), William London implied that time spent reading chapbooks was wasted. Although he thought people should read more substantial books, he did not condemn chapbooks as morally dangerous. "Too many," he wrote mildly, "idly sit down in the Chaire of Ignorance, travelling by the fire side, with the *Wandering Knight Sr John Mandevil,* or it may be *Bevis of Southhampton,* whilst the Laws of Nations, admirable foundations of Commonwealths, pass undiscovered or dived into." Instead of damning jest books out of hand as immoral, Thomas Fuller praised the therapeutic effects of good humor. "Harmlesse mirth," he wrote in *The Holy State*

(1642), "is the best cordiall against the consumption of the spirits: wherefore Jesting is not unlawfull if it trespasseth not in Quantity, Quality, or Season." According to Sir William Corne-waleys (1600), "all kinds of bookes" were "profitable, except printed Bawdry," which abused youth. Although one had to "beware of beeing familiar with them," there were intellectual and practical uses, he wrote, for reading "Pamphlets, and lying Stories, and News, and two penny Poets." His "custome," he explained, "is to read these, and presently to make use of thē, for they lie in my privy, and when I come thither, and have occasion to imploy it, I read them, halfe a side at once is my ordinary, which when I have read, I use in that kind, that waste paper is most subject too, but to a cleanlier profit." By the last quarter of the eighteenth century, the practicality of Corne-waleys, the tolerance of Fuller, and London's offhand dismissal were found wanting. Educational diagnosticians had looked deeper into the effects of chapbooks, and the few voices that earlier had condemned chapbooks now swelled to a chorus. If the little and almost insensible impressions made on tender infancies had lasting consequences, then what had once been passed off as meaningless or just harmless high spirits could not longer be tolerated as benign. Where a good education was designed, and this included moral education, something more innocent and profitable, Watts stressed, should be invented. This search for something more profitable led parents "in the middling stations of life" to conduct books and didactic moral tales.[13]

After chapbooks had been banished from the nurseries of the "intermediate orders," educational reformers turned their attention to the lower classes, particularly to those being educated in Sunday schools. Earlier in the century these new readers would have constituted a potential market for chapbooks. Now educators tried to steer them to more beneficial reading. Singlehandedly, Mrs. Trimmer, for example, wrote a series of instructive books for Sunday scholars, which she hoped would replace chapbooks and would help shape "good apprentices, and conscientious, faithful servants." "To counteract the pernicious Tendency of immoral Books etc. which have circulated of late Years among the inferior Classes of People," she began *The Family Magazine* in 1788. "Never was there a time," she explained, when reading "was so generally enjoyed in ENGLAND." Unfortunately, she thought, although young servants wanted to read things other than "immoral books and ballads," there were few publications which were suited to their capacities and which afforded "*useful instruction,* and *harmless amusement.*"[14]

In *The Servant's Friend* (1787), a novel-length tract Mrs. Trimmer also wrote to provide proper reading matter for the literate poor, servants were urged to avoid chapbooks. When his cook Betty left to be married, the Reverend Brown hired Susan Clarke as a replacement. Susan had unfortunately worked in a nobleman's family where she had acquired fashionable, and bad, reading habits. When she came to Mr. Brown's, she brought not only a fondness for novels but also a collection of ballads, all of which had been published as chapbooks. Some of these, like "Chevy Chase, the Cobler who lived in a Stall, the Children in the Wood, Black-eyed Susan, and a few others," were "pretty reading." Many, however, were "full of nothing but indecency," and Mrs. Trimmer's hero, Thomas Simkins, was so "ashamed" to read them that "he took the whole parcel and flung them into the fire, saying that his master would not suffer such things in his house." Even the *Children in the Wood* was not beyond Mrs. Trimmer's suspicion. Like a fairy tale, it appealed to the imagination rather than the understanding. Even worse, its dependence on the supernatural was liable, as Doddridge put it, to distract "tender Minds or infringe on those Regards, which are the incommunicable Perogative of the GREAT SUPREAM." Kitty, the house and dairy maid, whom Thomas eventually married, had just such a tender mind. Happily, however, Reverend Brown instructed his servants carefully, and Kitty was not deceived by the story. She did not believe it "could be all true," she explained, for Mr. Brown "had often told her there were no such things as spirits and apparitions." Kitty was lucky to work for Mr. Brown. Not all masters were so conscientious, and servants, Mrs. Trimmer implied, who read chapbooks, even those chapbooks which seemed harmless, risked being led astray.[15]

The French Revolution greatly increased concern over what the lower classes read. Convinced that jacobins were spreading seditious and immoral writings in hopes of fueling a revolution in Britain among the working classes, conservatives devoted much energy to providing safe reading materials. It was not a "time for indolence or indifference," the *Evangelical Magazine* (1795) stated, for "the Lord of Glory and the Prince of Darkness" were "more than usually active." Infidelity "dignified with the high-sounding titles of candour, rationality, and philosophy, assumes a formidable appearance, walking through the earth with gigantic strides, and threatening the destruction of every virtuous principle." "Since the aera of Printing" began, William Roberts wrote, "it seems as if a flood of learning has been progressively spreading over the human mind, checking its wholesome productions, and nourishing the growth of a worthless vegetation." On the side of the Lord of Glory and in hopes of grafting some appleless branches on to the Tree of Knowledge, Hannah More urged her evangelical Anglican friends at Clapham Common to assume "the laborious undertaking" of providing the poor with proper reading materials. "To teach the poor to *read,* without providing them with safe books," she explained, was "a dangerous measure." Prompted by Mrs. More, the Anglicans at Clapham began the enormous task of providing the poor with proper books. Realizing that the lower orders were familiar with chapbooks, that chapbooks were relatively inexpensive to produce, and that a network of peddlers already existed who could distribute chapbooks (the twenty thousand or so "hawkers" who vended "licentious publications" about "our cities, towns, and villages"), the Claphams put their writings into chapbooks and in the process invigorated a form that had fallen out of critical favor.[16]

The Clapham Sect, as they were later known, called their chapbooks the *Cheap Repository Tracts* (1795–1798). During this period over a hundred different tracts were published. Most of these sold for 1½d., 1d., or ½d., and were considerably cheaper if purchased in large numbers. The one-penny tract was usually sixteen or twenty-four pages long and sold, for example, for 4s. 6d. for one hundred, 2s. 6d. for fifty, and 1s. 6d. for twenty-five. The half-penny tract, which was usually eight or twelve pages, sold for 2s. 3d. a hundred, 1s. 3d. for fifty, and 9d. for twenty-five. The *Cheap Repository* was an overwhelming success. In its first year of publication, William Pitt the prime minister, the archbishop of Canterbury, and the bishops of Bristol, Bath and Wells, Chester, Durham, Exeter, Ely, Gloucester, London, Lincoln, Salisbury, and Worcester all lent their considerable prestige to the project by making token donations toward the publication costs.

To aid the distribution of tracts, "very respectable Societies" were formed throughout the country. These circulated the tracts among their members and in local schools and encouraged "Booksellers to supply themselves with them." To promote sales, "Retailers and Hawkers" were given tracts free "in the first instance." Fairs were canvassed and samples were given to the occupants of stalls. With such influential and zealous support from the upper and middle classes contributing to their success, some two million tracts, "besides great numbers in Ireland," were printed in a single year.

The tracts resembled traditional chapbooks, for they were comparable in size and illustrated by similar woodcuts. Conscious efforts to make them "entertaining" had been made, the Claphams explained, so that they would "supplant the corrupt and vicious little books and ballads" which were "so highly mischievous to the Community" and which were sold throughout the country "in the most alluring forms."[17]

There were three types of tracts. To lure readers away from the chapbook miscellanies of improper songs and ballads, the first kind of tract contained poetry. Inevitably, this verse hymned the virtues of sound morality and right religion. *The Carpenter; Or, The Danger of Evil Company* ended on a typically bleak instructive note: "*The Drunkard Murders Child and Wife, / Nor matters it a pin, / Whether he stabs them with his knife, / Or starves them with his gin.*" Tracts of poetry were the weakest kind of tract in the *Cheap Repository. The Contented Cobbler,* for example, was meant to be a happy poem teaching that "*all things work together for good to them that love God.*" However, it is doubtful if many readers would have shared the cobbler's belief that all things worked for the best. Despite being grindingly poor, the cobbler said that he did not envy any man's estate, for he had few needs and no debts. Although she was "neither pretty, / Nor smart, gay, nor witty," his "dear little Bess" was just what he wanted her to be: tidy, clean, and obedient. When she had a miscarriage shortly after marriage, the cobbler consoled her by observing that the child might have "prov'd a curse." Later, when Bess gave birth to triplets and lamented that the children would prove their financial undoing, the cobbler assured her "there's no use to fret and to stew." And "sure I was right," he complacently noted, "For before the next night, / The two eldest took leave and withdrew."[18]

The second kind of chapbook in the *Cheap Repository* was called "Sunday Reading." These were usually Bible stories or simple allegories told in homespun fashion. Implied in all "Sunday Readings" was the futility of consulting the traditional chapbook fortune-telling manual. Instead of putting one's trust in Mother Bunch or a deck of cards, "Sunday Readings" taught the necessity of putting one's "whole trust and confidence" in God. If men profited from the examples in the Bible and forsook their "evil courses, while the mercy of God" allowed them to do so, there would be no need to worry about the immediate future, or more importantly, that "dread hour" when "like the miserable mole, we shall blunder into light with all our dirt upon our heads."[19]

The best and most popular type of tract was the instructive tale. Like the chapbooks Steele's godson read, these "Histories," as they were called, taught discretion, virtue, and honor. Instead of leaping miraculously from the pages of medieval romances or fairy tales, however, the heroes and heroines of the histories trudged wearily from the backbreaking world of the laboring poor. Unlike Sleeping Beauty, the heroine of a tract did not doze in an enchanted castle for a hundred years until she was suddenly awakened by a handsome prince, who after some slight difficulty with his mother who "was of the race of the Ogrees," offered her a throne and a life of joy forever. Instead, like Betty Brown, the St. Giles orange girl who "was born nobody knows where, and bred nobody knows how," she lived in a five-story walk-up, three to a room. By struggling long hours on the London pavements, she was able to eke out a subsistence living. And if she were lucky and met no ogres—not the kind with "long teeth and claws," "a raw head and bloody bones," which ate "little boys and girls," but the avaricious kind which preyed upon the meager incomes of gullible working people—she might save enough so that someday she would be able to give up selling oranges and open a sausage shop at Seven Dials and marry an honest hackney coachman.[20]

Like the heroine of many fairy tales and romantic novels, Madge Blarney, "The Gipsey Girl," had an evil mother. Among a tribe of gypsies in the west of England, Madge's mother was "more daring in wickedness than her companions." "Hardened in iniquity," she "gloried in the number of crimes she had committed." During her "vagrant sinful life," she became the mother of Madge and Ben. When Madge was ten and Ben four, they were sent to beg at a farmhouse. While they stood before the open door, they heard a child in the house say the Lord's Prayer, answer questions from the catechism, and ask her mother's blessing. The next day Madge asked her own mother who made her. When her mother laughed and replied that she did not know, Madge responded that she was "very sorry for it." "The little girl," Madge explained, "where I got the victuals last night said God made her; I wish he had made me, for then I should, perhaps, have been as well off; not obliged to go a-begging in all weathers," but be "nice, and tidy, and clean as she was." The little girl, Madge continued, said that God made her to serve him in honor and truth. Although Madge said she did not know what honor was, she knew what truth was, for, she told her mother, "you have bade me not to tell truth, or you would be catched, so I have always told lies, and many is the blow I have got by people that did not believe me."

The prayers which Madge overheard influenced her, and she began to pray. Sometime later when she saw a village church, she entered and listened to the service. Thereafter, she contrived to attend church regularly. Madge wanted to obtain an honest job, but she did not know how to. Four years then passed, and Madge grew into a young woman. Religion kept her from falling into sinful ways, however. "As one vice naturally led" to another, Madge's "wicked male companions began to take liberties with her." Although she was young, "the good doctrines" which she had learned in church led Madge to "repulse them in so severe a manner" that she became "hateful to the whole gang." What was hateful to the world, however, was loved by God, and Madge's virtue was rewarded. When the gang planned to rob Farmer Thomson and then "silence" him and his family, Madge protested, whereupon her mother clubbed her to the ground. Although Madge was knocked out, not all the ears upon which her protest fell were deaf; one of Farmer Thomson's laborers overheard the quarrel. He warned his master, and a hardy band of neighbors surprised the gypsies when they attacked the farm. The beating Madge received almost killed her. Fortunately, though, she recovered; in gratitude Farmer Thomson offered her a job. She soon became a favorite, and because she was so industrious, her master took in Ben to teach him farming. Madge learned to read, and eventually she and Ben were baptized. The laborer who warned Farmer Thomson

CHEAP REPOSITORY.

MADGE BLARNEY,

The GIPSEY GIRL.

Printed and Sold by JOHN MARSHALL, at the Cheap Repoſitory, No. 17, Queen-Street, Cheapſide, and No. 4, Aldermary Church-Yard, Bow-Lane, London; and may be had of the Bookſellers, Newſmen, and Hawkers in Town and Country.

Great Allowance will be made to Shopkeepers and Hawkers.

PRICE ONE PENNY.

Or 4s. 6d. per 100.—2s. 6d. for 50.—1s. 6d. for 25.

[*Entered at Stationers Hall.*]

From *Madge Blarney, The Gipsey Girl.*

about the robbery inherited a farm and later married Mary, as Madge, who was now reborn in the church, "must be called." Thus, the history concluded, "the gipsey girl became a good wife, a tender mother, and a humane mistress; or more properly comprising all her qualities in a few words, a *good Christian*."[21]

The histories stressed religion. Not only did it satisfy one with his lot in life but it brought tangible rewards. In *The Two Soldiers* Robert Wells and Isaac Clark were granted three-month furloughs to visit relatives. On their way home, they stopped at the Green Dragon, famous for its ale and the meeting place of all the fives-and-skittle players in the county. So famous was the ale, the tract stated, "that it introduced beggary and famine amongst the Wives and Children in all the Neighbouring Cottages." Both Wells and Clark fell under the spell of the Green Dragon's monstrous brew. They became so drunk that they collapsed on the grass and were robbed. The next morning Wells vowed to give up ale and drink water in the future. The sober, religious education he had received as a child contributed to his decision and he urged Clark to follow his lead. Clark refused, adding that he had never bothered to learn the catechism when he was young. Instead, he bragged, he had been a "boy of spirit" who loved boxing, fives-playing, and robbing orchards better than his book. It was too late to change, and he would not, he declared, return to the regiment to be "sneered and jeered at by every one." Despite Wells's warning, Clark went his own way. Bad habits had long been woven into his nature, and he would seek money and pleasure, he said, wherever he could find them. Repentant, Wells was not too proud to ask for food, which farmers gladly gave him. "I love a soldier to my heart, because he fights for my Country," the mistress of one farm told him, "but when I find a Soldier to be a Christian, I love him to my soul, because our Country may stand a better chance to be preserved from the enemy in time of War, if our Soldiers are Christians." Virtue was again rewarded. When Wells returned to his regiment, he was promoted to sergeant. In contrast, Clark was caught in an alehouse after he attempted to rob the post-chaise, and the last Wells saw of him was "with his hands tied behind him, carried off to the County Jail, to take his Trial at the next assizes."[22]

The heroes of the tracts were often better-natured Nixons who could not foresee the future but who did their best to shape it through hard work and right religion. James Stock's father was so poor that the boy was bound out by the parish as an apprentice shoemaker. In contrast, Jack Brown's doting mother irresponsibly lavished money and affection on him. As a result, Jack did not form good habits and, always expecting something for nothing, he paid little attention to his trade, preferring instead to run after blind fiddlers, mountebanks, and ballad singers. From "the idle pastimes of the boy," it was not far "to the destructive vices of the man." While Jack gambolled his way to "Jail Fever," James worked steadily toward his own shop. When he married, it was not to Mr. Thompson's Nancy, the wealthy tanner's daughter and the local "fair Princess Angelica, Lady of the Golden Tower." Although Thompson offered him two hundred pounds with his daughter, Stock refused her because she was an "idle dressy, lass" and instead married penniless Betsy West, who had taken selfless care of her lame and blind mother.[23]

In the histories, the giants and wild beasts against which heroes tilted were the everyday living conditions of poverty and disease and common vices such as gaming, dishonesty, alcoholism, and atheism. Sorrowful Sam, for example, struggled against a nagging wife and the convivial company at the "Tennis-court" without much success until he fell out dead drunk on the highway and was run over by a wagon and lost both his legs. Although Sam's victory over strong drink seems Pyrrhic, for he spent the remaining two years of his life in "great pain and misery," it was nevertheless a victory—if not over a dragon from without, at least a demon from within.[24]

Although no St. George or St. James ever appeared in these dramas to save Sabra or kill a fire-drake, the main characters of these chapbooks were often heroic, albeit not in their martial talents but in their capacity for endurance. According to the Shepherd of Salisbury Plain, God honored poverty by choosing the disciples from among the poor. Consequently, the shepherd thought men should be satisfied with their lots in life, no matter how grim they were. To a gentleman farmer who noticed what a dilapidated cottage the shepherd and his wife and eight children were forced to live in, the shepherd replied stoutheartedly, "the house is very well, Sir, and if the rain did not sometimes beat down upon us through the thatch when we are a bed, I should not desire a better."

When compared, however, to the superhuman endurance of the Lancashire collier girl, the shepherd's tolerance of the cold winter rain was commonplace. Young Mary went down into the coal mines at nine years old. When she was between eleven and twelve, her father was killed in a mining accident. After the mishap her mother went crazy and with her four remaining children was put on parish poor relief. "Like a little independent woman," Mary continued working in the mines. Earning two shillings a day, she did not spend it "in vanity of dress, in nice eating and drinking, or other needless expence." Instead, she saved her money and at sixteen "released the parish from the burthen of maintaining her mother." Next she "relieved the parish officers from the charge of one of her brothers" and provided for him until he died. Later, she maintained and nursed another brother during a sixteen-week illness at her own expense. After his death, she paid the funeral costs herself; likewise, when her mother died after seven years' care, she paid the burial expenses "without any assistance from the parish." All this was accomplished by "extraordinary labour." Putting even "the Mighty Hercules of Greece" to shame, she often earned three shillings and sixpence a day "by taking what is called 'a double turn' in the coal pits." Perhaps even more astounding than her labors to maintain her family was her success in keeping her "virtue . . . safe." Unlike Hercules, though, Mary was mortal, and after the death of her mother, she began to "lose her strength" and to be troubled by "those strange and unpleasant imaginations, which are known by persons conversant with the diseases of the poor, to be no unusual consequence of bad food, and great bodily fatigue, joined with excessive grief." Happily, however, Mary's virtue received a fitting reward —not gold and silver or a throne and the hand of a prince—but a place "in a sober private family" in which after six years she recovered her health. Unlike the traditional "irresponsible" chapbook romance, Mary's tale was salubriously instructive, for it taught the poor, its author wrote, "that they can seldom be in any condition of life so low, as to prevent their rising to some degree of independence, if they chuse to exert themselves, and that there can be no situation whatever so mean, as to forbid the practice of many noble virtues."[25]

The Mother Bunch of the *Cheap Repository* was Mrs. Jones. Like Mother Bunch, Mrs. Jones was a widow, her husband having been a great merchant. But instead of dispensing recipes for discovering husbands, Mrs. Jones taught "the art of industry and good management" and along with her friend Mrs. White dispensed recipes for cheap dishes.[26] Throughout the *Cheap Repository* the characters and narrative devices of traditional chapbooks were turned to moral purposes. The sensational was not avoided, for tracts describing murders and criminal life were included in the *Repository.* These, however, did not romanticize crime, and criminals were always punished, usually by execution or transportation. Even ghosts appeared in the *Repository.* Unlike the spirit which carried off Isabella to the accompaniment of thunder, lightning, and screams, these were didactic ghosts bent upon saving souls from fiery torment. In *The Deceitfulness of Pleasure,* a farmer in Westmoreland sent his daughter Catharine as a servant to Lady Blithe. From Catharine's limited point of view, Blithe Hall was an earthly paradise. A garden "full of sweet flowers and fruit" stretched in front of the "fine tall oak trees" where the hall stood, while hidden in the pagan grounds about it lurked an arbor, a grotto, a canal, and a temple. Inside the hall, the curtains were made of silk and the floors covered with flowered carpets, while the rooms themselves were as large as a "parish church."

While growing up in the country, Catharine had read her Bible and said her prayers every day. She had been accustomed to get up at five in the morning and to go to bed at nine every night. At Blithe Hall she never opened her eyes "much before ten" and did not think of going to bed until "long after midnight." Although she was "very handsome, and knew a great many fine things, such as music, and dancing," Lady Blithe "troubled herself very little about religion" and, setting a bad example for her servants, cared only for pleasure, "fine cloaths," and jewels. Until her birthday, though, Lady Blithe enjoyed an idyllic life. Then, having become overheated while dancing, she strolled out into the chilly night air to see the fireworks display in her honor and caught a cold which rapidly turned into a fatal consumption. On the day of her mistress's funeral, Catharine was upset and, falling asleep that night, thought she heard the deep tolling of a funeral bell. "Hearkening to it, all shivering with cold," she saw the curtains of her bed part. Standing before her was a figure wrapped in a shroud. Speaking in a deep and hollow voice, the ghost of Lady Blithe, for this was she, preached a sermon on duty and the dangers of worldly ways. After warning Catharine that there was "no repentance in the grave," the apparition vanished amid the tolling of the bell, and "dreadful complainings and lamentations." Not surprisingly, when Catharine woke, she vowed from henceforth to be "pious, honest, and contented" in her "humble state."[27]

Sung to the tune of "Collins's Mulberry Tree," *Robert and Richard; Or, The Ghost of poor Molly, who was drowned in Richard's Mill Pond* told the sad story of Robert's "translation." Like the merry cobbler, Robert served the devil at night. By promising to marry Molly, Robert was able to seduce her. After having had his pleasure, however, he broke his word, and when Molly proved to be pregnant, he scorned her. After the birth of their child, Molly became so despondent that she drowned herself and the infant in the mill pond which belonged to Robert's friend Richard. Tormented not by witches but by a guilty conscience, Robert began to drink heavily. Each night Molly appeared in his dreams and warned him to "*Remember the End.*" She "talk'd of the woes and unquenchable fire / Which await the gay Sinner, the Drunkard, and Liar"; lest he "ruin'd more maidens she made him beware, / Then she wept, and she groan'd, and she vanish'd in air." Despite his dreams and Richard's warnings, Robert was unable to repent. His heart had become too hard. Beggared "by Gaming, distemper'd by Drink," he stared Death in the face but he "dar'd not to think." "Despairing of mercy, despising of truth," he "dy'd of old age in the prime of his youth."[28]

For the bawdy material that had been one of the mainstays of traditional chapbooks, the *Cheap Repository* substituted local color. If farmers and low mechanicals did not speak precisely the language they really spoke, they were nevertheless distinctly recognizable as characters often seen and often heard. "I wonder," Farmer Bragwell said to Mr. Worthy after meeting the latter's "sober girls," "they do not tiff off a little more. Why my girls have as much fat and flour on their heads as would half maintain my reapers in suet pudding." Cooks, household servants, postillions, publicans, beggars, in fact, all conditions and ages of men and women in the lower classes, could recognize themselves and characters they knew in the *Cheap Repository.* Not every small village had a shiftless Amy in the poorhouse, but every villager knew an Amy, and not a Hec-

CHEAP REPOSITORY.

ROBERT AND RICHARD;

OR, THE

GHOST of poor MOLLY, who was drowned in RICHARD'S MILL POND.

To the Tune of *Collins's Mulberry Tree*.

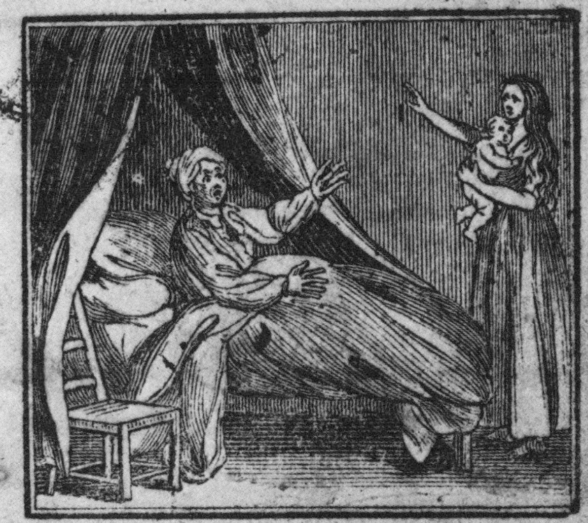

Sold by J. MARSHALL,
(PRINTER to the CHEAP REPOSITORY for Moral and Religious Tracts) No. 17, Queen-Street, Cheapside, and No. 4, Aldermary Church-Yard, and R. WHITE, Piccadilly, London.
By S. HAZARD, at Bath: J. ELDER, at Edinburgh, and by all Booksellers, Newsmen, and Hawkers in Town and Country.

Great Allowance will be made to Shopkeepers and Hawkers.

PRICE ONE HALFPENNY.

Or 2s. 3d. per 100.—1s. 6d. for 50.—9d. for 25.
A Cheaper Edition for Hawkers.

[*Entered at Stationers Hall.*]

From *Robert and Richard.* By permission of the British Library.

tor, prince of Troy. "Wherever there was a gossiping in the parish," *The Hubbub* read,

> thither ran Amy with her rags flying about her, like a scare-crow in a cherry tree. Her skin, which was quite tawny, was never washed; her hair had worked itself through the holes of her mob, half the border of which was lost, and the flags of it were always flying behind her; the pigs had one day eaten a hole through her hat as it lay on the ground, and a piece of it now hung over her eye like a black patch, her petticoats were all tatters, and her gown reached but little below her knees; it had been torn away bit by bit, till it was ravelled out to the above dimensions; her stockings had no feet, and her feet were slipped into a miserable pair of shoes, which she had not taken the trouble to draw up at heel, even when they were new; in one hand she clenched her rags together, whilst with the other, she held a short pipe in her mouth.[29]

Unlike the romantic and exotic worlds depicted in chapbooks like *Valentine and Orson* or Mandeville's *Travels,* the worlds described by the histories were often grimly realistic. After her father died, Alice Barnstable in *The Parish Nurse* went to live with her aunt, Nurse Flint. Alice's aunt took care of the parish orphans for a fee. Her heart, however, was as hard as her name, for Nurse Flint was a precursor of Dickens's Wackford Squeers. Not only did she starve the children so she could buy brandy, she also rented them to beggars at two shillings sixpence a week, "always," as she bragged, "paid in advance." When Alice arrived at her aunt's, she heard a child crying. She went to see what was the matter and discovered "the skin of several parts of the body was, for want of care, broken, and its little bones literally coming through." The child was in a bed "rotten with damp and filth"; its limbs were "almost stiff with cold," and it was "eat up with rickets." One day as Alice fed a child, "a most deplorable looking woman" came into Nurse Flint's house. Pointing to the child Alice held, Nurse Flint said, "Good-morrow to you Margery . . . there, take your bargain." "I would rather have the little black-eyed boy I had last week, mistress," the woman replied. "Oh," Flint answered, "Poor Jem dropt off the perch an hour ago; if you want him you must look in the box." "No, mistress," Margery answered as she took the child from Alice, "a living child will suit my turn better than a dead one—so good-morrow to you."[30]

The *Cheap Repository* did more than provide proper chapbook reading material, for some of the tracts contained criticism of traditional chapbooks. When approached for a contribution, Farmer Hoskins said in *The Sunday School* that the "new-fangled" idea of teaching the poor to read would ruin the country. On the contrary, Mrs. Jones replied, teaching "good principles to the lower classes" would save the country from turmoil. What was ruining the country, she said, was teaching people to read and then turning "them adrift to find out books for themselves." The farmer's own kitchen, she pointed out, was "hung round with loose songs and ballads." It was safer, she declared, for people not to read than to read the penny books which lay about the kitchen. In defense, the farmer, who was not familiar with Locke, replied that when he was hot and tired, he saw nothing wrong with enjoying a mug of cider and "a bit of a jest book or comical story."

The difference of opinion between Farmer Hoskins and Mrs. Jones would probably never have been resolved if Reverend Simpson, who had stayed out of the discussion, had not noticed two young dairymaids and the farmer's two daughters talking to a blind fiddler and the woman who led him. Having spread some books out upon the ground in front of the girls, the woman quickly gathered them up when she saw the minister approach and loudly asked the girls if they would buy "a godly book." Not fooled, Reverend Simpson snatched a book from one of the girls and after a brief examination pronounced it to be "poison for the soul." When faced with corruption of his own daughters, Farmer Hoskins saw the force of Mrs. Jones's arguments in a new light. And the girls themselves promised they would only deal with "sober honest hawkers" who sold "good little books, Christmas carols, and harmless songs"—just the sort of thing found in the *Cheap Repository*.[31]

After he became successful and owned his own shop, James Stock carefully watched his young apprentices to make sure that they would not go the way of James Brown. The most dangerous songs, he told Will Simpson after he overheard Will singing a gay ditty, were not those which contained vile words but those which were filled with "Wicked *thoughts.*" "Covered over with smooth words, and dressed out in pleasing rhymes," such songs did more harm to the principles of young people "than those songs of which the words are so gross and disgusting, that no person of modest decency can for a moment listen to them." Stock singled out drinking songs and verses which advised young people to live only for pleasure. "A man listens till the sentiment," Stock explained, "has so corrupted his heart, that his ear grows hardened too, and by long custom he loses all sense of the danger of prophane diversions."[32]

Tawny Rachel taught susceptible adolescents to avoid fortune-tellers and fortune-telling chapbooks. Cut from the tawdry cloth of Mother Bunch, Rachel traveled the country, pretending to make her living by selling laces, cabbage nets, ballads, and history books, and by buying rags and rabbit skins. All this, though, was just a sham enabling her to get into kitchens, tell fortunes, and practice upon the credulity of "silly girls." Not only was she adept at interpreting dreams but she read moles and as a result caused a great deal of mischief to ignorant and superstitious country folk. Because of her craft, "poor Sally Evans" met a sad end. Having inherited twenty pounds from her grandmother, Sally was a wealthy rural heiress. And until Robert "a rambling, idle young gardener" enlisted Tawny Rachel's help, she was happily engaged to Jacob, an honest laborer. Unfortunately, Sally did not put her trust in God but in "Dreams, Omens, and Conjurers." She "delighted in dream books, and consulted all the cunning women in the country to tell whether the two moles on her cheek denoted that she was to have two husbands, or only two children." If she found an old horseshoe while she walked to church, she was "sure that would be a lucky week." She never made a black pudding without borrowing one of the parson's old wigs to hang in the chimney so that the pudding would not burst. To avoid passing a churchyard at night, she would walk five extra miles. And "every seventh year she would not eat beans because they grew downward in the pod, instead of upward; and she would rather have gone with her gown open than have taken a pin of an old woman, for fear of being bewitched." Preying on Sally's superstitious nature, Rachel twisted her way into her confidence, then warned her not to throw herself away in marriage. She knew that Sally was about to make such a mistake, Rachel explained, because the two moles on Sally's cheek told her so. At all costs, Rachel told Sally, she was to avoid a man with brown hair and black eyes (honest Jacob), for she was "*fated*" to marry a man worth a

CHEAP REPOSITORY.

TAWNY RACHEL,

OR,

The FORTUNE TELLER;

With ſome Account of Dreams, Omens and Conjurers.

Sold by J. MARSHALL,
(Printer to the CHEAP REPOSITORY for Religious and Moral Tracts) No. 17, Queen-Street, Cheapſide, and No. 4, Aldermary Church-Yard, and R. WHITE, Piccadilly, LONDON.

By S. HAZARD, at Bath, J. ELDER, at Edinburgh, and by all Bookſellers, Newſmen, and Hawkers, in Town and Country. Great Allowance will be made to Shopkeepers and Hawkers.

PRICE ONE PENNY,
Or 4s. 6d 100.—2s. 6d. for 50.—1s. 6d. for 25.
A Cheaper Edition for Hawkers.

[Entered at Stationers Hall.]

From *Tawny Rachel, or The Fortune Teller.* By permission of the British Library.

hundred times more. This ideal suitor had blue eyes, Rachel informed her, light hair, the initials R.P., "a stoop in the shoulders," and "money beyond sea." Last, Rachel advised Sally to walk to the churchyard on Sunday. If she met a man in a blue coat "with a large posy of pinks and surthernwood in his bosom" sitting on the church wall at seven o'clock, she could be assured that he was her future husband. The following Sunday, Sally walked to the church and, sure enough, met such a man. With her fate obviously controlled by an outside force, Sally threw over Jacob and married Robert Price. Once he had her inheritance in his hands, Robert left for beyond the sea, and poor Sally, suspected of stealing a silver cup which Rachel had pocketed while telling her fortune, fell "into a deep decline" and died shortly thereafter from "a broken heart."[33]

In 1798 the Clapham Sect stopped publishing the *Cheap Repository.* The tracts themselves, though, had enjoyed a remarkable popularity. Not only had they been widely circulated, but they also provided the model for a score of societies which began publishing tracts within the next decade. Most prominent among these was the Religious Tract Society, which was founded in 1799. Having studied the *Cheap Repository*'s success, the society emphasized the necessity of making narrative "the medium of conveying truth," and among the five hundred million items which they published by 1850 were many of the "new chapbooks."[34]

Tracts did not, of course, completely replace traditional chapbooks. In *The Parish Register* (1807), Crabbe described the library of a poor villager. On a shelf next to the cuckoo clock, Crabbe recounted, were found "pious works for Sunday's use," a Bible "bought by sixpence weekly saved," and John Bunyan's *Pilgrim's Progress.* Next to these were chapbooks, "humbler works" supplied by the "pedlar's pack." A few like those poor Sally Evans read revealed a science "never taught in schools" and enabled cottagers to determine their futures from "moles and specks." Others, Crabbe said, were "the peasant's joy," and while "half his delighted offspring" climbed about his knees, he read accounts of "Thumb the great," "Hickerthrift the strong," and "Jack, by whose arm the giant-brood were quell'd." In part, Crabbe's parish was old-fashioned, mirroring what Wordsworth thought an earlier, better reading time. In Sunday and charity schools, in private academies, and in middle-class homes, and indeed in the homes of most members of the lower classes, particularly those in and near large cities, the popularity of traditional chapbooks had declined greatly. Wordsworth lamented this because he believed that the appeal to the imagination of old wives' and fairy tales broadened children's sensibilities and indirectly prepared them for the challenges which lay ahead. As a child, he wrote in *The Prelude,* he had been free to wander across the "open ground of Fancy." As a result, when he saw the dead man with the "ghastly face" rising "bolt upright" out of Esthwaite's Lake, he was not frightened, he explained, because he had seen such sights before in "the Forests of Romance" and "among the shining streams / Of Fairy Land." Those "mighty" educational "workmen" who had banished chapbooks, however, believed they had done children an important service. Disciplining the luxuriant imagination, they thought, was a good thing. By shielding the empty cabinets of children's minds from Puss in Boots's traveling companions —the Jolly Tar, Wanton Tom, Mother Bunch, Nixon, and Little Jack Horner with his hands full of something other than plums—they knew they were making children the fathers and mothers of moral, and indeed politically safe, men and women.[35]

CHAPTER FIVE

From Godly Books to Godly Poetry: Natural Theology and Tender Infancies

At the beginning of the eighteenth century, few books had been published specifically for children. Aside from chapbooks and Aesop's fables, the only other children's books seem to have been "Godly books." Written mostly by divines with Calvinistic leanings, these books relentlessly preached right religion as the one thing necessary for life. The unsaved child was not merely the potential father of a demonic man, but he was also "Satan's Brat" or "the degenerated Bough of the wild Olive tree" whose "grapes" were sure to ripen as "*Sodom*'s pride and lust." Before children's hearts hardened in sin, Hezekiah Woodward (1649) urged "Parents and Tutors" to "look to the preventing of evils, which, while they are but in the seed, may be crushed, as it were, in the egge, before there comes forth a flying Serpent or Cockatrice." At a time when large numbers of children died young, writers of godly books felt duty-bound to hurry their readers toward salvation. The cockatrice of original sin lurking within the human breast had to be crushed before the fragile egg cracked and the young soul took flight. Nothing was more important than eternal life, and godly books urged children to concentrate their energies on attaining salvation. "What are the Toyes, of wanton Boyes," Abraham Chear (1708) asked, "to an immortal Spirit?" Death, John Bunyan (1686) wrote, was "a cold Comforter to Girls and Boys" who were "wedded" to "their Childish Toys." When the "Reckoning" was cast on "Judgment Day," each child would be far better off if his "time and strength" and "every thought" had been devoted to "How Christ may be injoy'd." Certain that right religion was the only educational imperative, Richard Baxter began his *Compassionate Counsel To All Young-Men* (1681) by fervently stressing the frailty of human life and the horror of damnation. "The youngest have not assurance of Life for a day, or an hour," he wrote; "Thousands go out of the World in youth. Alas, the Flesh of young men is corruptible, liable to hundreds of Diseases, as well as the old. How quick may a Fever, a Pleurisie, an Impostume, or one of a thousand Accidents, turn your Bodies to corruption? And O that I knew how to make you sensible how dreadful a thing it is to die in an unholy state, and in the guilt of any unpardoned sin? An unsanctified Soul, that hath lived here but to the flesh, and the world, will be but fewel for the fire of Hell, and the wrathful Justice of the most holy God."[1]

As eighteenth-century commercial prosperity greatly enriched the middle classes, parents began to envision their children's futures in more worldly terms. As people were no longer forever trapped by the circumstances of their birth and as opportunities arose for them to move up through society, both socially and economically, the youthful pilgrim's progress was not simply limited to the road between hellfire and heavenly bliss. What seemed suitable reading for children in 1680 was often thought inappropriate by 1750. Reflecting the age's greater concern with worldly matters, writers of children's books in the mid-eighteenth century put more emphasis, for example, on food for the body than did seventeenth-century godly books. For Arthur Dent (1601) the body was but "wormes-meat, dust and ashes, durt and doong." Locke, however, placed a lengthy section on proper diet at the beginning of *Some Thoughts,* long before he considered religious education. Following Locke's lead, Newbery began *A Little Pretty Pocket-Book* with a discussion of "the Nurture of Children." Discussions of diet and warnings against improper eating habits became an integral part of children's books. Typically, *The Pretty Play-Thing* (1759) included a section entitled "A few MAXIMS for the Improvement of the MIND." Although the maxims began with the head, like Little Bear's porridge they quickly sank to lower, more vital regions, warning that "he who is always feeding shall soon make a Harvest-home for the Worms." In her *Easy Lessons For Young Children* (1786), Mrs. Trimmer described the misfortunes of six-year-old Miss Page, who grazed upon sweetmeats until she foundered. When her baby teeth fell out, Miss Page ignored her aunt's warnings against eating sweetmeats. Consequently, within "a short time," her new teeth "had holes in them, for she would pick them with pins, and they grew quite black." Eventually she was forced to have all her teeth pulled, "and then she could not chew her meat, but had it all to mince and sop; and if she got a bit of crust in her mouth, she mumpt and mumpt with her bare gums like an old man." In frightening the age's Little Miss Muffets away from sweetmeats, Mrs. Trimmer was actually a kindly spider. Her particular emphasis on care of the teeth, like Newbery's success with Greenough's Tinctures for Teeth, is understandable when one realizes that "Teeth" killed large numbers of people in the eighteenth century. According to *Payne's Universal Chronicle,* some 17,576 people died in London during the year 1758. Consumption and convulsions were the great killers, responsible for the deaths of 3,411 and 4,417 people, respectively. But "Teeth" killed 649, a figure which is half that of smallpox and only 33 less than dropsy and 47 less than measles. In a typical week, 6–13 January 1759, some 514 people died. Teeth killed 26, while consumption killed 91; dropsy, 18; measles, 15; smallpox, 27; and old age, 63.[2] In the eighteenth century, one might not be what he ate, but if he ate wrongly, the chances were good that soon he would not be.

Godly books, however, made few concessions to children's physical health and instead played upon their emotions. Relying heavily on fear, they attempted to shock children into awareness of the parlous state of their souls. When children's emotions had been thoroughly harrowed and they were ready for the gospel seed, godly books tried to lead them through repentance to Grace, Christ, and life everlasting. One of the best and most popular of these books was James Janeway's *A Token For Children: Being An Exact Account of the Conversion, Holy and Exemplary Lives, and Joyful Deaths of several young Children* (1671).

In a preface containing "Directions to Children," Janeway addressed his young readers, asking them if they were "willing to go to Hell to be burn'd with the devil and his angels?" Did they want, Janeway continued, to "be in the same Condition as naughty Children," for hell was "a terrible place . . . worse a thousand times than whipping." To avoid this painful fate, Janeway urged children to read *A Token* "over an hundred times." Then, when a "pretty *Lamb*" began to cry, he ought, Janeway taught, retire to his garret, fall upon his knees, "weep and mourn," and beg Christ for "Grace and Pardon," pleading with Him to "make thee his Child." To bring children to this repentant and receptive spiritual condition, *A Token* was filled with the inspirational biographies of young Christians, all of whom went to heaven at an early age "in an Extasie of Joy and holy Triumph."

When she was only a little over eight years old, Sarah Howley heard a sermon which convinced her of "her Need of a Christ." From this time forward, she was "very much in secret Prayer as," Janeway wrote, "might easily be perceived by those who listened at the Chamber-door, and was usually very importunate, full of Tears." She spent her free time reading the Bible and holy books, until at fourteen, she was, almost happily, stricken with consumption. "Like a continued Sermon," Janeway recounted, "she was full of Divine Sentences, in almost all her Discourse, from the first to the last." Even more instructive was the life of "A Certain little Child," whose mother dedicated him to the Lord while he slumbered in her womb. As he grew up, he became "more and more affected with the Things of another World," and while other children played, he prayed. He was so "exceeding importunate with God" that he pled "with God at a strange rate . . . with great Reverence, Tenderness and Groans." Sometimes he wept so that he disturbed those about him, once piercing not merely the rest but the conscience of a neighbor, who cried out in agony, "The Prayers and Tears of that Child" will "sink me to Hell" because by his acts he condemns my "Neglect of Prayer."

Although the intention of writers like Janeway was noble, their methods slammed down like a sledgehammer, crushing not merely the cockatrice but the frail egg itself. The vast majority of children probably eagerly swallowed the sensationalism of godly books, enjoying it in the same way they marveled over those orthopedic boots Little Poucet stole from the hungry ogre. Indeed, the appeal of spiritual biographies of dying children was not unlike that of romances and fairy tales. In spiritual biography, Sin replaced the ravenous ogre or fabulous monsters against which Jack the Giant-Killer and Bevis struggled. A child's victory over Sin, a beast who dwelt within rather than without, resembled the triumphs of chapbook heroes. Moreover, God, who watched over and rewarded good little children, resembled the fairy godmother who protected spotless Cinderellas from the sullying world. Cinderella herself was an archetypical character whose counterpart appeared in many spiritual biographies. Within each child, Janeway seemed to preach, a beautiful Cinderella waited to be born. Washed in the blood of the Lamb, she would appear beautiful, not in a golden dress but in robes immortal. Instead of tripping a light, evanescent dance with a prince in a fantastic earthly palace, she would dance eternally amid the splendors of heaven in the arms of the real King's son. For Janeway's good child, life resembled Sleeping Beauty's hundred-year sleep. When the good child awoke from life's fitful fever, however, she found herself embraced, not by a prince whose mother was an ogre, but by a prince whose father had banished all ogres from his kingdom.

The typical hero of a fairy tale was a wanderer who, because he was outside conventional society, was able to establish relationships with anybody or anything. Janeway's children were similarly outside conventional society. If they were not wanderers drifting through life, they were pilgrims struggling to escape life. With heightened religious sensibilities, they, like fairy-tale heroes, were able to communicate with a world rarely, if ever, glimpsed by their playmates. In contrast to Janeway's spiritual biographies, however, fairy tales usually focused on the worldly rather than the other-worldly. Cinderella, Sleeping Beauty, the Marquis of Carabas, and Little Poucet all lived happily and affluently in this world. Moreover, criticisms which were applied to fairy tales were in part applicable to spiritual biographies. For a parent concerned about his child's secular success and not immediately worried about Baxter's fire of hell, spiritual biography seemed to contain "Bug-bear Thoughts." Once "into the tender Minds of Children," these might do more than simply haunt them with "Strange Visions." If education determined the characters and futures of nine men out of ten, then spiritual biography might harm children. "'Tis Knowledge," James Burgh wrote in *Youth's Friendly Monitor* (1754), "that makes the Difference between one Man and another and raises some to the Rank of Angels." Despite their miraculous paraphernalia, fairy tales did not raise heroes to the rank of angels but usually left them enjoying the earthly pleasures of riches and matrimony. In contrast, the heroes of spiritual biographies were invariably elevated to the angelic host. Instead of educating children for ordinary daily life, spiritual biography prepared them for life eternal; some children, into whose systems such enthusiasms invaded, must have found them incurable. If fairy tales and romances could fill the mind's empty cabinet with poison for the spirit, then spiritual biography could fill it with poison for the body.

Janeway's book itself lends substance to this view. A "certain beggar boy" seems to have been physically healthy while he roamed the streets "running to Hell" as "a very Monster of Wickedness." Taken into service, however, by a well-meaning Christian, he was happily transformed by "the Glory of God's free Grace." Unfortunately, while his spirit thrived, the beams supporting his clayey tenement gave way and he fell into religious melancholia. His "former Sins stared him in his Face, and made him tremble," and the "Poyson of God's Arrows" drank "up his Spirits." His "Self-abhorrency" grew so great that "he could never speak bad enough of himself" and the only "Name he would call himself" was "Toad." Not surprisingly it was not long before Toad hopped "into the Arms of Jesus." That a particular "poor Child's Thoughts were very much busied about the Things of another World" cannot have contributed to his physical health, particularly when he took "heavenly Conference to be sweeter than his appointed Rest." Tabitha Alder's religious enthusiasm probably contributed little to her decline. But by the same token, her longing for "Robes immortal" did not help her regain her health. On her deathbed her ecstasy was unbounded, as she cried out, "Anon . . . I shall be with Jesus, I am married to him, he is my Husband, I am his Bride; I have given my self to him, and he hath given himself to me, and I shall live with him for ever." "This strange Language," Janeway noted, "made the Hearers even stand astonished."[3]

The most influential writer of children's books to follow along Janeway's theological path was Isaac Watts. Although Watts's Calvinistic beliefs resembled those of Janeway, Locke had taught him the practical necessity of cozening children into knowledge, not simply of letters but of spiritual truth. Watts was also aware that educational expectations and literary taste were changing. In a metaphor anticipating the emphasis which would be put upon proper diet in children's books, he proposed changing children's spiritual food. Was it, Watts asked in his *Cate-*

chisms (1730), "the best Method for the feeding and nourishing the Bodies of young Children to bestow upon them Nuts and Almonds in hopes that they will taste the Sweetness of them when their Teeth are strong enough to break the Shell?" Would "they not be far better nourished," he wrote, "by Children's Bread, and by Food" which they could "immediately taste and relish?" Watts by no means went so far as Newbery's "Be Merry and Wise" approach to children's books. But he did palliate the bite of Janeway's didacticism. Moreover, he adapted that "strange language" to the capacities of young children and to the inclinations of middle-class parents. "He was," as Dr. Johnson put it, "one of the first authors that taught the Dissenters to court attention by the graces of language. Whatever they had among them before, whether of learning or acuteness," Johnson wrote, "was commonly obscured and blunted by coarseness and inelegance of stile."[4]

Watts's famous children's book was entitled *Divine Songs, Attempted in Easy Language For The Use Of Children* (1715). In his preface to all "concerned in the Education of CHILDREN," Watts explained as a good Lockean that children found that "*the very learning of Truths and Duties*" was "*a greater Delight*" when they were written in appealing verse form. As Locke had thought that a man who had studied Aesop's fables as a child might "retain them all his life after" and draw "useful Reflections" from them, so Watts believed that "*What*" was "learnt in *Verse*" was "*longer retain'd in Memory.*" These poems, he thought, would "*be a constant Furniture for the Minds of Children.*" When they were alone and their minds were furnished with ideas, he hoped the poems would "*give their Thoughts a divine Turn, and raise a young Meditation.*"[5]

Although Watts muted Janeway's Calvinism, water from "the Lake that burns with Brimstone and with Fire" steamed throughout the *Songs.* "Young Sinners" were taught that "One stroke of his Almighty Rod" could send them "quick to Hell." Careless infants learned that "a thousand Children young" as they were "call'd by Death to hear their Doom." There was "no Repentance in the Grave," and if one were "a wretched Slave to Sin" when he died, he would have to dwell with devils "in Darkness, Fire, and Chains." The heat rising from Watt's Calvinism, however, did not reach an uncomfortable level—at least not from an eighteenth-century point of view. In the preface Watts stressed that he had tried to avoid doctrinaire religion. Readers, he hoped, would find "*nothing that favours of a Party.*" Children "*of high and low Degree,*" from "*the Church of* England *or Dissenters,*" whether "*baptized in Infancy or not,*" he wrote, would be able to "*join together in these Songs.*" To this ecumenical end, most of the songs were moral poems teaching right conduct and were typically entitled "Against Lying," "Against Quarrelling and Fighting" (the famous "Let Dogs delight to bark and bite"), "Love between Brothers and Sisters," "Against Idleness and Mischief" ("How doth the little busy Bee"), "Against Evil Company," and "Against Pride in Clothes." Other poems were songs of praise thanking God for his general kindness to man, "Praise to God for our Redemption," and for his particular kindness to the reader, "Praise for Birth and Education in a Christian Land." Some poems directed readers' senses to the natural world and its creator, "Praise for Creation and Providence," while others stressed the importance of weaving good habits into the "very Principles" of a child's nature, "The Advantages of early Religion," "The Danger of Delay," and "Examples of early Piety."[6]

The *Divine Songs* were an extraordinary success. The chord Watts struck sounded not just during his generation but reverberated down through the next one hundred and fifty years. Twenty editions were published during Watts's lifetime. By 1929, J.H.P. Pafford reckoned, at least eight million copies had been printed, and some three hundred and eighty editions had been published in Britain, while another three hundred and forty-five had appeared in the United States. On Watts's death in 1748, eulogists wrote that "WATTS is a Name that Nations know; a sacred Name that Nations love." There was "no Man now living of whose Works so many have been dispersed," David Jennings wrote, "both at Home and Abroad, that are in such constant Use, and translated into such a Variety of Languages." In his *Life of Watts,* Dr. Johnson praised him for condescending "to lay aside the scholar, the philosopher, and the wit, to write little poems of devotion, and systems of instruction," adapted to children's "wants and capacities." In 1789, Mrs. Trimmer stated that "of all the Religious Books which have been written for Children, I know of none that is committed to memory with so much delight, as the DIVINE SONGS OF DR. WATTS." In 1795 an edition of the *Songs* was published in the *Cheap Repository* as a poetry tract, and short years later another edition was the fifth publication of the Religious Tract Society.[7]

There were several imitations of the *Songs.* None, however, was more successful than Anna Barbauld's *Hymns in Prose for Children* (1781). In 1778 Anna Barbauld published her first children's books, *Lessons for Children, from Two to Three Years Old* and *Lessons for Children of Three Years Old.* These were followed in 1779 by "part II" of *Lessons for Children of Three Years Old* and by *Lessons for Children from Three to Four Years Old.* Important not for what they said but how they said it, the *Lessons* began, as Fanny Burney put it, the "new walk" in children's books. Printed on good quality paper in big type with large spaces between words, the *Lessons* were, Mrs. Trimmer wrote, the "first of their kind." Before they appeared, "everything for *little folks,*" and this included not only books but also the type used in them, had been "*diminutive.*" Furthermore Mrs. Barbauld introduced "a species of writing, in the style of *familiar conversation,*" which was "much better suited to the capacities of young children than any thing that preceded it." Mrs. Barbauld's "hints," Mrs. Trimmer judged in 1802, had "been generally adopted by her cotemporaries." As a result, "many books" had been "supplied to the nursery, by means of which children at an early age have acquired the rudiments of useful science, and even of the first principles of Christianity, with delight to themselves, and ease to their instructors." The *Lessons* had a catalytic effect upon Mrs. Trimmer herself. After reading them, she wrote her *An Easy Introduction to the Knowledge of Nature, and Reading the Holy Scriptures* (1780) as in part a continuation of the *Lessons* for older children and thus began her distinguished career as a practical educator and writer of books for children. "I cannot pass over this opportunity of mentioning a very useful Publication, entitled *Lessons for Children from two to three or four Years old,* written by Mrs. Barbauld," Mrs. Trimmer declared in the preface to *An Easy Introduction.* "Free from all formality," the *Lessons,* she wrote, were the best she "ever met with" for teaching children to read. "I have endeavoured," she continued, "to adopt a similar mode of expression, and to build upon the ground work which the ingenious author has laid for the Education of Children." In 1798 Maria Edgeworth noted that the "first books" which were "usually put into the hands of a child" were the *Lessons*. They were "by far the best books of the kind" that had "ever appeared" and those who knew "the importance of such compositions in education" sincerely rejoiced, she wrote, that "the admirable talents of such a writer" had "been employed in such a work." In 1869 Charlotte Yonge estimated that Mrs. Barbauld had helped teach reading to "three-quarters of the gentry of the last three generations."[8]

Originality of style and innovations in layout were not entirely responsible for the popularity of the lessons. "To lay the first stone of a noble building" or "to plant the first ideas in a human mind" could not, Mrs. Barbauld wrote, dishonor "any hand." It was essential, however, if the building were to withstand the storms of temptation, that its foundation be laid in a proper manner. Since she joined the bricks of knowledge with mortar mixed from Locke's writings, educators approved Mrs. Barbauld's methods. In the first volume of the *Lessons*, she attempted to furnish the empty cabinet of her main character's mind by directing his senses to "*external sensible objects*." In the second volume, this process was intensified as a lesson was devoted to each month of the year. Thus, in May, young Charles first saw the bright hawthorns, daisies, crowflowers, and cowslips and afterward made a sweet-smelling nosegay. Later he felt some "little birds" which Billy had taken from their nest high in a tree. In the last two volumes of the *Lessons*, Mrs. Barbauld tried to link sensation to reflection, as Charles's experiences in external nature often led to instructive tales appealing to his "internal sense."[9]

Artistically and pedagogically the *Lessons* were an apprentice work preparing Mrs. Barbauld for the *Hymns in Prose*. At the conclusion of his *Divine Songs*, Watts included two poems, "Innocent Play" and "The Sluggard" ("Tis the Voice of the Sluggard"). These, he said, were "A Slight SPECIMEN of MORAL SONGS," such as he wished "*some happy and condescending Genius would undertake for the use of Children, and perform much better.*" The "Sense and Subjects," he thought, could be borrowed "from the *Proverbs of Solomon*" or "from all the common Appearances of Nature, from all the Occurrences in the Civil Life, both in the City and Country." The "Language and Measures," he suggested, "should be easy and flowing with chearfulness, and without the Solemnities of Religion, or the sacred Names of God and Holy Things: that Children might find Delight and Profit together."[10]

Watts's hints were well taken, and Mrs. Barbauld became the happy genius for whom he wished. In the preface to the *Hymns,* she praised the *Songs,* saying that it was one of the few books calculated to assist children in the devotional part of religion. As Watts, however, had dissociated himself from the blunter Calvinism of writers like Janeway, so Mrs. Barbauld distinguished herself from Watts. In making suggestions for the contents of the "Moral Songs," Watts almost seemed to envision latitudinarian poems. These, he thought, would appeal broadly to parents and children of varying theological stripes. By suggesting such a format for the "Moral Songs," Watts effectually precluded later writers from establishing the rationale for their children's books on criticism of his Calvinism. Consequently, although she was a Unitarian and as such was unsympathetic to Calvinism, Mrs. Barbauld did not criticize the contents of the *Songs.* Instead, she closely followed Watts's directions for the substance of the "Moral Songs" and parted with him only on form. Although the *Divine Songs* were "in pretty general use," it was doubtful, she wrote, "*whether poetry ought to be lowered to the capacities of children.*" It was better, she decided, to keep them from reading poetry until they were "*able to relish good verse.*" To this end, the *Hymns* were written in "*measured prose*" which she thought, was "*nearly as agreeable to the ear as a more regular rhythmus*"—a form which today might be labeled prose-poetry.

After this explanation of why she thought prose more suitable for a child than poetry, Mrs. Barbauld discussed her didactic intentions. In hopes of forming children's characters, she had raised the *Hymns* upon Locke's theories of the origin and association of ideas. These she used in the service of natural theology to lead children to God, much as Watts suggested in his *A Treatise on the Education of Children* but which he did not attempt in the *Divine Songs.* "*To feel the full force of the idea of God,*" she explained, a child "*ought never to remember the time when he had no such idea.*" The person "*who has early been accustomed to see the Creator in the visible appearances of all around him,*" she stated, "*has made large advances towards that habitual piety, without which religion can scarcely regulate conduct.*" Therefore, the design of the *Hymns,* she continued, was "*to impress devo-*

tional feelings as early as possible on the infant mind" by "*connecting religion with a variety of sensible objects; with all that he* [a young child] *sees, all he hears, all that affects his young mind with wonder or delight; and thus by deep, strong, and permanent associations, to lay the best foundation for practical devotion in future life.*"[11]

The discrepancy was often great between educational theory and embodiments of it in eighteenth-century children's books. In this case, however, theory and practice complimented each other gracefully, and the *Hymns* were a land of pure delight. No other eighteenth-century children's book wed natural theology to Locke's account of human development so well. Indeed, in the world of children's books, natural theology was sometimes suspect. Although it ultimately led children to reflect on God, it appealed to the imagination before the understanding. By the end of the 1780s, many children's books stressed dampening rather than awakening the imagination. Despite this trend in children's books, the *Hymns* were rarely criticized by educators. They were so superior to other children's books that they were not measured by the same critical standard. Educators like Mrs. Trimmer, whose first book relied heavily on natural theology but whose later books betrayed a growing distrust of the imagination, continued to commend them uncritically. "Come, let us go forth into the fields," Mrs. Barbauld wrote simply,

> let us see how the flowers spring, let us listen to the warbling of the birds, and sport ourselves upon the new grass. The winter is over and gone, the buds come out upon the trees, the crimson blossoms of the peach and the nectarine are seen, and the green leaves sprout. The hedges are bordered with tufts of primroses, and yellow cowslips that hang down their heads; and the blue violet lies hid beneath the shade. . . . The butterflies flutter from bush to bush, and open their wings to the warm sun. The young animals of every kind are sporting about, they feel themselves happy, they are glad to be alive—they thank him that has made them alive. They may thank him in their hearts, but we can thank him with our tongues; we are better than they, and can praise him better.[12]

Like the *Divine Songs,* the *Hymns* was a great success. In 1877 Jerom Murch asked, "where, in the long catalogue of children's books, shall we find any to be compared with them? Many who heard them the first time at their mother's knee can trace to them their deepest, most precious convictions. A century has now passed since they were written; they have been largely used by all classes from the palace to the cottage; and still what a freshness and beauty in every page!" At Mrs. Barbauld's death in 1825, the *Christian Reformer* wrote that the *Hymns* were "beyond all praise" and accused the parent who did "not familiarize his children" with "these exquisite effusions of pious taste" of being "deficient in the first of duties." During Mrs. Barbauld's lifetime, individuals were hardly less restrained than eulogists after her death. In her *Thoughts On The Education of Daughters,* Mary Wollstonecraft praised the *Hymns*, saying that she could not "help mentioning a book of hymns, in measured prose, written by the ingenious author of many other proper lessons for children. These hymns, I imagine, would contribute to fill the heart with religious sentiments and affections; and, if I may be allowed the expression, make the Deity obvious to the senses." In "On the Living Poets," William Hazlitt wrote that the "first poetess" he could recollect was Mrs. Barbauld. Recalling that she strewed "the flowers of poetry most agreeably round the borders of religious controversy," Hazlitt declared nostalgically, "I wish I could repay my childish debt of gratitude in terms of appropriate praise." In 1797 Coleridge called her "that great and excellent woman," and on the publication of the second edition of the *Lyrical Ballads* in 1800 instructed Thomas Longman to send her a complimentary copy. For Henry Crabb Robinson, meeting Mrs. Barbauld was like meeting the Angel Gabriel.[13]

Not all opinions of the *Hymns* were favorable, but even the criticisms indicated the book's influence. In 1802 Lamb complained to Coleridge that "Mrs. Barbauld's stuff" had "banished all the old classics out of the nursery." Like Dr. Johnson, Lamb believed that "wild tales" which appealed to the imagination rather than the understanding were better for children, and he criticized Mrs. Barbauld's didacticism. Knowledge as "insignificant and vapid as Mrs. B.'s books convey" limited, Lamb argued, rather than expanded children's capacity for learning and encouraged them to have a false "conceit" of their "own powers." "Damn them!" he concluded, "I mean the cursed Barbauld Crew, those Blights and Blasts of all that is Human in man and child."[14]

In starting the "new walk" in instructive children's books, Mrs. Barbauld's writings served as examples for her contemporaries, a "Crew" whose books were usually highly didactic. This was particularly true of Mrs. Trimmer's later works, many of which were written as elementary religious and educational manuals for grossly ignorant children from the lower classes.[15] With some justification, Lamb's strictures could be applied to Mrs. Trimmer's writings, and perhaps even to Mrs. Barbauld's *Lessons.* But when applied to the *Hymns,* Lamb's criticism was ill-founded. In condemning them because of the narrowness of Mrs. Barbauld's admirers and imitators, Lamb ignored the beauty of the *Hymns* and failed to recognize that their reliance upon Locke's theories and natural theology expanded rather than limited children's imaginations.

In *Some Thoughts* Locke warned parents and teachers against forcing children to learn "their Lessons by heart, as they happen to fall out in their Books, without Choice or Distinction." Such methods, he said, gave "them a Disgust and Aversion to their Books." Locke did not, however, proscribe selective memorization, for he believed the "Custom of frequent Reflection" kept children's "Minds from running adrift." To call "their Thoughts home from useless unattentive roving," he suggested that it might "do well, to give them something every day to remember." He stipulated, though, that this something should be "in it self worth the remembering." Many late eighteenth-century educators believed that the *Hymns* were ideally suited for such beneficial memory work. Their literary merit was such that it appeared unlikely that they would disgust children with books, and since they filled "the heart with religious sentiments and affections," they were clearly worth remembering. Consequently, children were often encouraged to learn them. Not all children, of course, enjoyed the task. In describing his unhappy childhood in *The Way of All Fresh,* Ernest Pontifex angrily recalled that he had been forced to memorize the *Hymns.* Ernest's resentful recollection seems, however, to have been exceptional. Probably little George Pembroke's attitude toward them in Priscilla Wakefield's *Juvenile Anecdotes, Founded on Facts* (1795) was more typical. Miss Lambert, the Pembroke children's governess, kept a journal in which she described the behavior of her young charges. At the end of each week, she read her entries aloud so that the children could learn from their mistakes and receive rewards for good behavior. One Monday's entry gave George the place of honor because he had memorized "a hymn of Mrs. Barbauld's," not at Miss Lambert's suggestion, but "at his own request." Three generations of George Pembrokes memorized the *Hymns.* In 1803 Mrs. Trimmer observed that she had frequently heard them "recited by young children, with such intelligence of countenance, and emphasis of delivery, as evidently proved that the sentiments of the writer were transfused into the minds of the little speakers." The extent to which such transfusions enriched children's minds can never be known. But if impressions made on "tender Infancies" had "important and lasting Consequences," then the *Hymns* may have had an influence which reached beyond the shelves of "Infant Libraries." In particular, the *Hymns*' dependence upon natural theology had interesting parallels in later poetry written for adults.[16]

Natural theology was so much a part of eighteenth-century Christianity that it often seems a habit of thought woven into the "very Principles" of the age. Although its taproot stretched back to antiquity, it absorbed its immediate nourishment from the soil of the seventeenth century. Popular physico-theologians taught that the existence and attributes of God could be inferred from the study of nature. The "Works of this visible world," John Ray wrote, afforded "a demonstrative Proof of the unlimited extent of the Creators Skill, and the fecundity of his Wisdom and Power." If, he added, "a curious Edifice or Machine" necessarily implied the existence of an intelligent architect or engineer, did not the "Grandeur and Magnificence" of nature, which far transcended human art, "infer the existence and efficiency of an Omnipotent and All-wise Creator"? Study of "the divine Excellencies display'd in the Fabrick and Conduct of the Universe, and of the Creatures it consists of" led, Robert Boyle wrote in *The Christian Virtuoso* (1690), "directly to the acknowledgement and adoration of a most Intelligent, Powerful, and Benign Author of things, to whom alone such excellent Productions may, with the greatest Congruity by ascrib'd."[17]

Latitudinarians also contributed to the popularity of natural theology. In the seventeenth century, leading Church of England divines like Samuel Clarke and John Tillotson attempted to direct Anglicanism away from dogma and toward good deeds. Charity and benevolent feelings were emphasized more than the Trinity and original sin. In the process, attention shifted in part from finding religious truth in the book of law to discovering it in the book of nature. At the end of the eighteenth century, the Church of England's most celebrated latitudinarian, William Paley, published *Natural Theology: or, Evidences of the Existence and Attributes of The Deity, Collected from the Appearances of Nature* (1802). According to Paley, natural theology was "the foundation of every thing which is religious" and caused the world to become "a temple" and "life itself one continued act of adoration." Latitudinarians, it should be stressed, were not the only churchmen strongly influenced by natural theology. In 1763 John Wesley published *A Survey Of The Wisdom of God in the Creation,* in which he discussed natural theology in great detail. Like a good Lockean, Wesley denied the existence of innate ideas and argued that "Our Senses" were "the only Source of those Ideas, upon which all our Knowledge is founded." Without ideas, he wrote, man could have no knowledge, and without senses, no ideas. "Properly speaking," he explained, men had "no Idea of God" but came to "Knowledge of his very Existence" through "Reasoning upon the Works of the Visible Creation." Accordingly, these works were very important. The "World around us," he wrote, was "the mighty Volume wherein God hath declared himself." Although men spoke different languages, the "Book of Nature" was "written in an universal Character." Consisting of things rather than words, it pictured "the Divine Perfections." The "whole Universe," he maintained, displayed not merely God's existence but "his Unity, his Power, His Wisdom, his Independence, his Goodness."[18]

In his writings Locke generally sympathized with the latitudinarians and physico-theological argument from design, typically observing that "the wisdom and goodness of the Maker plainly" appeared in all parts of and creatures found in "this stupendous fabric." In analyzing the imperfections of words in *An Essay,* Locke praised physico-theology at the expense of revealed religion. Too often, he implied, enthusiasts abused words and interpreted revealed religion highly subjectively. God, he wrote, had "spread before all the world such legible characters of his works and providence" and had given man "so sufficient a light of reason" that people who never saw the "written word" could not doubt God's existence or their duty to him. Since "the precepts of natural religion" were "plain and very intelligible to all mankind" whereas "other revealed truths" conveyed by books and languages were "liable to the common and natural obscurities and difficulties incident to words," it would become us, he concluded, "to be more careful and diligent in observing the former, and less magisterial, positive, and imperious in imposing our own sense and interpretations of the latter."[19]

In discussing natural philosophy in *Some Thoughts,* however, Locke took a slightly different position, one which stood out against the general philosophic and educational flow of both *An Essay* and the remainder of *Some Thoughts.* In an earlier discussion of religious education in *Some Thoughts,* Locke warned parents against zeal. By "gentle degrees," he taught, "an Idea of God" should be settled in a child's mind. But "any Discourse of other Spirits," he stressed, should be avoided, for it would clutter the child's head with false or unintelligible "Notions." In counseling moderation, Locke seemed to have the abuse of religious education in mind: the enthusiasm of men like Baxter and Janeway who singlemindedly swaddled children with "Curious" and sharp doctrines and prematurely bundled them off to paradise. On the other hand, however, when teaching natural philosophy to children, Locke focused on the abuses of scientific study. As narrow devotion to early religious education could lead to false views, so an unbalanced scientific education could fill a child's head with incomprehensible notions. In *The Excellency Of Theology, Compar'd With Natural Philosophy, (as both are Objects of Men's Study)* (1671/72), Robert Boyle anticipated his friend's strictures. The "Book of Nature," Boyle explained, resembled "a well contriv'd Romance." Like a romance, nature was intellectually seductive. Its parts had "such a connection and relation to one another," he wrote, "and the things we would discover are so darkly or incompleatly knowable by those that precede them, that the mind is never satisfied till it comes to the end of the Book." Unfortunately, unlike a romance, nature had no end, and the reader was condemned to burn in a fitful and distorting fever throughout his life. The other "great" book by "the same Author," that "of Scripture," would enable the student, Boyle suggested, to put natural philosophy into proper perspective. Studying the Scriptures did not hinder, he wrote, "an Inquisitive man's delight" in the study of nature. Instead, it contributed to it. The man who looked "upon the wonders of Nature, not onely as the Productions of an admirably wise Author of things, but of such an one as he intirely honours and loves, and to whom he is related," would not only enrich his understanding but would find contentment.[20]

Locke prefaced his remarks on teaching natural philosophy to children with the Boyle-like warning that although sciences produced an expectation of "Truth and Certainty," such could not be found in natural philosophy. "The Works of Nature," he wrote, were contrived "by a Wisdom" and operated "by ways too far surpassing our Faculties to discover, or Capacities to conceive, for us ever to be able to reduce them into a Science." Natural philosophy itself he divided into two categories: "*Spirits*" or metaphysics, and "*Bodies*" or matter. Believing that only children past infancy, beyond the time when they were most liable to be frightened by talk of spirits, would study natural philosophy, Locke urged that they be taught "some Notion of Spirits" before they studied matter. Since our senses were constantly conversant with matter, he explained, it was "apt to possess the Mind." Like the exclusive enthusiasm of some educators for religious truth, enthusiasm for matter could lead to the exclusion of "all other Beings." Both reason and revelation led, he held, "our Minds towards a truer and fuller comprehension of the intellectual World." To insure that children embarking on the study of nature did not become wholly absorbed in it, as in Boyle's romance, and lose perspective, Locke proposed they be acquainted with that other great book. To this purpose he suggested the composition of "a good History of the Bible, for young People." Like the playthings which cozened children into a knowledge of the letters, the Bible should be adapted to a "Child's Capacity." Only incidents "fit" for children should be included, and "several things" suited "only to riper Age" should be omitted. If this were accomplished, not only would children be prepared for "study of Bodies," but also, Locke added, "that Confusion, which is usually produced by promiscuous reading of the Scripture, as it lies now bound up in our Bibles" would be avoided.[21]

Locke's comments on the method of teaching natural philosophy should not be taken as an attack upon natural theology but should instead be seen as commonsensical suggestions for tempering scientific study with religious study. Directed only at the education of older children, Locke's remarks did not apply to the education children received in their "tender Infancies." Physico-theology, like that explained by Watts which "by gentle degrees" led from the sensible world to God, was useful in impressing "a true Notion of *God*" and his attributes upon young children. So that readers would not misinterpret his suggestions and neglect the study of matter, Locke concluded his discussion of natural philosophy by saying he would "not deter any one from the study of Nature." Although all the knowledge man had or would ever have could not "be brought into a Science," there were "very many things in it," he said, which were "convenient and necessary to be known."[22]

Locke's point was understood, and his remarks on natural philosophy did not deter educators from relying on natural theology in books for young children. First books were not so analytical as the scientific studies of matter that Locke seemed to envision. Instead of rejecting the book of nature, educators used it until the late eighteenth century in the manner Isaac Watts recommended. Ellenor Fenn, for example, included a quotation from the *Hymns in Prose* on the title page of *The Rational Dame; Or, Hints Towards Supplying Prattle For Children* (1790). In her preface she said that she hoped her "little volume" would "be the pocket companion of young mothers" when they walked "abroad with their children." She believed it would assist them in teaching children "To look from nature, up to nature's God."[23] Among other educators who linked physico-theology to Locke's theories on the understanding and of association were, of course, Anna Barbauld and Mrs. Trimmer. The latter, it will be remembered, said she began *An Easy Introduction* after reading Watts's explanation how a survey of the "Works of Providence" could be "very useful" in opening "the Mind by gradual steps to the Knowledge" of God. On the title page of *The Mosaic Creation,* the first part of which was "intended to give Children an Idea of the wonderful Works of the Creation, and to lead their Minds to a Contemplation of the Power and Goodness of the Almighty," Newbery included an epigraph from Watts. "Nature *is nothing but the art of* GOD," the epigraph read, "*a bright Display of that Divine Wisdom, which demands our Eternal Tribute of Wonder and Worship.*" At the end of the century, perhaps the most popular writer of children's books who used natural theology extensively was Priscilla Wakefield. In the preface to *Mental Improvement:*

Or The Beauties and Wonders Of Nature And Art (1794), she praised Watts and revealed the great influence his writings had upon her ideas on education. "The art of exercising the faculty of thinking and reflecting upon every object that is seen, ought to constitute a material branch of a good education," she wrote, "but it requires the skill of a master's hand, to lead the minds of youth to the habit of observation." "Dr. Watts," she continued, "says that there are four methods of attaining knowledge. Observation, reading, conversation, and meditation. The first lies within the compass even of children, and from the early dawn of reason, they should be accustomed to observe everything with attention, that falls under their notice. A judicious instructor will find matter for a lesson among those objects, that are termed common or insignificant."[24]

Although Watts showed how natural theology could be put to good use in children's books, many dissenters and evangelicals were uncomfortable with it, particularly when adults embraced it. In contrast to the Locke of *Some Thoughts* who implied that rigorous scientific analysis of nature might undermine a child's ability to accept biblical truth, in effect limit the flexibility of his imagination, these people distrusted natural theology's appeal to the imagination. Intead of suggesting biblical reading in order to expand the imagination and to enlarge comprehension "of the intellectual World," such people often prescribed revealed religion as an antidote for an active imagination. In discussing "the book of Creation," John Newton, a Calvinist and friend of Hannah More, expressed typical evangelical reservations about natural theology and criticized those who preferred Locke's "legible characters" to "other revealed truths." God, Newton wrote, was "revealed in the least as well as in the greatest of his works. The sun and the glow-worm, the fabric of the universe, and each single blade of grass," he thought, were "equally the effects of divine power." Unfortunately, the "lines" of the book of creation, he continued, although beautiful and expressive in themselves, were not immediately legible to fallen man. "The works of creation," he asserted, could be compared "to a fair character in cypher, of which the Bible" was "the key." Without this key, the book could not be understood. As proof, Newton cited the example of the heathens, observing that, although the book was always open to them, they could neither read it nor discern the proofs of God which it afforded. As a result, they became "vain in their own imaginations, and worshipped the creature more than the Creator." The case, Newton stated, was "much the same at this day." Many people were thought wise whose hearts were not "subjected to the authority of the Bible." "The study of the works of God, independent of his word, though dignified with the name of *philosophy,*" he summed up, was "no better than an elaborate trifling," and it was to be feared that none were "more remote from the true knowledge of God, than many of those who" valued "themselves most upon their supposed knowledge of his creatures." For William Jones of Nayland, the book of creation was in itself "dull and insipid." Revealed religion, however, infused "a new spirit into common things" and disciplined and directed the imagination. Devout reading of the Scriptures transformed "the objects of the natural world" into "objects of revelation." "The touch of a devout mind," Jones explained, had a "magical effect." Living as a Christian, he said, was "the next thing to living in a spiritual world."[25]

With the publication of *A Vindication Of The Rights of Woman* (1792) and *The Age Of Reason* (1794), substance was given to the view, for those looking for it, that people who valued themselves on their knowledge of the book of creation and neglected revelation were remote from true knowledge of God. The "extravagent doctrines" of *A Vindication* could be interpreted as the unnatural outgrowth of natural theology. The religion of the heroine of *Mary* (1788), Mary Wollstonecraft's novel for adolescent girls, was founded on natural theology. After gazing at the moon, rambling along gloomy paths, watching the changing shapes of the clouds, listening to the sea, and taking the "wandering spirits" which she imagined "inhabited every part of nature" as her "constant friends and confidants," the heroine "began to consider the Great First Cause" and "formed just notions of his attributes." More damaging was Thomas Paine's scrutiny of Christian institutions and advocacy of a return to untainted natural theology. "All national institutions of churches," Paine argued, were established "to terrify and enslave mankind, and monopolize power and profit." Christianity had abandoned "the original and beautiful system of theology . . . to make room for the hag of superstition." Paine lamented no longer did men study "God himself in the works" which he made but in "the works or writings" that man made. "THE WORD OF GOD," Paine stressed like a good natural theologian, was "THE CREATION WE BEHOLD."[26]

Such radical support undermined natural theology. This was particularly true during the French Revolution and the first years of the Napoleonic Wars, when English Christianity swung to the theological right. During this period most writers of children's books drew closer to Newton's position, that without a knowledge of the Bible one would misread the book of creation. In their *Cheap Repository Tracts,* the Anglican evangelicals at Clapham stressed reading the Bible in preference to reading nature and they printed Watts's *Songs,* not Mrs. Barbauld's *Hymns,* as a poetry chapbook. Although she recommended that the "Christian Mother" examine "the *great book* of NATURE" with her children, Mrs. Trimmer warned that "this measure alone" did not provide an adequate religious education and should be used in conjunction with revealed religion. "Natural and experimental Philosophy," she wrote, frequently deified nature and denied the existence of "the almighty and all-wise Creator of all things." In *Letters Addressed To A Young Man* (1801), Mrs. West, who wrote several outstanding novels for young people, emphasized the educational importance of moral tales and biblical narratives for children. The "rising generation," she wrote, had received "considerable benefit" from the general use of "little apposite instructive histories of good and naughty children." These had "very deservedly" supplanted stories of fairies and goblins and supplied the juvenile library "with really *valuable* literature." "Example," she explained, was the best means of instruction "at a volatile, thoughtless age." Instructors were "little acquainted with the infant mind," she argued, who believed it could "only be awakened by sensible objects." To replace not merely the objects which awakened children's imaginations but also Watts's educational method which linked physico-theology to Locke's theories on the understanding and of association, she like Newton suggested a biblical key, albeit one adapted to children's limited understandings. "Scripture narratives," she declared, were "proper" for "the purpose of instruction" and would remedy what she thought was the "neglect" of religious studies "in modern education."[27]

If the tide had turned to a slight degree against natural theology in children's books at the end of the eighteenth century, with the prominent exception of Priscilla Wakefield's books, it was running with natural theology in romantic poetry, particularly in that of William Wordsworth. In *Wordsworth's "Natural Methodism",* Richard Brantley argues that Wordsworth's literary world was built "upon the foundation of spiritual and natural theology." Brantley's study shows the great extent to which Wordsworth's poetry was indebted to religious, specifically evangelical, idiom. However, in a discussion of Wordsworth and the Book of Nature, he says little about evangelicals' Newton-like distrust of nature's appeal to the imagination—a distrust which Watts did not communicate to those writers of children's books who learned educational technique from him, and which was not present in Wordsworth's early poetry. Moreover, in Wordsworth's first poetry, as in many of the "first" books written by educators influenced by Watts, there was a strong reliance on Locke's theories of understanding and of association.[28]

Whether or not Watts influenced Wordsworth is speculative. Wordsworth did, however, write much about childhood and growth, and there were parallels between Watts's suggestions for the educational use of natural theology and Wordsworth's use of it in his early poetry. Furthermore, similarities existed between Watts's explanation and emendation of Locke's theory of the understanding in his *Philosophical Essays* and Wordsworth's poetic adaption of the theory that he relied on to explain the mental development of children. Finally, there were marked parallels between Wordsworth's poetry about childhood and Anna Barbauld's poetic prose for children, *Hymns in Prose.* Although a discussion of these similarities cannot establish definite links between Wordsworth and educational theory or children's books, and Wordsworth and Mrs. Barbauld, whom he judged "the first of our literary women," it can at least take children's books in general and the *Hymns* in particular off the narrow shelf of the infant library and place them in the greater literary world where they rightfully belong.[29]

Walter Pater maintained that "the sense of a life in natural objects," which was rhetorical artifice in most poetry, was almost a "literal fact" for Wordsworth. "To him," Pater wrote, "every natural object seemed to possess more or less a moral or spiritual life, to be capable of a companionship with man, full of expression, of inexplicable affinities and delicacies of intercourse." Pater was right. For Wordsworth and Mrs.

Barbauld, natural objects did possess a spiritual life. They revealed the existence and attributes of the deity and emblematically taught those "precepts of natural religion" which Locke said were "intelligible to all mankind." To understand the truths taught by natural objects, or in Newton's words to read the book of creation, people, and most particularly children, did not need the "authority of the Bible." Understanding was reached through sensation and reflection. Wordsworth stressed that impulse, sense perception leading to understanding, played a major role even in the mental development of adults. An impulse could invigorate "the discriminating power of the mind." Unfortunately, the harsh ways of the world, he wrote in the "Preface of 1800," often reduced men's minds to "almost savage torpor"—in effect dulled their sensibility to natural objects. However, an epiphanic moment replete with sense impressions, as when the poet stood upon Westminster Bridge in the early morning light, could bring sudden understanding. The overwhelming wealth of sense impressions pushed through the blackened "white Paper" of a person's mind and unconsciously led his vision beyond the actual object perceived to spiritual understanding. In contrast to adults, who had endured the callousing experience of getting and spending, children found understanding easier. The great birthright of our being, Wordsworth like Locke concluded, was "infant sensibility." As a result, the "common face of Nature spake" to children, and they "held unconscious intercourse / With the eternal Beauty, drinking in / A pure organic pleasure."[30]

In the first book of *The Prelude,* Wordsworth stressed the formative importance of such unconscious sensations. In his youth, he wrote, he felt "hallo'd and pure motions of the sense." These seemed "to own / An intellectual charm," which he thought must belong "To those first-born affinities that fit / Our new existence to existing things, / And, in our dawn of being, constitute / The bond of union betwixt life and joy."[31] In educational terms, the joy Wordsworth described was not secular emotion. Instead, he described the process by which Locke's sensible perception of natural objects ("life") was transformed into spiritual joy. This process was aided by what he called "first-born affinities," a phrase which revealed the similarity between Wordsworth's ideas of natural theology and human development and those of Isaac Watts.

Watts accepted Locke's arguments that ideas originated in sensation and reflection. With his denial of innate ideas and principles, however, Watts, like Sherlock, was slightly uncomfortable. As a strongly religious man, he was sensitive to the possibility that Locke's theories could be construed as offering an explanation of mental and moral development in which God played no significant role. Consequently, he tried to make the deity central to the growth of the understanding. After stating that he was in general agreement with Locke's contention that no ideas were innate, he backtracked, writing, "and yet I believe still that many *simple Ideas* are innate in some Sense, tho' not actually formed in the Mind at the Birth; and perhaps also some *general Principles* both of *Truth* and *Duty* may be called in some Sense innate, tho' not in the explicite Form of Propositions." Examples were the sensible qualities of light, color, sound, taste, and smell. "'Tis only God the Author of our Nature," he continued, "who really forms or creates these Sensations and all these Ideas of sensible Qualities in a Soul, united to a Body." God "appointed" these ideas to arise when particular impressions were made on the brain by sensible objects. Yet, he explained, turning back to Locke, "Man may be said to form them, because what hand soever God has in it, 'tis by one uniform Law of Creation or original Appointment, which has a lasting Efficacy thro' all Generations of Men."

From this discussion of innate ideas of sensible qualities, Watts moved to consider in "*what Sense some Truths may be innate.*" Here, he said, certain truths were self-evident, such as the whole is greater than the part and nothing could be the cause of itself. These were "so interwoven with the very Constitution and Nature of a Reasoning Being" that they became constant principles "of all its Assent or Dissent in particular Enquires" and could also be called innate. Therefore, he concluded, "the Mind or Soul of Man" was not "so perfectly indifferent to receive all Impressions as a *Rasa Tabula,* or *white Paper.*" It was framed by its creator "as not to be equally disposed to all sorts of Perceptions, nor to embrace all Propositions, with an Indifferency to judge them true or false." But "that antecedently to all the Effects of Custom, Experience, Education, or any other contingent Causes," the mind was "ordained" to have "appointed Sensations or Ideas raised in it by certain external Motions." Moreover, it was "also inclined and almost determined by such Principles as are wrought into it by the Creator, to believe some Propositions true, others false; and perhaps also some Actions good, others evil."[32]

The "Soul" which was "the Eternity of Thought," Wordsworth wrote in the first book of *The Prelude,* gave "to forms and images a breath / And everlasting motion." Affected by this breath and motion, the senses enabled children to understand God's immanent presence and his moral truths. The "first-born affinities" or, in Watts's words, those ideas which were appointed to be raised in the mind "by certain external Motions," aided children in reading the book of creation without Newton's biblical key. Unfortunately, reading this particular book became more difficult as children grew older. They accommodated themselves to the unnatural world, or as Wordsworth wrote in the "Intimations" ode, the shades of the prison-house closed upon the growing boy and he became a "little Actor." Throughout man's life, however, the spirit, to bring Emerson to mind, conspired with nature to emancipate man and free him from the roles in which he had become trapped. God's "original Appointment" had a lasting efficacy. No matter how tarnished it was by "evil Influences," the mind was still susceptible to Watts's "external Motions." This predisposition toward virtue gave the mind, Wordsworth wrote, "certain inherent and indestructible qualities" which made the reformation of the worst sinner always possible. For such a reformation to occur, man had to escape from the "blank confusion" of modern life to some "pleasant lea" where he would be more susceptible to simple sense impressions. Washed by the "gentle breeze" of sense impression, he would become receptive to apocalyptic impulse and perhaps rediscover the "Wisdom and Spirit of the universe."[33]

Watts's modification of Locke's theories was not central to the construction of the *Hymns in Prose.* The close similarity between Wordsworth's and Watts's views of innate ideas is significant in a discussion of the *Hymns,* however, not because Mrs. Barbauld adopted it, for she did not, but because it indicates that she and Wordsworth wrote in the same educational tradition, that which originated with Locke and which was popularized by Watts. Moreover, in comparing the *Hymns* with Wordsworth's early poetry, one should not forget that Wordsworth and Mrs. Barbauld had different audiences and consequently different intentions. As a practical educator, Mrs. Barbauld emphasized directing sense experience and tried to reinforce whatever "appointed" inclinations children had toward seeing "the Creator in the visible appearances" of all about them. Written as a "first" book for very young children, the *Hymns* attempted, in Locke's words, to turn "flexible Waters into Chanels" and make lasting impressions on tender infancies. Although Wordsworth's poetry illustrated and stressed the importance of sense experience, it was not explicitly an educational tool. In describing the growth of children, Wordsworth preached to his audience. Because his readers were adults, he could not shape their characters by leading them through a world of formative sense experience. Instead, he appealed to their conscious intelligence. In showing them the importance of sense experience, he implicitly urged them to better, if not reform, their lives by confronting nature much as a child does, but not as a child, for that would be impossible.

The *Hymns* immersed readers in description as Mrs. Barbauld tried to invigorate children's senses with lush pictures of nature. After "infant sensibility" had been marked by sense experience, she directed attention to the God who lay beyond the visible natural garment of the universe. For any natural theologian like Watts, all "lines" of the book of creation yielded meaning. Wordsworth began *The Prelude* metaphorically by stating that he had just been set free from "prison." He compared himself to the ancient Hebrews after they escaped slavery in Egypt and implied that an uncharted wilderness stretched before him. This did not frighten him, however, for he had put his trust in God. Alluding to "the pillar of the cloud" which led the Hebrews by day, he wrote, "should the guide I chose / Be nothing better than a wandering cloud, / I cannot miss my way." Similarly, Mrs. Barbauld encouraged her young readers to put their trust in God. Once they did so, it would be impossible for them to miss the way, for the "sensible objects" which surrounded them revealed God's presence and taught spiritual truths for the conduct of life. "Every field," she wrote, was "like an open book." "Every painted flower" had "a lesson written on its leaves," and "every murmuring brook" had "a tongue." For Wordsworth and Mrs. Barbauld, the decay of the "meanest flower" provoked joyous thoughts which lay "too deep for tears" because, like the rainbow to Noah, the death of a flower revealed God's promise of immortal life. "I have seen," Mrs. Barbauld wrote, "the flower withering in the stalk, and its bright leaves spread on the ground.—I looked again, and it sprung forth afresh; the stem was crowned with new buds, and the sweetness thereof filled the air. I have seen the sun set in the west, and the shades of night shut in the wide horizon: there was no colour, nor shape, nor beauty, nor music; gloom and darkness brooded around—I looked, the sun broke forth again from the east, and gilded the mountain tops; the lark rose to meet him from her low nest, and shades of darkness fled away. . . . Thus shall it be with thee, O man! and so shall thy life be renewed. Beauty shall spring up out of ashes, and life out of the dust."[35]

Both Wordsworth and Mrs. Barbauld celebrated democracy. To a large extent, natural theology of the sort which did not rely upon an authoritarian book or complex religious structure was responsible for their attitudes. It taught the importance of the ordinary appearance of sensible objects. Simple sense impression aided by the "first-born affinities" or Mrs. Barbauld's observations were enough to lead a child to God and to moral truth. In contrast, complexity, best epitomized in *The Prelude* by the city as a type of Bartholomew Fair, confused people. Instead of elevating what at first seemed trivial by showing how it led to God, complexity trivialized all things by reducing them to "blank confusion." The only person not confused by the city's multiplicity was he, Wordsworth wrote, "who hath among least things / An under-sense of greatest," the person who could distinguish the whole from the parts. This ability came, Wordsworth explained, "From early converse with the works of God." Since such familarity was best obtained in the simpler natural world, Wordsworth eschewed the city's deceptive complexity. Moreover, as the modern city was not a type of the heavenly city, so civilized man had strayed far from original simplicity and moral truth. Consequently, as Wordsworth took his readers to the countryside to confront untrammelled nature, so he democratically celebrated the simple man unconsciously close to moral truth. Mrs. Barbauld's egalitarianism was similar to that of Wordsworth, although it was not the same. Early converse with the works of God was, however, for both poets socially leveling, and natural theological criticism of complexity was implicit in the *Hymns,* as Mrs. Barbauld directed attention to simple sensible objects. In teaching children to love "all beings" because they were "the creatures of God," she approached Wordsworth's celebration of Cumberland beggars and old leech-gatherers as ready vehicles of instructive truth. Nature taught, she stressed, that all humans, from the "Negro woman, who sittest pining in captivity" to the "monarch, that ruleth over an hundred states," were equally members of "God's family."[36]

Wordsworth's and Mrs. Barbauld's attitudes toward the use of language were close. Like Locke, both were aware of the abuses of words. Wordsworth's attack on poetic diction in the preface of 1800 stemmed from the same concern as his criticism of the blank confusion of life in London and Locke's criticism of revealed religion in the *Essay.* As poetic diction imposed artificial complexity on language and erected an unnatural barrier between sense experience and spiritual understanding, so revealed religion neglected the "legible characters" of God's "works and providence" and instead focused on the confusing obscurities of words. So that readers would feel the full force of poetry, Wordsworth advocated a "natural" poetical language and stripped poetry of what he called its "gaudiness and inane phraseology." To this end he stressed that the poet was "a man speaking to men" in the "language really spoken by men." Although Mrs. Barbauld followed Watts's suggestions for the subject of the *Hymns,* she rejected the Calvinistic tone of his *Songs.* As Wordsworth criticized poetic diction, so she in effect criticized religious diction. The precepts of natural religion, Locke taught, were "plan and very intelligible to all mankind." Consequently, she used the "easy" language of a man speaking simply in hopes of leading children to "the shepherd's shepherd."[37]

As educators, albeit with different "students," Wordsworth and Mrs. Barbauld emphasized growth in their writings. As Wordsworth referred to *The Prelude* as "Growth Of A Poet's Mind," so the *Hymns in Prose* could have been subtitled "Growth of a Child's Mind." In her preface Mrs. Barbauld emphasized that she wanted to control the "Fair seed-time" of a child's mind in order to lay the "*best foundation for practical devotion in future life.*" Although her instructive intentions resembled "the art" of the "mighty workmen" who were able to "manage books, and things," Mrs. Barbauld's practice did not repress the imagination of children. To be sure, her young readers were not allowed to wander freely through the "open ground / Of Fancy" which Wordsworth celebrated in *The Prelude.* Their lessons were directed, but on the other hand, they were not confined like "engines" to a set didactic "road," and it seems probable that their knowledge was "not purchas'd with the loss" of imaginative "power." In *The Prelude* Wordsworth taught that natural beauty and irrational fear contributed greatly to the development of his imagination and understanding. Unfortunately, the "Tutors of our Youth," he thought, had banished fear from the educational experience and had thereby limited the mental development of their young charges. In the *Hymns* Mrs. Barbauld did not banish fear. Instead, she used it as Wordsworth did, to foster growth and understanding. After attempting to invigorate children's imaginations with rich descriptions of sensible objects, Mrs. Barbauld introduced them to mortality in order to encourage them to reflect on themselves and the state of man. Although the concept of mortality was not fear, it could lead to bleak fears of death, and then, Mrs. Barbauld hoped, to spiritual knowledge of immortality. Resembling the poet's development in *The Prelude,* the imaginative and spiritual growth of Mrs. Barbauld's young readers was in a sense fostered by beauty and by fear. "The rose is sweet," she wrote, "but it is surrounded with thorns: the lily of the valley is fragrant, but it springeth up amongst the brambles. The spring is pleasant, but it soon is past. The rainbow is very glorious, but it soon vanisheth away: life is good, but is quickly swallowed up in death. There is a land, where roses are without thorns, where the flowers are not mixed with brambles. In that land, there is eternal spring, and light without any cloud. The tree of life groweth in the midst thereof; rivers of pleasures are there, and flowers that never fade."[38]

Both Wordsworth and Mrs. Barbauld stressed that imagination was more important to a child's early development than reason. It was reasonable educators, Wordsworth implied in *The Prelude,* who had banished Fortunatus from the nursery. These "too industrious times," he wrote, had engendered a "monster birth," a child who was not a child but who was a "dwarf Man." This child's mind had been crammed with factual, useful knowledge, and he had little sympathy for the natural wonders surrounding him. The "playthings" which "old Grandame Earth" had lovingly designed for him lay "Unthought of." Although Mrs. Barbauld did not regret Fortunatus' absence from the nursery, or more to the point, the absence of Tom Hodge and his tale-telling school fellows, she did champion the imagination. In a catechistical section of her sixth hymn, she urged children to use their imaginations to discover the presence of God beyond sensible objects. What Wordsworth called a dwarf man was Mrs. Barbauld's "child of reason," and she began her instructive catechism by asking the child of reason where he had been and what he had seen. Lacking imagination, he answered that he had been in the meadow looking at cattle and wheat. "Didst thou see nothing more?" Mrs. Barbauld asked.

> Didst thou observe nothing besides? Return again, child of reason, for there are greater things than these. —God was among the fields; and didst thou not perceive him? his beauty was upon the meadows; his smile enlivened the sun-shine. I have walked through the thick forest; the wind whispered among the trees; the brook fell from the rocks with a pleasant murmur; the squirrel leapt from bough to bough; and the birds sung to each other amongst the branches. Didst thou hear nothing, but the murmur of the brook? no whispers, but the whispers of the wind? Return again, child of reason, for there are greater things than these. —God was amongst the trees; his voice sounded in the murmur of the water; his music warbled in the shade; and didst thou not attend?[39]

Mrs. Barbauld was not, as Matthew Arnold called Wordsworth, "one of the very chief glories of English Poetry."[40] She was, however, one of the glories of eighteenth-century English children's books, and her writings deserve more recognition. The literary way from early eighteenth-century godly books through Locke and Watts to the *Hymns in Prose* is winding. Nevertheless, the way to Anna Barbauld can be traced, and although it is impossible to obtain a clear view, for time has grown tall and leafy, this path from the world of Lockean education and children's books may wind through romantic poetry itself.

CHAPTER SIX

John Marshall's Literary Associates and Disciplining the Natural Temper

Writers and publishers of children's books readily adopted Mrs. Barbauld's "hints" on style and layout. They did not, however, frequently imitate the gentle natural theology of the *Hymns.* Like John Newton, many seemed convinced that the "study of the works of God, independent of his word" was "no better than an elaborate trifling." Instead of reading the book of creation to children, they often wrote "scripture narratives" and those "apposite instructive histories of good and naughty children" praised by Mrs. West. While keeping the imagination within proper bounds, these histories stressed discipline and taught right behavior. In *Some Thoughts,* Locke urged parents to use examples in instructing children. Set "before their Eyes," he wrote, "the *Examples* of those Things you would have them do, or avoid." Nothing, he stated, sank so deeply and so gently into "Men's Minds, as *Example.*" Instructive histories provided parents with a wealth of examples. These, authors stressed, were not so much fiction which appealed to the imagination as they were fables appealing to the understanding. In reading such books, children were encouraged to pay "chief attention" to the advice they gave rather than to the amusement they provided.[1]

By the 1780s Locke's educational ideas had long been "universal," and the malleability of children was "holy writ." The "Influence, which Parents and Tutors may have over the Minds of Children," David Fordyce had written thirty years earlier, "is almost incredible. They may sow Errors and Prejudices, or Truth and Knowledge, and fix right or wrong

Habits so deep in their Constitution, that it shall be almost impossible ever to extirpate them." In the preface to *The First Book for English Schools; Or The Rational Schoolmaster's First Assistant* (1787), John Parsons stated that he wanted to teach children to read and to "furnish their memories" with tales and verses "as may afterwards, by returning to the mind, be as so many monitors against vice, and constant prompters, to virtuous actions." Although at first view it might seem impossible for very young children to be furnished with lifelong monitors and prompters, Parsons reminded readers of Locke's ideas on human development. "The mind," he wrote, was "at first, a meer blank, on which may be inscribed, what characters you please." Because "the first particulars inscribed upon it" made "deep impressions" which were "hardly to be eradicated during life," there was an opportunity "strongly to imprint, on the minds of youth, such principles of virtue, and religion; as may probably have, a happy influence." The "bettering of the next generation," Parsons explained, depended "greatly, on the education, of the youth" of the present generation, and he urged parents "to take care, what Books they give their children to read."[2]

In the last quarter of the eighteenth century, the publication of children's books became a serious business—serious not merely because it was profitable but because it was taken for granted that children's books, like Fordyce's parents and tutors, could greatly influence "the Minds of Children." The person who had discovered "the true Secret of Education," Locke wrote, was he who "found a way" to keep "a Child's Spirit, easy, active and free" while simultaneously restraining "him from many things he" had "a Mind to" and drawing "him to things" that were "uneasy to him." Instead of restraint, Newbery's books emphasized keeping children's spirits active and free. The shortest path to knowledge and proper conduct lay, he thought, across a landscape pepperminted with laughter. With smoke from the Gordon Riots, violent sectarian disturbances in London in 1780 that seemed to indicate instability within the nation, lingering on the horizon and with commercial growth and the spread of education beyond the upper and middle classes straining the oligarchic fabric of society, unrestrained merriment did not seem the ideal mate for wisdom in the 1780s. Although entertainment was recognized as a necessary ingredient of children's books, educators frequently pointed out the abuses of seductive playfulness. "When we speak of rendering literature agreeable to children," Richard Edgeworth wrote in *Practical Education,* we should avoid "the error of those who in their first lessons accustom their pupils to so much amusement, that they cannot help afterwards feeling disgusted with the sobriety of instruction." "It has been the fashion of late to attempt teaching every thing to children in play," Edgeworth explained, "and ingenious people have contrived to insinuate much useful knowledge without betraying the design to instruct." "This system" could not, however, "be pushed beyond certain bounds without many inconveniences." The habit of being amused made unfortunate impressions on children, for not only did it increase the desire for amusement but it so lessened "the relish for pleasure" that "a course of perpetually increasing stimulus" was "necessary to awaken attention."[3]

Edgeworth's criticism of the extent to which play and recreation had become essential to children's books was not an attack upon Locke's profit-and-delight formula. Instead, it underlined a slight shift in educational emphasis that occurred in many children's books published near the end of the century. Although authors continued to appeal to that "Natural Temper of Children" which disposed their minds to wander, some tried to prevent children's minds from wandering too far. Newbery's success taught the importance of weaving play into children's books. By the 1780s, however, some educators believed Newbery had emphasized delight at the expense of profit. For them, profit included instruction and discipline, and attempts were made, most particularly by some of John Marshall's authors, to blend profit and delight into a healthier whole. In *Some Thoughts,* Locke had emphasized the importance of discipline. The "great Principle and Foundation of all Vertue and Worth," he wrote, lay in a man's power "to *deny himself* Desires, cross his own Inclinations, and purely follow what Reason directs as best, tho' the Appetite lean the other Way." A good education, he stressed, enabled a child to master his inclinations. One could weave such mastery into children's natures, Locke explained, by reasoning with them. The "plainest, easiest, and most efficacious" way of reasoning with children, he taught, was to set examples of good and bad behavior before them. These, he asserted, had "more force to draw or deter their Imitation" than "any Discourses" that could be directed to them.[4]

At the same time that Locke taught the importance of example and provided an apologia for Mrs. West's little apposite histories, he strongly criticized attempting to weave discipline into children's natures through the use of rewards and punishments. Esteem and disgrace, he granted, were "powerful Incentives to the Mind," but other rewards and punishments which depended on the "Pains and Pleasures of the Body" were, he added, "*ill-chosen.*" Flattering children "by *Rewards* of things" should be avoided. "He that will give his Son *Apples,* or *Sugar-plumbs,*" he wrote, "to make him learn his Book does but authorize his Love of Pleasure, and cocker up that dangerous Propensity, which he ought by all Means to subdue and stifle in him." The playthings or baits which Locke suggested to cozen children into knowledge were not rewards but lures. Although they made learning pleasurable, they were used to attract children to learning rather than to "flatter" them afterward. Although the distinction between a reward and a bait was real, it was not great, and it was not something to which Newbery paid much attention. In cozening children into knowledge, Newbery's books sometimes seemed, from the point of view of the mid-1780s, to encourage children to indulge rather than cross their inclinations. In *The Renowned History of Giles Gingerbread* (1764), learning was linked to appetite as much as to ambition and reason. The foundation of Giles's virtue and worth, and he was well on the way to riding in a coach and six, did not lie in his power to deny himself. If Giles had crossed his inclinations, he would not have been a success. He might not have even been, for he was, as Newbery put it, "A Little Boy who lived upon Learning."[5]

At the beginning of *Giles Gingerbread,* "Old Gaffer Gingerbread" saw his son Giles, "who was a ragged as a Colt," trying to climb up behind Sir Toby Thompson's coach. Gaffer Gingerbread told his son that he should try to go in through the door instead of climbing on top. Giles answered that the door was not for poor people. "Not for poor Folks, replied the Father, yes, but it is. A poor Man, or a poor Boy may get a Coach, if he will endeavour to deserve it. Merit and Industry may entitle a Man to any thing." Gaffer Gingerbread then described how Sir Toby

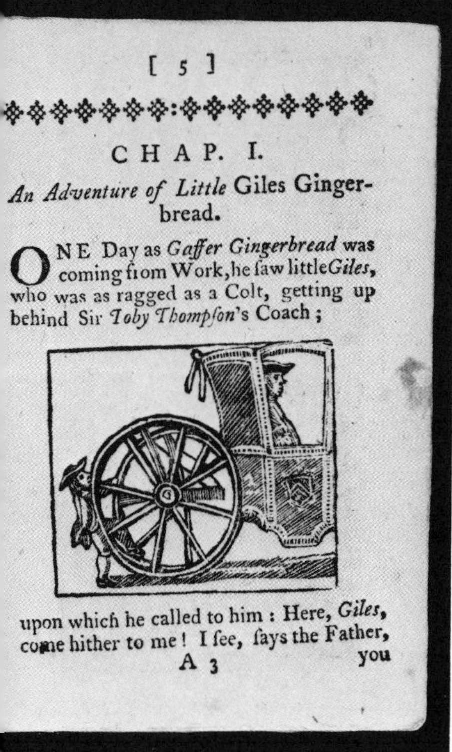

[5]

CHAP. I.

An Adventure of Little Giles Gingerbread.

ONE Day as *Gaffer Gingerbread* was coming fiom Work, he ſaw little *Giles*, who was as ragged as a Colt, getting up behind Sir *Toby Thompſon*'s Coach;

upon which he called to him: Here, *Giles*, come hither to me! I ſee, ſays the Father,

A 3 you

From *The Renowned History of Giles Gingerbread.* Copyright Bodleian Library Oxford.

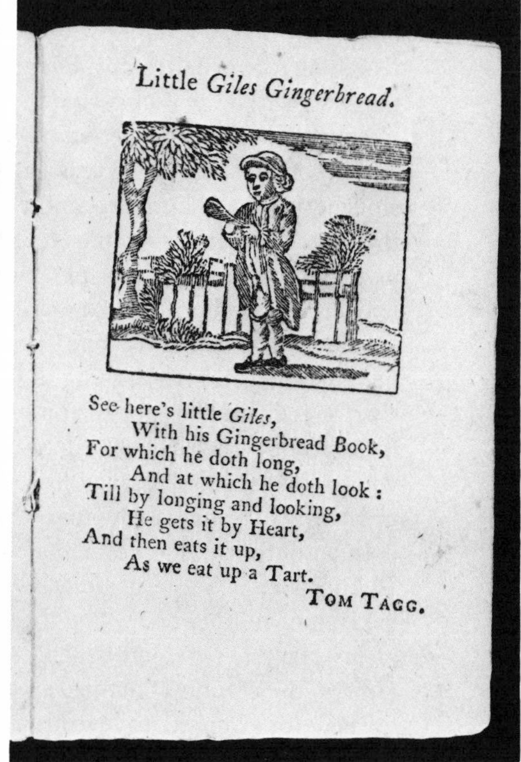

Little *Giles Gingerbread.*

See here's little *Giles*,
With his Gingerbread *Book*,
For which he doth long,
And at which he doth look:
Till by longing and looking,
He gets it by Heart,
And then eats it up,
As we eat up a Tart.

TOM TAGG.

From *The Renowned History of Giles Gingerbread.* Copyright Bodleian Library Oxford.

himself had risen from poverty. Toby was the son of a poor widow with three children. She took in washing, but often ends didn't meet and the children went without meals. One day, when Mr. and Mrs. Goodwill passed the widow's house, they saw all three children crying. Two of the children were crying because they were hungry; Toby cried because he had no food to give the other two. A wealthy London tradesman, Mr. Goodwill took pity on Toby and made him his servant. Later, Toby returned the good deed by exposing another servant who had been robbing Mr. Goodwill. Industrious and honest, Toby soon became Mr. Goodwill's favorite servant. Eventually he became Mr. Goodwill's business partner and was able to ride in a coach and six.

Sir Toby's success appealed to Giles, and the boy decided to learn to read when his father, who was a gingerbread baker, baked a gingerbread alphabet to cozen him into knowledge. After Giles learned the letters, the alphabet quickly became an edible reward. Next, Old Gingerbread baked a hornbook on which he wrote a syllabary. This did not last very long either. When Gaffer Gingerbread returned from his rounds, he discovered Giles "had eat up one Corner of his Book." "Hey day *Giles,* says he, what do you love learning so well as to eat up your Book? Why Father, says *Giles,* I am not the only Boy who has eat his Words. No Boy loves his Book better than I do, but I always learn it, before I eat it. Say you so, says the Father, pray let me hear you say your Lesson" – whereupon Giles "sung the whole Cuz's Chorus," which the publisher pointed out, "the sly Rogue had got out of Mr. *Newbery's* pretty Play Thing." Gaffer Gingerbread was so pleased with Giles's progress that he baked him another book, "on the learning of which, he told him, much of his Happiness would depend." Entitled *How to be Happy and go to Heaven,* the volume contained six rules from the New Testament. Giles learned, for example, to love his neighbor as well as himself, to pray for his enemies, to go to church on Sunday, and to be charitable to people in distress. Once these were, if not woven into his nature, at least part of Giles's very being, his father baked another book. This taught him to obey his parents, listen to good advice, keep animals in their proper place, and not to lie. A short instructive history and a wood or gingerbread cut accompanied each of these lessons. Thus, when Tom's father bought a lion "for a show," he warned his son that the animal was dangerous. Tom, alas, paid no attention; when his father was away, he went to the lion's hutch to play. There "the Beast caught hold of him with his Paw, and chopt his Head off." Each day Giles received new books, "all of which he eat up," so Newbery concluded, "it may truly be said, *he lived upon Learning.*"[6]

Giles Gingerbread was an entertaining book. However, the parent who used it as a teaching plaything was pretty well obligated to have a supply of gingerbread on hand. Although it encouraged learning and contained biblical rules of conduct and instructive tales, it did not consciously teach self-denial and its stress on play could be interpreted as authorizing love of pleasure. Although Newbery taught religion, loyalty, and good morals while he "gratified" curiosity, his "engaging books," Mrs. Trimmer wrote in 1802, were "in some respects objectionable." Mrs. Trimmer did not specify what aspects of Newbery's books were objectionable. Her own books were, however, generally more serious than those of Newbery. In them she put greater emphasis upon profit, particularly the profit of discipline, and it seems probable that she, like Richard Edgeworth, found the fashion of playing children into knowledge fraught with many inconveniences. In a review of *Mince Pies for Christmas,* a collection of riddles and charades "Intended to Gratify the Mental Taste, and to Exercise the Ingenuity of Sensible Masters and Misses," Mrs. Trimmer genially extended the eating and learning metaphor and warned parents against letting children feed upon books indiscriminately. "So much *cookery*" was going on "amongst the Editors of Children's Books," she wrote, that booksellers' shops resembled the shops of pastry cooks. Along with the "good and wholesome," one could find "some things . . . fit only to corrupt the taste of the plain eater, or gratify the vitiated appetite of those who, by luxurious indulgence" had "lost all relish" for the "simple and nutritive." This comparison, she continued, could be extended to "the commodities of the *Literary Cook's Shop*" with "its plain wholesome *biscuits,* its *buns,* its *diet-bread,* its *rich plum-cakes,* its *mince pies.*" All these, childish and youthful curiosity "devoured with greediness, when not restrained by parental care." "The art of the apothecary" could remedy the consequences of indulging in things bought in "*the Pastry Cook's Shop*" and "restore nature to itself." But who, she asked, "can answer that the poison which the *mind* receives in infancy, or early youth, will ever be eradicated?"[7]

When he criticized the works of Mrs. Barbauld and those of the crew who followed her, Lamb noted that *Goody Two-Shoes* was "almost out of print." In the mid-1780s, books published by or similar to those published by John Marshall helped push *Goody Two-Shoes* onto a relatively neglected shelf of the juvenile library. Like those of Mrs. Trimmer, many of Marshall's books were more serious than Newbery's, placing greater emphasis upon discipline and less upon play and recreation. Unlike Newbery, who became a celebrated public character, even whirling into *The Vicar of Wakefield* to succor Dr. Primrose while he lay ill at "the Wells," Marshall has remained faceless. While Newbery's good humor sprawled beyond the covers of his books, often overwhelming their instructive contents and calling attention to the publisher himself, Marshall did not let his personality edge into his publications, much less divert attention from their contents. In 1785, in an advertisement attached to A.C.'s *The Footstep to Mrs. Trimmer's Sacred History For the Instruction and Amusement of Little Children,* Marshall listed thirty of his books. These, he informed "Ladies, Gentlemen, and the Heads of Schools," were all "*original,* and *not compiled*" and had been "written to suit the various Ages for which they" were "offered." Moreover, he continued, they were composed "on a more liberal Plan, and in a different Style from the Generality of Works designed for Young People: being entirely divested of that prejudicial Nonsense (to young Minds) the Tales of *Hobgoblins, Witches, Fairies, Love, Gallantry, etc.* with which such little Performances heretofore abounded." By *liberal,* Marshall meant educationally progressive. His books were tools, he implied, which the "mighty workmen" of the 1780s would find useful in shaping children's personalities and fashioning that instructive regimen which Lamb said "banished all the old classics out of the nursery."[8]

Like Woglog the giant, Marshall seemed to have started his career with a hankering for more adventuresome things. But as Woglog stumbled against Tommy Trip, so Marshall may have met Mrs. Trimmer, or some of the crew associated with her. At the back of *The History Of The Good Lady Kindheart, Of Hospitable-Hall. Near The Village of Allgood* appeared a "catalogue" of Marshall's books "for the Instruction and Amusement of CHILDREN." Although the *History* did not have a date on the title page, an edition appears to have been published in 1780. On page 47 of the copy in the Victoria and Albert Museum is the inscription, "Elizabeth Mitchell Her Book sent her from Miss Nuns of Portsmouth by her sister Polly January 1781." Only two of the thirty books advertised in A.C.'s *Footstep* were listed in the catalogue: *The First Principles of Religion* and *The History of a great many Little Boys and Girls.* Some of the other books in the catalogue, *The Careful Parent's Gift* and *A Compleat Abstract of the Holy Bible,* for example, seemed to emphasize instruction more than amusement. Many of the books, however, stressed amusement and were markedly less didactic than the volumes Marshall advertised in the *Footstep* and whose publication he trumpeted in the middle and late 1780s. Among the books in the catalogue were *Goody Goosecap*—6d., Solomon Sobersides' *Christmas Tales*—6d., *The Friends; or, the History of Billy Freeman and Tommy Truelove*—3d., *A Choice Gift and Pretty Toy; with the Story of Little Red Riding Hood*—2d., *The Pleasant Gift; Or, a Collection of New Riddles*—2d., *Nancy Cock's Song Book By Nurse Lovechild*—2d., *Gaffer Goose's Golden Plaything*—1d., *The New Year's Gift*—1d., Nurse Allgood's *Whitsuntide Present*—1d., *The House that Jack Built, with some Account of Jack Jingle*—1d., *The Life, Death, and Burial of Cock Robin*—1d., *Tom Thumb's Play-Thing*—1d., and *Jackey Dandy's Delight*—1d..[9]

Less expensive and not so "*original*" as the instructive books which Marshall was soon to publish, the volumes in the catalogue constituted a relatively safe group with which to begin trading in children's books. The *Abstract* of the Bible was, if not exciting, certainly safe, and *Goody Goosecap* as an imitation of *Goody Two-Shoes* could be expected to sell fairly well. Tom Thumb, Cock Robin, and Little Red Riding Hood were well-known nursery characters, while the house that Jack built was one of the most famous estates in Lilliputia. In publishing this list of books, Marshall closely followed, if not in the footprints, at least in the printmarks of Newbery the master. Gaffer Goose was a kinsman of Jack the Giant-Killer. Like Jack, Goose was concerned about children's behavior. British commercial growth, however, had enabled old Goose to reward the children who followed the rules contained in his *Golden Plaything* more handsomely than Jack rewarded pretty Miss Polly or little

Master Tommy. Instead of a penny for being good, Goose said he would give a bag of gold and half a brick of silver, which he assured readers he kept locked up for that purpose, "to any little girl or boy" who could furnish proof that he had not broken any of the *Plaything*'s rules "in thought, word, or deed, for the space of one whole twelve-month and a day."

Nancy Cock and Nurse Lovechild were also familiar characters, having first appeared in the 1740s, while Nurse Allgood was a relative of Newbery's Nurse Truelove. The main characters of *The Whitsuntide Present* closely resembled those in Newbery's *The Whitsuntide–Gift.* In this latter book, because Master Billy and Miss Kitty Smith were the best children in the whole county, the Duke of Goodwill presented them with two small horses and invited them to spend part of the summer with his son and daughter, the Marquis of Goodwill and Lady Mary, at his family seat in Yorkshire. In a "pretty neat country Village" in the west of England, Nurse Allgood similarly recounted in *The Whitsuntide Present,* the "first thing seen in the morning" was "Master and Miss Goodchild going to school hand in hand, where they always came before any of the other scholars." Although his family estate Mannerly Park was perhaps not so old as the Duke of Goodwill's seat in Yorkshire, the Duke of Goodmanners was just as distinguished a nobleman. When he came down from London, he invited George and Charlotte Goodchild to visit Mannerly Park and meet his two children, Lady Maria Dutiful and the Marquis of Wellbehave. At Mannerly Park, the Goodchilds, like the Smiths, were given presents. From the duke, Master Goodchild received some books while the marquis gave him a fiddle. The duchess gave Miss Charlotte a gold watch and her picture set in diamonds, and Lady Maria presented her with "a fine green Parrot, lately arrived from abroad," and a gilt cage in which to keep him.[10]

Most of these books which Marshall initially published contained a modicum of digestible instruction. Through hard work and virtue, Jack Jingle rose from a cottage to his fabled mansion. He began life humbly as the son of Gaffer Jingle. His industry, however, drew him to the attention of the benevolent Sir Luke Loveall, whose favorite he soon became. Sir Luke sent him to school, after which he presented him with a fine coach and six and that estate on which Jack constructed his famous house. In *Jackey Dandy's Delight,* Billy Froward was not allowed to see the birds and beasts depicted in the book because he had told a lie. The punishment, and shame it made him feel, so upset Billy that he promised never to lie again. The heroine of *Nurse Dandlem's Little Repository,* a book advertised at the end of *Goody Goosecap,* told instructive stories to the "Chickabiddy Generation." The son of a wealthy miller in Yorkshire, Wake Wilful, she recounted, was a naughty boy who often skipped school. One day while he was truant, a press gang seized him and carried him aboard the *Dragon.* When the *Paul Jones,* an American pirate ship, sank the *Dragon,* Wake was captured, then imprisoned in the hole with rats and mice for companions. Because the pirates did not want a bad boy on board their ship, Wake was marooned on an island belonging to the giant Grumbolumbo. The brother of "*Raw-head-and-bloody-bones,*" Grumbolumbo had three heads, nine eyes, and seven toes "besides his great one on each foot." At first, Wake was happy to be abandoned on the island. Trees hung heavy with fruit, and he ate greedily until he fell asleep on a couch of flowers. While he slept, however, the couch changed into a car drawn by fiery dragons and escorted by six hobgoblins. They carried Wake to Grumbolumbo's cave, where the giant imprisoned him. Grumbolumbo wanted to fatten Wake and serve him as a delicacy at the feast which was to be held in honor of his marriage to the giantess Unavilda. Happily though, Fairy Starbright decided to help Wake, who by now had determined to be a good boy. Starbright poisoned Grumbolumbo and then enabled Wake to return home, where he behaved superbly.[11]

Because she was "a hundred years old," all Nurse Dandlem's little pupils had "a great reverence for her." Not having read Locke, however, they were not able to judge what constituted a good children's book. Like that in Nurse Dandlem's stories, the instruction found in many of the books advertised in Marshall's catalogue seemed to be fashioned out of rubbish and lumber. Where a good education was intended, to bring Watts to mind, many educators were now certain something more substantial was necessary. In *A Storehouse of Stories* (1870), Charlotte Yonge said that one of Dorothy Kilner's nieces informed her that Mrs. Trimmer "overlooked [examined] many of her works in MS." Dorothy Kilner's *First Principles of Religion* was advertised at the end of *The History of Good Lady Kindheart.* Mrs. Trimmer was familiar with the *First Principles* and in 1784 made an abridgment of it for Marshall entitled *Sunday School Dialogues.* Perhaps she, or she and Dorothy Kilner together, urged Marshall, as Tommy Trip did Woglog, to change his ways and make his publications more original and instructive. By the time of the appearance of *The Footstep* in 1785, Marshall had reformed his list. He was a shrewd publisher and, reading the market well, he saw that instruction would sell. While keeping a selection of old-fashioned, amusing books in print, he now concentrated his energies on children's books "entirely divested" of what he called "prejudicial Nonsense." Marshall harvested golden dividends from his new crop of publications. Not only was his list popular, but he established a reputation as a printer of moral works. In 1795 he was made "Printer to the CHEAP REPOSITORY for Moral and Religious Tracts," a post he held until November 1797, when J. and C. Evans and Hatchard succeeded him.[12]

In shifting emphasis away from amusement to instruction, Marshall acknowledged the shortcomings of his first publications. One of the volumes which he advertised in 1785 was *Poems On Various Subjects, For The Amusement of Youth.* Of the thirty-one poems in the book, ten were written by Dorothy Kilner. In "Convesation [*sic*] between Master Tommy and Miss Jenny on Reading," Tommy asked Jenny, who was rushing past him in a great hurry, to stop and toss a ball. Jenny refused, saying that she preferred to read "pretty books." Tommy was startled. He did not like reading, and he asked her "pray where / In your life, did you meet with a book, / Deserving the title of *pretty* to bear, / Or worthy receiving a look?" Her mother, Jenny replied, always called upon Mr. Marshall when she went to town, and he sent "great numbers of pretty books down," which, Jenny added, she studied with pleasure. Not all Marshall's books were good, however, and Jenny noted, "Some with nonsense indeed, more than others abound, / Which mamma shortly throws in the fire; / Whilst those which exhibit instructions more sound, / With rapture I read and admire." Books properly filled with sound instruction appealed to Tommy, and he told Jenny that in the future "Mr. *Marshall*" could send him books too.[13]

Jenny's mother would not have found much fuel for her fire among the books which Marshall advertised in *The Footstep* in 1785. The only books whose tone occasionally echoed Newbery's light-hearted instruction were Marshall's didactic histories. These included *The Adventures of a Pincushion, Memoirs of a Peg-Top,* and *The Life and Perambulation of a Mouse.* Even here, however, amusement seldom got in the way of instruction. The entertaining "perambulations" of Brighteyes were exceptional, as the biographies usually were skeletal narratives fleshed out with somber examples. The account of John Active and his family was grimly typical. However, it taught an important lesson to the young hero of *William Sedley: or, the Evil Day Deferred.* Through hard work, Active had "got a pretty fortune." A large sum was spent, however, on medical expenses for his daughter Susan, who broke her leg when she disobeyed her parents and jumped off the top of a gate. In carrying Susan about until she was able to walk, Mrs. Active "got a hurt in her back, which never could be cured, and occasioned her to be lame all the rest of her life." On a later occasion, when Susan and her sister Nancy did not want to help their mother make a bed curtain, they pretended to be sleepy. Sent to bed, they immediately lit a candle and began reading. When they thought they heard their mother on the stairs, they hid the candle in the closet and pretended to be asleep. Soon, however, their pretence became reality, and they fell asleep without extinguishing the candle. Left unattended in the closet, the candle burned a hole in the shelf and caught the house on fire. Although Mr. Active rescued the girls from the flames, he lost all his possessions and "one of his legs" was so badly burned that he was unable to work for a long time. Moreover, the fire had "such an effect" on Mrs. Active "that she was never well after." Despite this calamity, Active's "perverse and disobedient" daughters did not mend their ways and as a result the family's fortunes deteriorated further. All was not lost, however, for the ashes of the Actives' family fortune nurtured young Sedley's awareness of the consequences of disobedience.[14]

In the 1750s and 1760s, Newbery published several religious books for children. Four of these were advertised as a set: *The History Of the Lives, Actions, Travels, Sufferings and Deaths Of The Apostles And Evangelists* (1763), *An History Of The Life Of Our Lord and Saviour Jesus Christ. To which is added, The Life of the Blessed Virgin Mary* (1764), *An History Of the Lives, Actions, Travels, Sufferings, and Deaths of the most eminent Martyrs, and Primitive Fathers of the Church, in the first four Centuries* (1764), and *The New Testament Of Our Lord and Saviour Jesus Christ, Abridged and harmonized in the Words of the Evangelists* (1764). Costing a shilling a volume, the books were comparatively long. *An History Of . . . Jesus Christ,* for example, was 192 pages long, while there were 311 pages of text in *The New Testament . . . Abridged and harmonized.* Although Newbery advertised that the books were "For the Use of Children," little was done to suit them to "a Child's Capacity and Notions." In *The New Testament,* the four gospels were blended into a single continuous narrative. As a youth "in the Country among People of little Learning, and less Speculation, without proper Books for my Assistance," Newbery explained, he had been confused by the fact that four historians drawing upon the same sources had not recorded the same events. Therefore, as soon as he was able, he recounted, he determined "to set the Matter in a light, and adapt those glorious and important Truths to the Capacities of Children, so that no other weak Minds might labour under the same Difficulties." Although the unified narrative cleared up the particular difficulty which Newbery remembered, no effort was made to simplify the biblical language or make the account of Christ's life appeal specifically to children. *The New Testament* was simply a scissors-and-paste job. Newbery seems to have recognized that the book was not really suited for tender minds, and later he published the shorter *An History Of The Life Of Our Lord,* in which he said the obscure allusions present in *The New Testament* were effectively explained. Unfortunately, this too was not an appealing children's book. Newbery took little pains with the religious books he published for children. As an entrepreneur of patent medicines, perhaps he was more interested in curing bodies than saving souls. Be that as it may, however, only one of his religious books for children today seems a success.[15]

The Holy Bible Abridged: Or, The History Of The Old and New Testament was first published in 1758. In 1768 Newbery and Carnan printed a seventh edition. In contrast to Newbery's other religious books, in this one care was taken to appeal to children. In *Some Thoughts* Locke warned against using the Bible as a primer and forcing children to read selections they could not understand. "The promiscuous reading of it through, by Chapters, as they lye in order" inhibited the acquisition of reading skills and gave children "an odd jumble of Thoughts . . . concerning Religion." The "Law of *Moses,* the Song of *Solomon,* the Prophecies in the Old, and the Epistles and *Apocalypse* in the New Testament," he wrote, were beyond "a Child's Capacity." Although "the History of the Evangelists, and the Acts" were somewhat easier, these were also "very disproportionate to the understanding of Childhood." To "ingage" a child to read while insuring that he would not become confused about religion, Locke suggested that young children's biblical studies be limited to "easy and plain moral Rules" taken from the New Testament and to stories selected primarily from the Old Testament. As examples of the latter, he cited "the Story of *Joseph,* and his Brethren, of *David* and *Goliath,* of *David* and *Jonathan.*"[16]

Biblical stories suited the educational spirit of the late eighteenth century. Unlike spiritual biography, they taught a child how to live in this world and were not liable to sow fatal "*Bug-bear* Thoughts" in children's minds. In being filled with the marvelous and the improbable, they resembled fairy tales and romances. Unlike fairy tales, which conventional wisdom condemned for presenting false views of life, biblical stories were thought true. The careful parent who protected his child from fiction, including instructive histories, probably encouraged his reading the Bible and studying revealed religion. "What reading can be so pleasing as the Bible?" Mrs. Trimmer's Thomas Simkins asked Kitty the housemaid. "I like," he continued, "Robinson Crusoe, and the other book of travels my master lent us, very well, but they are not half so entertaining as the stories in the bible and testament; besides how do we know the first are true? and we are sure the latter are so, because they were written by holy men, who were taught by God himself what to write."[17]

Unlike that of fiction, any appeal which biblical stories made to the imagination was not considered dangerous. The imagination, Hannah More wrote, was "an enemy of peculiar potency" until it was "employed in the cause of God." Religion was "the only subject" in which the imagination could "safely stretch its powers and expand its energies." In teaching children the Bible, she urged parents to appeal to the imagination. "It is a lion," she explained, "which though worldly prudence indeed may *chain* so as to prevent outward mischief, yet the malignity remains within; but when sanctified by Christianity, the imagination is a lion *tamed;* you have all the benefit of its strength and its activity, divested of its mischief." Children's fondness for narrative was, Mrs. West wrote, "one of their most active passions," and she urged teachers to illustrate their observations with stories from the Old and New Testaments. Children's "sparkling" eyes would, she said, prove the effects of such instruction.[18] Marshall, who made much of the assertion that his children's books were free of the dangerous nonsense found in romances and fairy tales, published several collections of biblical stories in order to "*introduce Young Minds to an early Acquaintance with the Bible.*" For many children such an acquaintance must have differed little from an acquaintance with fairy tales. God, or God through his son, resembled the fairy godmother who watched over and rewarded the good but neglected child. Like Puss in Boots who obtained an estate for the Marquis of Carabas, Jacob was a trickster who obtained a blessing through craft. As a large fish swallowed Tom Thumb, so a whale swallowed Jonah. The Joseph saga which Locke recommended had several parallels with fairy tales. Although he was the youngest and weakest of his brothers, Joseph was the only dreamer. Like Little Poucet, he saved his stronger brothers from destruction. Sold into slavery, or forced to endure hardship like Cinderella, he became the typical wanderer, journeying to a far country and experiencing fabulous adventures which tested him. Similarly, David was the youngest and to all appearances the weakest son, yet, behaving like Jack the Giant-Killer, he killed Goliath, the Philistine ogre.[19]

In the preface to *The Holy Bible Abridged,* Newbery explained that his design was to give "Children such a Taste of the Writings of the Holy Pen-men, as may engage them earnestly and seriously in the Study of the Sacred Books of the *Old* and *New Testament.*" To forward "this laudable and pious Pursuit," he followed the spirit of Locke's suggestions and adapted the most famous biblical stories to a child's capacity. From the Old Testament he included, for example, accounts of David and Goliath, Joseph, the deluge, the fall of Jericho, Jonah, Shadrach, Meschach, and Abednego, and Daniel in the lions' den; from the New Testament, he took the stories of Lazarus, the Good Samaritan, the Prodigal Son, and so forth. "Such Portions of the Scriptures," he wrote, were "both *instructive* and *entertaining.*" Not only would they "feed the Fancy" but they would "mend the Heart, and establish in the Mind those unalterable Laws of the DEITY, which lead us to the Knowledge of Himself, which cement us together in Society, and on which our Happiness both in this Life and the next must absolutely depend."[20] *The Holy Bible Abridged* contained many illustrations which contributed to its appeal. Filled with wonderful anachronisms, these must have fed children's fancies even if they did not necessarily help establish the unalterable laws of the deity in the mind. A full-rigged British merchantman stood off shore in the background of the plate which showed Jonah's escaping from the sea monster's mouth. No hint of barren waste appeared in the depiction of the pharaoh's host's being swept to their deaths in the Red Sea. Instead, the landscape was comfortably English, filled with shrubs, small trees, and rolling hills. Crumbling Jericho resembled a medieval castle, and Sodom was not a baked village beside the Dead Sea, but an eighteenth-century market town.

Newbery's handling of religion differed greatly from the way Marshall handled it. Although *The Holy Bible Abridged* enjoyed much success and although Newbery taught religion throughout his books, religious instruction did not play so big a role in his publications as it did in Marshall's. Constituting only part of the miscellaneous contents of Newbery's most popular children's books, religious matter was reduced by its surroundings and seemed to carry no more didactic weight than the jumble of alphabets, fables, humorous and moral tales, poems, and letters from Jack the Giant-Killer which filled the rest of Newbery's pages. In *Giles Gingerbread,* for example, "How to be Happy and go to Heaven" was sandwiched between Giles's recitation of Cuz's chorus and the woodcut showing Tom lying headless under the lion's paw. The *Lilliputian Magazine* (1751) told readers who wanted to become members of the "*Lilliputian Society*" that they had to promise to say their prayers twice daily, keep the Sabbath, and to serve, worship, love, honor, and give thanks to God. The text of the *Lilliputian Magazine* contained Old Testament stories, hymns, prayers, and discussions of Christianity. Because he had "*innocency and God Almighty*" on his "side," Master Tommy Trusty rushed in where few children would have trod and rescued Miss Biddy Johnson from the clutches of two thieves who planned to murder her.[21] Yet, despite this wealth of religious matter, the dominant impression left by the *Lilliputian Magazine* was not the importance of religion, but rather the importance of good nature and warm, generous behavior.

In teaching "the young Idea how to shoot," Newbery often directed it upward toward religion. But since he rarely bound it carefully, it soon tumbled down. The epigraph attached to *The Newtonian System of Philosophy* was taken from the Psalms and directed children's attention to the "Riches" of the earth and to the "Wisdom" of God who "made them all." In his lectures on "Natural Philosophy," Tom Telescope often fell into raptures as he discussed "the skirts" of God's "glory." Just as often, however, he fell into "a *pet*" and had to be reminded "that patience ought to be a principal ingredient in the character of a Philosopher." He became quite upset, for example, when "Lady *Caroline*" refused to believe that the center of the earth was hot and quizzed him, saying, "so you are going to turn the earth into a hotbed, and I suppose we, who are its inhabitants, are by and by to be complimented with the title of mushrooms and cucumbers, or perhaps pumpkins."[22]

Like Master Tom's lectures, Newbery's books frequently directed readers' attentions to the skirts of glory. However, the heavens rarely held their gaze for long and within a few pages, readers were usually rolling happily about with Lady Caroline in the commonsensical, everyday world of cucumbers and pumpkins. On other occasions, readers' descent from the heavens was not just to the secular but to the commercial, as Newbery enlisted religion in the good cause of selling his books. Near the end of *Nurse Truelove's New-Year's-Gift* (1759) appeared a short catechism in which *M* asked *S* questions on religion. To *M*'s asking what Jesus Christ required of one for his "abundant Love," *S* answered "that we should believe, and do as he has directed us in the New Testament, which I am to learn by and by." "Very well, my Dear," *M* responded, "and if I give you one of the little Spelling-Books, and some of the other pretty Books which are sold at the *Bible* and *Sun* in St. *Paul's* Churchyard, will you learn them so as to be able to read and understand the New Testament."[23]

In *Letters From A Mother to Her Children, on Various important Subjects,* Dorothy Kilner addressed "Young Readers," writing, "Whoever you are, that have now taken this little book into your hand, I hope you intend to read it with a sincere desire of being instructed in your duty, both towards God and man; and a fixed determination to endeavour to practice what shall therein be taught you." A solemn tone similar to Dorothy Kilner's and far from the gaiety of "YOU KNOW WHO" pervaded many of the children's books Marshall published in the 1780s. When Tom Telescope and his friends met at the Marquis of Setstar's to discuss natural philosophy, "his Lordship" was "so well pleased" that he "ordered them to be elegantly treated with tarts, sweetmeats, syllabubs, and such other dainties" as he "thought were most proper for youth." Unlike his lordship, Marshall knew that rewards which appealed to pleasure were "*ill chosen*" and he rarely sweetened instruction, particularly religious instruction, with dainties. Most of the books he advertised in 1785 were serious vehicles for teaching children "the principles of piety and morality." When taken as a group, the volumes practically constituted a course in religious and moral education. To some extent the instructive focus of Marshall's books reflected their composition. Many of Newbery's books may have been cooperative efforts. With several people contributing to a volume, consistency was difficult to achieve, and as a result his books often sprouted and grew in all directions. In contrast, Marshall's books were written by individual authors who were able to exercise more than just an overseer's control over their manuscripts. Moreover, in the 1780s a small group of authors wrote many of Marshall's children's books. Of the thirty books mentioned in the advertisement, fourteen were written by Dorothy Kilner (M.P.), six by her sister-in-law Mary Ann (S.S.), and eight by Ellenor Fenn (Mrs. Teachwell).[24]

In pruning Newbery's exuberance and returning to what they thought was the foundation of all learning, "M.P. and Co.," as the *Monthly Review* labeled Marshall's "literary associates," carefully followed the path Locke had marked out for religious education. They seemed to agree that the "promiscuous reading" of the Bible led to confusion over religious beliefs and made learning to read unnecessarily difficult. As Locke had suggested that a history of the Bible be written for young people, so they composed several, each suited to the "Capacity and Notions" of a slightly different age group. The adaptation for very young children was A.C.'s *The Footstep to Mrs. Trimmer's Sacred History.* Published in six volumes, Mrs. Trimmer's *Sacred History* (1782–1786) consisted of selections from the Scriptures "Suited To The Comprehension Of Young Minds." She had adapted the Bible to the comprehension of young persons, she explained, because both Locke and Watts had pointed out the danger of "*indiscriminate* use of the SCRIPTURES." Each selection from the Bible was accompanied by a long section of "Annotations and Reflections." These, she hoped, would encourage biblical studies "in SCHOOLS and FAMILIES" and would make religious "EDUCATION easy to the TEACHER, and pleasing to the PUPIL." The *Sacred History* was a useful educational tool. It filled a gap in middle-class homes, and even at three shillings a volume it sold well enough to make a second edition necessary in 1788. Reviewers praised Mrs. Trimmer herself and said that the *History* deserved the attention of all "Protestants," "Christians," and "friends to the sober and religious education of youth." Finding the *History* beyond the understanding "*of* VERY YOUNG *children,*" however, A.C. produced the "FOOTSTEP, *to lead them to Mrs.* TRIMMER'S *more improved work.*" Selecting "several pretty histories" from the Old Testament, A.C. wrote them "in an easy style" suited "to the confined understanding of a child." Histories like those of Joseph, David and Goliath, Samson, and Elisha and the Bears, A.C. hoped, would enable children to understand "lessons at church" and to realize they attended church "to pray" and "not to play and look about." In contrast to *The Holy Bible Abridged,* whose pages overflowed with prose printed in small type, *The Footstep* benefited from Mrs. Barbauld's hints. Marshall's typescript and margins were larger than Newbery's, and A.C.'s text was more familiar and less biblical. *The Footstep,* however, did not contain illustrations. Although it was easier to read and perhaps easier to learn from than *The Holy Bible Abridged,* the book did not feed children's visual fancy.[25]

Although *The Footstep* did not contain illustrations, both Marshall and Mrs. Trimmer realized that pictures appealed to children. In the middle and late 1780s, they joined forces and produced a series of influential illustrated educational playthings. In 1783 Thomas Holcroft translated Countess de Genlis's *Adelaide and Theodore; or Letters on Education: Containing All the Principles relative to three different Plans of Education; to that of Princes and to those of young Persons of both Sexes.* Although the book contained much that was sensible and judicious, the *Critical Review* said it could not recommend *Adelaide and Theodore* to English readers. "*Tares,*" Mrs. Trimmer wrote, were "*mixed with the wheat*" and care had to be "taken to sift it throughly." From the harvest, Mrs. Trimmer winnowed out a single grain, the fertility of which was remarkable and which grew to be such a part of English education that Clara Balfour stated in 1854 it was "employed in all infant schools."[26]

To protect their children from the corrupting impressions of life in Paris, Adelaide and Theodore's parents, Baron and Baroness d'Almane, moved their family from the metropolis to a castle in Languedoc. Possessing extensive means, they devoted themselves to their children's educations and meticulously decorated the castle with "objects of instruction." The "eating parlour" contained frescoes depicting scenes from Ovid's *Metamorphoses.* The salon focused attention on Rome; along one wall were hung medallions on which were portraits of every king, emperor, and famous man from Roman history while opposite were medallions depicting the empresses and other celebrated Roman ladies. On the two remaining sides of the room and on the doors were painted striking scenes from the history of Rome. The long gallery and the baroness's chamber were decorated with scenes from Greek history and Scripture, respectively. Colored prints which illustrated French history and which had explanations printed on their backs lined the walls of Adelaide's bedroom. The prints were removable and were often taken down and replaced by new ones. The study housed four hundred carefully chosen books and a cabinet containing minerals, corals, and shells. In the conservatory was a selection of plants, each of which had been classified. Paintings illustrating "military art" hung in Theodore's bedroom while portraits of the kings and queens and all the great men and ministers of France adorned the baron's apartment. Large maps decorated the colonnades of the grand staircase, and in a marble closet were six screens on which were written the chronologies of England, Spain, Portugal, Germany, Malta, and Turkey. The baroness even had four hundred panes of glass specially stained. Each illustrated a famous historical event, and four times a week they were inserted into magic lanterns for "diversion."[27]

Mrs. Trimmer pared Baron and Baroness d'Almane's Gallic extravagance down to the size and cost of Marshall's children's books. She praised Countess de Genlis for thinking to ornament "those apartments in which children receive the first rudiments of their education, with objects calculated at once to delight and to improve." Instead of decorating an entire house, however, she suggested that the ornamentation be limited to "the *nursery* or *teaching-room.*" On the walls of the nursery could be hung a set of prints. This initial set, she thought, should depict scriptural history. Like the prints in Adelaide's bedroom, they ought to be accompanied by proper commentary. Once children were thoroughly familiar with them and the commentary upon them, another set could be added. The process of adding sets and reading commentaries would continue until the children completed a course in "UNIVERSAL HISTORY."[28]

In 1786 Marshall published the first part of Mrs. Trimmer's universal history, *A Description Of A Set of Prints Of Scripture History: Contained In A Set of Easy Lessons.* Dedicated to Countess de Genlis, *A Description* was ninety-six pages long and contained thirty-two lessons. Printed in large type and written in simple prose, the lessons retold the most entertaining and instructive stories of the Old Testament. Each lesson was accompanied by a three-by-three-inch print. These, however, were published separately. Appealing to people who possessed different means and who would use them in slightly different ways, the prints came in three prices. An unbound set of sheets cost only 8d. while that bound in red leather cost 1s. 2d. and that mounted "*on boards,* to hang up in Nurseries" was priced at 1s. 6d. *A Description* itself was sold at two prices: 6d. for a sewn volume and 10d. for one bound in red leather. *A Description* could have been read simply as a history of the Bible for young people, and it was not necessary to buy the accompanying prints in order to enjoy it. The various forms in which the sets were published broadened their use. The parent who wanted to decorate those apartments in which children received the first rudiments of their education could purchase the mounted set. For those who preferred books, the bound set was available. Moreover, the prints were not identified by titles or explanatory captions. A Roman numeral at the top of each print corresponded to the number of the appropriate lesson. Thus it was possible to play several educational games. Unbound prints, for example, could be shuffled like cards, and children could try to match prints and lessons. Since biblical stories were "true," care was taken to make the prints appear accurate and to eliminate anachronisms of the sort which frequently cropped up in Newbery's illustrations. As a general rule, Marshall's inhabitants of the Holy Land dressed like Arabs rather than eighteenth-century Englishmen, and desert towns did not resemble English villages. The playfulness and rough-hewn primitivism which often gave Newbery's illustrations a charm that extended beyond the text rarely appeared in Marshall's prints. Like good supporting actors, Marshall's prints lent verisimilitude to the text; only infrequently did they draw attention away from the narrative.[29]

The attempt to fit Countess de Genlis's elaborate educational plan into plain English dress was successful. Mrs. Trimmer and Marshall soon produced four additional sets of "Easy Lessons" and prints. These taught the *New Testament* (1786), *Ancient History* (1787), *Roman History* (1789), and *English History* (1792). Instead of thirty-two, each of these histories contained sixty-four prints. Moreover, each book of lessons was considerably longer than *A Description Of . . . Scripture History.* The New Testament history was, for example, 239 pages long while the English history filled two comparable volumes. In the preface to *Ancient History,* Mrs. Trimmer explained that she wanted to show "*the connection between Sacred and Prophane History.*" She was not wholly successful and often the connections between the two were tenuous. If the various volumes were not, however, joined by a clear historical continuity, they were linked by Mrs. Trimmer's moral purpose. The instructive accounts which filled the books provided innumerable examples "of those things" which parents would have children "do, or avoid." Moreover, unlike the little histories praised by Mrs. West, these stories were true and consequently less liable to lead the imagination astray. From *Ancient History* children learned that if Xerxes had been a good man, God would have watched over him and would not have allowed him to have been murdered in his sleep. Alexander's drinking illustrated that intemperance killed more people than the sword. If the Thracians had been Christians, they would have celebrated rather than mourned the birth of children. Sesostris's suicide was "an example to the world, that neither *riches* nor *power* can confer *happiness* when *humility* is wanting." In *Roman History* children discovered that "killing flies" by sticking them through with a bodkin first hardened Domitian's heart and eventually led to his practicing "the most horrid barbarities upon mankind." Had Lucretia been a

Christian, children learned, she would not have killed herself but would have recognized that she was duty-bound to bear slander patiently.[30]

The Footstep was not the most elementary book advertised by Marshall in 1785. If Marshall's conservative approach to playing children into knowledge made his books duller than Newbery's, he compensated by trying harder to appeal to particular stages of childhood. The success of Mrs. Barbauld's graduated *Lessons* made publishers more aware of the differences between the mental capacities of children of different ages. Marshall realized that there was not one market for children's books but several; unlike Newbery, many of whose books were cut from a similar intellectual cloth, he varied the fabric of his books, making it light or heavy depending on the ages of the children to whom he wished to appeal. The most elementary books listed in the advertisement were four of Ellenor Fenn's volumes, which were written in "*infantine prattle*" suited "to the *gradual program* of the young scholar." Two of these were adaptations of Aesop, *Fables In Monosyllables By Mrs. Teachwell; To Which Are Added Morals In Dialogues, Between A Mother and Children* and *Fables, By Mrs. Teachwell: In Which The Morals Are Drawn Incidentally In Various Ways.* The former was written for children aged three to five. The fables were very simple, and the dialogues which supplied the morals consisted of discussions between Mam-Ma and Wil-li-am, aged three and a half, and five-year-old George. The latter volume was for children aged five to eight and told the same fables in more complex language. Instead of explanatory dialogues, the morals appeared in the text of the fables themselves. In 1758 Newbery himself had published a children's edition of Aesop. *Fables in Verse* was not, however, written for young children. It began with a sketch of Aesop's life that contained complex language. This was followed by a playful biography of Woglog, the great giant. Parts of Woglog's life, such as his penchant for *bons mots* and his scorn for "fops and coxcombs," must have appealed more to parents than to children. Only children whose reading was well advanced could read Newbery's Aesop without help. In contrast, after a child had progressed only a short distance beyond his letters, he could piece out Mrs. Teachwell's adaptations with little help.[31]

"My Dears," Ellenor Fenn wrote at the beginning of *Cobwebs To Catch Flies: Or, Dialogues In Short Sentences,* "Do not imagine that, like a

40 COBWEBS TO CATCH FLIES.

The R A T.

(In Words of Three Letters.)

B O Y.

I Saw a rat; and I ſaw the dog try to get it.

From Mrs. Teachwell, *Cobwebs to Catch Flies.* By permission of the British Library.

great spider, I will give you a hard gripe, and infuse venom to blow you up.—No—I mean to catch you gently, whisper in your ear." Unlike Tom Telescope's lectures, which contained "a few hard words" and which Tom advised his "good company" to learn "from Mr. *Newbery's* pocket dictionary," the prose in the *Cobwebs* was simple, if not gentle. For children aged three to five, the first volume contained stories written in words of three, four, five, and six letters. For children aged five to eight, the second volume contained stories written in words of one, two, three, and four syllables. The initial story in words of three letters was entitled "The Cat" and discussed such things as whether or not the cat could get a rat or get on the bed. "One day," children learned, the cat was "bit by an old rat"; another day, a dog "bit her jaw." A later story about "the Rat" ended abruptly when he met the cat, and "pop! she got him." Although Mrs. Trimmer praised Ellenor Fenn's "benevolent labours" and in 1802 said she thought the *Cobwebs* had been in constant circulation since they first appeared, contemporary reviewers handled her books with less care. Stooping "to lead an infant by the hand" could provide satisfaction and delight, as Ellenor Fenn wrote in the preface to *Fables In Monosyllables,* but it could also be treated scornfully or humorously. According to the *Monthly Review,* the *Fables in Monosyllables* lacked "consistency in the characters; variety in the incidents; vivacity in the expression; and brevity in the application." Buzzing through the *Cobwebs,* the *Critical Review* briefly observed that "what she says of herself is very true: 'she is the mistress of the infantine language.'"[32]

In comparison to its unimaginative contents, however, the form of the *Cobwebs* was interesting. Instead of relying heavily on discipline, Locke advised, parents should "admit" children "into serious Discourses" as "fast" as "Age, Discretion, and Good-Behaviour" allowed it. Familiar discourse, he thought, would "put Serious Considerations" into a child's "Thoughts, better than any Rules or Advice" and would raise his "Mind above the usual Amusements of Youth, and those trifling Occupations which it is commonly wasted in." "Rules" went down "easier" and sank deeper, he thought, if children bore "a Part" in instructive "Conversation." In the 1780s Marshall's "literary associates" tried to raise children's minds by using the dialogue and adaptations of dialogues as the structure of many of their books. Since the dialogue necessarily elicited participation by giving parents and children parts to read, the form seemed able to hold children's attentions without descending to the seductive gimmickry of Newbery's "nonsensical trifling." Moreover, its resemblance to the church catechism and the catechism's frequent use by parents in instructing their children lent the form respectability. In reviewing Ellenor Fenn's *School Dialogues for Boys. Being an Attempt to convey Instruction insensibly to their tender Minds, and instill the Love of Virtue,* the *Critical Review* observed that "the scheme of conveying instruction, by the conversaion [*sic*] of boys" was "in a great measure new." "Advice, in this form," the journal continued, was "perhaps more commodiously insinuated than in any other" as it was "conveyed to the young reader with an air of disinterestedness and impartiality."[33]

Such disinterest, however, lay light on the surface of Marshall's books; opening his dialogues quickly dispelled it. That "so little pains" had been taken "*properly* to ingraft" the "purest religion upon earth" upon "the ductile heart of youth" was a matter of "sorrow," Dorothy Kilner wrote in the preface to her *Clear and Concise Account of the Origin and Design of Christianity,* two books which formed a sequel to the two volumes of her *The First Principles of Religion, and the Existence of a Deity, explained in a Series of Dialogues.* "Set to read the holy scriptures by way of its daily *lesson,*" the "lisping *infant,*" she wrote, agreeing with Locke, was "suffered to annex what ideas its *narrow* mind" thought "most applicable to the sacred passage." To remedy this abuse of religious education and thereby help young children form "clear and Distinct Thoughts" about religion, she wrote dialogues.[34] In them Mamma and Maria discussed such things as Old Testament stories, prayers, baptism, the sacraments, angels, the attributes of God, and the abuses of Catholicism.

In the same form Dorothy Kilner wrote *Dialogues and Letters on Morality, Oeconomy, And Politeness, For the Improvement and Entertainment of Young Female Minds* and *Short Conversations; or, an Easy Road to the Temple of Fame; which All May Reach who Endeavour To Be Good,* while Mary Ann Kilner wrote *Familiar Dialogues for the Instruction and Amusement of Children.* Concerned more with practical morality and correct behavior than with particular religious matter, these three books tried harder to mix amusement with instruction. However, in relying upon original instructive anecdotes and not drawing upon biblical stories, these dialogues, as the *Critical Review* wrote of *School Dialogues for Boys,* were "attended with some prolixity and puerilities." Thus, in *Familiar Dialogues,* while Mamma and Mary were chatting intimately, Pompey their pet dog trotted into the room wagging his tail. Seeing that he was thirsty, Mamma told Mary, "He puts out his tongue; he is thirsty, fetch him some water." "But he should not put out his tongue," Mary answered like a clever little girl, for "you tell me it is not pretty. You must not have any water, if you put out your tongue, Pompey." Patiently Mamma repeated her instructions, explaining, "Yes, give the little dog some drink. Pompey cannot speak. If you are dry, you can say, Pray, Ma'am, let me have some water? But dogs put out their tongues to show they are hot and thirsty." Not grasping the difference between her pet and herself, Mary replied, "I shall put my tongue out now then, for I am very hot." Not so patient as perhaps she should have been, Mamma exclaimed, "No Mary! put in your tongue, it will not make you cooler; and you do not want any drink; you are a little girl. Pompey is a little dog. Little girls must not do the same things as little dogs do. Sit quiet, and you will be cool. Exercise has made you hot."[35]

Because it seemed capable of holding children's attention while it provided them with serious instruction, the dialogue was a major part of Marshall's educational curriculum. Only one series of lectures, for example, was advertised in 1785, and this, Mary Ann Kilner's *A Course of Lectures for Sunday Evenings Containing Religious Advice to Young Persons,* had been carefully adapted to the "weak and puerile ideas of children." Although other books on Marshall's list were not dialogues, they oftentimes resembled them. In their efforts to hold attention and to avoid the soporific dangers of lectures, some books leaned heavily on "Familiarity of Discourse" and became dialogues in all but name.[36] In *Letters From A Mother to Her Children,* although Mrs. Ord was away from home for a short time, she systematically wrote and received letters from young Master Thomas, Miss Mary, and Miss Hanna and was able to continue their religious education almost as if she had never traveled beyond the range of familiar conversation.

The dialogue was used not only to teach children from middle-class families; it was also used to drill lessons into children from lower levels of society. Often such lessons had political as well as moral and religious overtones. Most of the discussions in Mrs. Trimmer's *Sunday School Dialogues* explored religious matters. A few, however, urged children to be satisfied with their lots in life, regardless of how grim they were—a position which by the late 1780s seemed as much political as religious. When Mary said she did not want to be either sick or poor, her teacher quickly answered, "Nobody likes to be sick or poor; but if God chuses that we should be so, to punish us for having been wicked, or to make us think more of Heaven, and prevent our setting our minds too much on the things of this world, we must be good-humoured and patient, and bear whatever he thinks proper. It will not be a vast number of years before we shall go to Heaven, and then all our troubles will be at an end, and we shall never have any thing more to make us uneasy." Because large numbers of the lower classes were children, insofar as their formal education was concerned, several of the *Cheap Repository Tracts* were published in simple dialogue form. The pamphlet which served as a trial balloon for the *Cheap Repository* was Hannah More's *Village Politics. Addressed To All The Mechanics, Journeymen, And Day Labourers, In Great Britain. By Will Chip, A Country Carpenter* (1792). Consisting of "serious Discourses" between Tom Hod, a mason who had become dissatisfied with his lot in life after reading Thomas Paine, and Jack Anvil, a God-and-country blacksmith, *Village Politics* used the catechistical method to teach truth about "Liberty and Equality, and the Rights of Man." A typical section read: "*Tom.* What then dost thou take French *liberty* to be? *Jack.* To murder more men in one night, than ever their poor king did in his whole life. *Tom.* And what dost thou take a Democrat to be? *Jack.* One who likes to be governed by a thousant tyrants, and yet can't bear a king. *Tom.* What is *Equality? Jack.* For every man to pull down every one that is above him, till they're all as low as the lowest. *Tom.* What is the *new Rights of Man? Jack.* Battle, murder, and sudden death. *Tom.* What is it to be an *enlightened people? Jack.* To put out the light of the gospel, confound right and wrong, and grope about in pitch darkness."[37]

In reviewing the *Letters From A Mother,* the *Monthly Review* wrote that "if an objection might be hinted," it was "that their cast" was "something too much of the grave kind." When compared to the godly books published at the beginning of the eighteenth century, Marshall's books were sunny and lighthearted. But when put alongside Newbery's books, they appeared grave. In the *Letters* themselves, religion cast a threatening shadow over life as Dorothy Kilner preached that it was "*God* who changes the milk and bread which babies eat, into *blood,* and *flesh,* and *bones,* and *hair,* and *nails.*" After describing the "*dreadful*" state of idiots, she stressed that only through God's kindness were children blessed "with *sense* and *understanding.*" Although she did not say that God would turn bad children into idiots, she warned them that He watched them "*constantly*" and knew all their "*thoughts, words,* and *actions.*" In other books listed in Marshall's advertisement, such gravity often stemmed more from an emphasis on the beneficial effects of early discipline than it did from somber Christianity. Although Locke taught that parents corrupted "the Principles of Nature in their Children" by "humoring and cockering them when *little*" and that "Liberty and Indulgence" did "no Good to *Children*" because their "Want of Judgment" made them need "Restraint and Discipline," Newbery did not stress the importance of discipline in education. This is not to say, of course, that Newbery did not expose the wages of disobedience. Many instructive stories of disobedient and willful children appeared in his books. In *Giles Gingerbread,* for example, one of Giles's hornbooks described the misfortune of a self-willed little boy who "lived at a Farm House where there was an unlucky Bull, that often ran at People who were going by." Although he had been told repeatedly not to call the servants to his aid when he did not need them, the little boy often cried out "*the Bull, the Bull, oh the Bull*" when the bull was far away in the fields nibbling grass. When the inevitable event occurred and the bull did chase the little boy and he screamed for help, the servants thought he was lying as usual and did not rush to help him. As a result the boy was "tossed by the Bull till he was almost dead." Although this was a somber tale, Newbery did not dwell on discipline, and his books did not usually contain extended accounts of the evils of disobedience. In contrast, Marshall's books frequently focused on discipline. In *Short Conversations* Mamma threatened to tie a handkerchief over Mary Ann's eyes if she cried and said that if she ever lied, she would be "whipt very hard," "shook," and have her "mouth tied up" so she could not eat or speak. In her enthusiasm for laying the foundation of virtue on the threat of physical punishment, Mary Ann's mother was overzealous, for Locke had warned that "Children should very seldom be corrected by Blows." There was "one Fault," however, for which he said "Children should be Beaten" and that was "*Obstinacy* or *Rebellion.*" "For this," he wrote there was "no other Remedy." In depicting obstinate children, Marshall's books took Locke at his word and mastered them if not "with Force and Blows," at least with uncomfortable physical ordeal. In *The Holiday Present,* after Charles refused to apologize for throwing rocks at his brother George and for taking his brother Tom's apple, Charles's father put him to bed with his arms and legs tied together behind his back and left him there until the next morning when he was ready to beg forgiveness. While reading to his mother in *The Histories of More Children than One,* young John Strictum stumbled over the word *thought.* When his mother asked him to spell it, he refused and stood like a dunce crying and sobbing. Although she did not want to punish him, Mrs. Strictum "wisely considered how sad a thing it would be to let him continue so obstinate." Consequently, she took him into the garden "a great way from the house" and tied him to a tree with a piece of rope which had been wrapped around a sugar loaf. She told him he would stay there "without victuals or drink, and without going to-bed till he would be good and spell the word." At first John refused to ask her pardon, but as night approached, he became tired and hungry. Moreover, the longer he was tied up, the more time he had to think about his obstinate refusal to spell. Before nightfall he realized he was wrong, and he apologized. In refusing to humor him, Mrs. Strictum had done John a service, for never again was he ill-tempered. He became a happy, much-loved child who grew up to be a happy, much-loved man who gave "great pleasure" to all who knew him.[38]

In the books in Marshall's advertisement the responsibility for providing learning shifted from Newbery's the Countess of Twilight and the Marquis of Setstar and their playfully informed but often harum-scarum ways to somber schools conducted along proper lines. In Marshall's schools, students and readers learned more about proper conduct than they did natural philosophy. In *School Occurrences,* Miss Sprightly was placed "in various situations," Ellenor Fenn explained to young readers, "as an example to you, how you ought to acquit yourself in similar circumstances." Sent to "the *Grove,*" Miss Sprightly was immediately exposed to the inspiring sermons of Mrs. Teachwell and the instructive foibles of her schoolmates, Miss Pert, Miss Cheat, and Miss Pry. While visiting "*Simpleton-hall,*" for example, Miss Pert broke one of Mrs. Teachwell's rules and paid a servant to take a letter secretly to Miss Cheat. When Mrs. Teachwell discovered the letter, she dismissed the servant and explained to her students how Miss Pert had not only been "guilty of indelicacy" in "trafficking" with a footman but how in corrupting a servant she had done a disservice to another human being. Of Miss Pert's letter, which mocked the absurdities in the characters of Louisa and Tom Simpleton, Mrs. Teachwell remarked primly that "to receive pleasure, the mind must be formed to enjoy it." Terribly spoiled by their parents, the young Simpletons themselves provided Mrs. Teachwell with subjects for an instructive lecture. "Spoiled children," she told her pupils, were "the most disagreeable animals in the world." "The whole duty of a child," she stressed, consisted in "a contented resignation" to his parents' "regulations."[39]

In stating that his publications were composed on "a more liberal plan," Marshall implied that children's books had improved since the days when Newbery began publishing. When Mrs. Sprightly visited the Grove, her daughter took her and an unidentified lady for a tour of the school. In the library Miss Sprightly pointed out "the infant books" and "*Mrs. Barbauld's* lessons for little children," explaining, when she led the visitors along the shelves, "as you advance this way" the books "rise gradually." Before the Sprightlys could reach the advanced books for older children, the lady recognized a book which she had read as a child and exclaimed, "Here is my old friend *Goody Twoshoes!* Don't you often read that?" "No, indeed, Ma'am," Miss Sprightly answered quickly, "I leave that to the little ones." Miss Sprightly's pert response did not please her mother, who asked her rhetorically, "My dear! is that a proper manner of speaking to a lady?" Although Miss Sprightly's manner was improper, her answer was apt. Composed according to a more progressive plan, his books, Marshall implied, were as much beyond Newbery's as Miss Sprightly was beyond *Goody Two-Shoes.* The lady who recognized *Goody Two-Shoes* on the shelf was not well educated. She thought, for example, that Shakespeare instead of Racine wrote "*Athaliah*" and "*Esther.*" Newbery's publications, Marshall implied, represented an unsophisticated first generation of children's books. As educational practice progressed, so, many educators believed, children's books advanced. Proper books published in the 1780s would take sprightly children far beyond the ignorance which marked many a lady of the previous generation who read Newbery's books.[40]

Occasionally Marshall openly criticized Newbery for being too simple and making learning too amusing. *The Wisdom of Crop the Conjurer* (1780?) described "the celebrated Tom Trot, who Rode before all the *Boys* in the *Kingdom* till he arrived at the *Top* of the *Hill* called LEARNING." Tom's diligence and studious habits, Crop explained, drew him to the attention of Jack's father. Young Jack himself was a dunce, and his father hoped Tom would be able to interest him in books. Try as he might, however, Tom was unsuccessful, and he finally suggested that Jack be apprenticed to Blackbrush the chimney sweep. Although Jack would not "burden his head with sense," Crop related, he could carry "a good load of soot upon his back." Jack's father took Tom's advice, after which he treated Tom like a son, buying him "all the books in the world." Making "very good use" of his books, Tom proved an apt and progressive scholar. He never ate them, Crop emphasized, "as *Giles Gingerbread* did his; nor did he tear them in pieces, or put them in his drawer and never look on them, as many ignorant boys and girls do, who love the gilt or fine covers, better than the inside." "No, no," Crop continued, "*Tom* made very good use of them, he read them all through; and if he did not understand or remember what they contained, he would enquire of those who knew more than himself, and would read them over again."[41]

Despite the "*despicable* tricks" played by some of the students, the Grove was a happier school than that attended by Dorothy Kilner's Martha Beauchamp. In great part Mrs. Teachwell must have been responsible. She was not an ordinary schoolmistress, and Mr. Sprightly said she reminded him of Dr. Johnson's character of Watts. Like Locke, Dorothy Kilner believed that the "evils" which accompanied "a boarding-school education" counterbalanced the advantages, but she also believed, as she wrote in *Anecdotes of A Boarding-School; Or, An Antidote to the Vices Of Those Useful Seminaries,* that there were some situations which rendered "them very proper places for girls to pass some few years of their time at." Because her mother was sick, Martha Beauchamp was sent to Miss Steward's school. Surrounded by unpleasant schoolmates like Miss Creedless and Miss Grumpton and taught by Miss Starch, who refused to let her say her prayers in English, Martha was soon homesick. However, her mother refused to let her leave the school, explaining, "if, my dear, you suppose that the children whom you are now with, are worse than those you would meet elsewhere, I fear you are much mistaken; for in every school I have ever heard of, there are always numbers to be found, who perversely will practice every kind of naughtiness." Forced to remain at school, Martha was exposed to many instructive examples; she learned antidotes for every kind of naughtiness and eventually became a good scholar and the best girl in the school.[42]

Unlike evenings at the Marquis of Setstar's when the Duke of Galaxy was likely to drop by and throw everything "into some confusion," Marshall's books describing school life were seldom confused. Rarely were Marshall's lessons subject to misunderstanding, and reviewers approvingly labeled the books "judicious," "natural," and "highly proper." On occasion, however, Marshall's literary associates strained too hard for instruction and, instead of enlightening their readers, plunged them into the ludicrous world of the inappropriately didactic.

Until its conclusion, Dorothy Kilner's *The Village School* was an ordinary collection of instructive stories about the students who attended Mrs. Bell's school in Rose Green, "a clean pleasant village, about forty miles from London." The account of Ralph Breakclod's misfortunes, for example, typically attempted to teach readers the dangers of lying. Poor Ralph was an habitual liar, so much so that when a chaise ran over him and hurt his back no one believed him. At school he was beaten for crying, and at home he was punished for complaining about his health. Finally, when he became bedridden, people realized that for once he had been telling the truth. "I am sorry, as you did happen to speak the truth this time," his father told him, "that I did not look at your back sooner; but, indeed it is your own fault, for having been so wicked, and given me reason to think, that you were falsifying. I do not think that you can ever be cured; but, if you should live, I hope it will teach you never to deceive any body again." His father's advice was well-taken, but unfortunately Ralph had little time in which to put it to use, for he died within the week.[43]

Like a long school day, *The Village School* was filled with a series of lessons. Like classroom assignments, the stories of Master William Crafty, Roger Riot, Jacob Stedfast, Philip Trusty, John Sneak, Jane Liptrap, and Benjamin Heady followed one after another until the end of the day when school was dismissed and all instruction went up in smoke, both figuratively and literally. Concluding a book describing boarding-school life was not difficult. The narrative was usually unified by the presence of a main character who saw, heard about, took part in, or learned from its diverse stories and incidents. Such a book reached a natural conclusion when the main character either became the school's best pupil or returned home. In *The Village School,* there was no main character around whom the narrative was unified, except for the dully benevolent Mrs. Bell, with whom it was almost impossible for young readers to identify. Moreover, unlike the boarding school which surrounded students' lives with walls, the village school did not limit or contain its pupils' possible experiences. Before school began and at the end of the day, Mrs. Bell's students roamed over Rose Green and through a potentially infinite series of instructive experiences. When confronted by the dilemma of how to conclude *The Village School,* Dorothy Kilner became a narrative arsonist and burned up not only the school and Mrs. Bell but a poverty-stricken woman on whom Mrs. Bell had taken pity. The son of this poor woman had been arrested for robbery. In attempting to follow him to jail, she had twisted her ankle and become ill. Like the Good Samaritan, Mrs. Bell volunteered to care for the old woman and took her home. That night as Mrs. Bell sat by the old woman's bed watching over her and knitting a shirt for a neighbor whose wife was ill, the heavy labor of good deeds weighed her down and she fell asleep. The candle she had lit to knit by tumbled onto the bed, and the house was soon ablaze. All was not lost, however, for these melancholy circumstances provided Dorothy Kilner with a unique didactic opportunity. "Some bones were the next day found in the rubbish," she concluded, "but the flesh was so entirely consumed as to make it impossible to distinguish Mrs. Bell from the poor woman she had so charitably assisted. Thus concluded the life of that most valuable member of society; much lamented, and much beloved, by all the inhabitants of Rose Green; and an irreparable loss to all the rising generation of that place. From this fatal accident it is to be hoped, that every body will learn to be extremely cautious not to leave candles burning near linen, nor, indeed, any where, without constantly watching, that they may not do mischief."[44]

The reviewer of *The Village School* in the *Critical Review* wrote that although such "little books" were "in themselves scarcely objects of criticism," they ought to be "perused . . . with some care," because "their design" was "important" and "their influence" probably "extensive."[45] Today most of Marshall's books lie like Mrs. Bell, forgotten in the ruins of time past. With the exception of *The Life and Perambulation of a Mouse, The Adventures of a Pincushion, Memoirs of a Peg-Top,* and one or two other individual favorites, the books Marshall advertised in 1785 are interesting primarily to the devotee and the scholar. However, like the sugar and spice with which Newbery seasoned his volumes in the middle of the century, Marshall's switches and ashes reveal much about education in the late eighteenth century.

Locke provided the theoretical and practical foundation for the books of both publishers. It was clear to both that the child was the father of the man and that children's books served an important educational purpose. Unlike Newbery's books, however, the books Marshall advertised in 1785 were more serious and didactically more consistent. "The dogs of Egypt, when thirst brings them to the Nile," Dr. Johnson wrote in his description of Newbery, "are said to run as they drink for fear of the Crocodiles. Jack Whirler always dines at full speed. He enters, finds the family at table, sits familiarly down, and fills his plate; but, while the first morsel is in his mouth, hears the clock strike, and rises; then goes to another house, sits down again, recollects another engagement, has only time to taste the soup, makes a short excuse to the company, and continues through another street his desultory dinner." Newbery's books resembled Jack Whirler's meals. Almost all the dishes were home-cooked in Locke's kitchen. Rarely, though, did Jack finish a single course. As a result, his dinners consisted of a tasty mixture of morsels, much as Newbery's books consisted of a seemingly haphazard blend of instructive and amusing matter. By the end of the century, some educators were stressing the importance of a balanced diet and became more selective. Before they bought any biscuits, buns, diet-bread plum-cakes, or mince pies from the "*Literary Cook's Shop,*" they considered what effects such food would have upon children's characters.[46]

The rapid spread of literacy and the phenomenal growth of the Sunday school movement turned many educators' attention toward the social implications of Locke's educational ideas. As large numbers of people began receiving educations, albeit elementary ones, the manner and matter of education came to be thought more important not merely for the individual but for the state. If nine people out of ten were formed "Good or Evil, useful or not, by their Education," then the general stability of a society which was beginning to instruct large numbers of people rested in great part upon the content of the education which it supplied. "Wisdom and knowledge," Thomas Sheridan wrote, "are the parents of religion and virtue; folly and ignorance, of vice and impiety: where wisdom and knowledge are wanting in a nation, virtue and religion will hardly be found; and when ignorance and folly reign, vice and impiety will be seen triumphant. The only way to bring about a reformation of manners, is to restore wisdom and knowledge. This can be effected only by a right system of education." By the late eighteenth century, many people thought education too serious a process on which to waste much time seducing children into knowledge. Instead of appealing to children's fleeting thoughts and utilizing that natural temper which disposed their minds to wander, many educators tried to discipline children's imaginations and to settle them into safe "habits of thinking." In her *Strictures On The Modern System of Female Education* (1799), Hannah More implicitedly criticized publishers like Newbery who baked gingerbread books to lure children to learning. Like Marshall's "literary associates," she believed a new balance should be struck between profit and delight, one which would raise the latter higher in the air. The "multiplicity" of "alluring little books" published for children, she argued, increased their "natural reluctance" to apply themselves to serious study. "Do what we will, she wrote, "we cannot *cheat* children into learning or *play* them into knowledge." "The tree of Knowledge, as a punishment perhaps, for its having been at first unfairly tasted," she explained, "cannot now be climbed without difficulty."[47]

As Hannah More looked around her in the 1790s, she saw many ill-instructed people climbing part of the way up the tree of knowledge and then falling off, not simply into the gulf of ignorance but into the chasm of "Liberty and Equality, and the Rights of Man." The only way to insure that people would be strong enough to climb to the top of the tree and be able to see truth unobscured by branches and leaves was, she and many educators like her believed, to see that children received a highly disciplined education. Wordsworth's "mighty workmen" had not listened to Tom Telescope's lectures but instead had been Mrs. Trimmer's and Mrs. Teachwell's apprentices. Toward the end of the eighteenth century, many educators neglected Tom Trapwit's favorite saying, "Be Merry and Wise." Instead, they echoed Mrs. Teachwell's emphasis on obedience and tried to confine children's imaginations within a hedge of responsibilities. To the children who read her *Fables,* she preached, "Your duties lie in a narrow compass. A ready and cheerful obedience; as inviolate in the absence of your parents as when they are present; a strict adherence to truth; a contented submission to the will of your superiors; and a readiness to comply with the innocent wishes of your equals—or, in other words, to do to them as you would wish they should do to you—these comprise the chief duties of a *child*—these will remain your duties through life: practice them *now* and they will be easy to you when you grow up: practice them when you are a *Man,* and you will be happy."[48]

Afterword

In 1818 Benjamin Tabart published *Popular Fairy Tales; Or, A Lilliputian Library; Containing Twenty-Six Choice Pieces Of Fancy And Fiction, By Those Renowned Personages King Oberon, Queen Mab, Mother Goose, Mother Bunch, Master Puck, And Other Distinguished Personages At The Court Of The Fairies.* Despite stating in the introduction that he had attempted "to elevate the language and sentiments" of the tales "to a level with the refined manners of the present age," Tabart actually did little to the stories. Although Tom Thumb's bovine excursion went no farther than the Red Cow's mouth, Little Red Riding Hood disappeared as usual between her grandmother's canine incisors. Blue Beard's closet remained clotted with gore and Sleeping Beauty's mother-in-law still had ogreish tendencies. Reviewers greeted Tabart's traditional tales enthusiastically and used the occasion to survey the state of children's books. In the *Quarterly Review,* Francis Palgrave observed that "the literature of the nursery" had undergone "a mighty alteration" since his "boyish days." Nurse, he wrote, had become "strangely fastidious in her taste." The books which now pleased her were, he wrote, quite different from those over which "she used to pore, when she put on her spectacles, and took such desperate pains in leading us onwards from great A and little a, and bouncing B, even down to *Empesand* and Izzard." Like Wordsworth, Palgrave mourned the passing of chapbook romances. The ancient heroes of chivalry "who defended their posts so long and sturdily" had, he noted, been "fairly fibbed out of the ring by modern upstarts and pretenders." Peddlers, he claimed, burned "their ungodly story-books like sorcerers of old" and filled "their baskets with the productions sanctified by the Imprimatur of the Tabernacle." Swept along by memories of childhood reading past, Palgrave recalled Marshall's books fondly. Marshall, he lamented, had "been compelled to shut up his shop long ago" and his "cheap and splendid publications" had disappeared. His penny books were out of print, and "not a soul in the trade would bid for the copy-right and back stock of Tommy Two Shoes."[1]

In the *London Magazine,* a reviewer struck a similarly sentimental chord, beginning an essay on "The Literature Of The Nursery" with an epigraph from Wordsworth's "Ode: Intimations of Immortality," "where is passed the glory and the dream!" For the reviewer, splendor had vanished from the pages of children's books. In earlier, better, bookish times, he exclaimed, "what enchanting details lurked under the variegated cover of Mother Goose! How exquisite the perfume of Mother Bunch's darling nose-gay! Our literary horizon in those days was peopled with dragons, was lit up with chariots of fire and beautified with magical rainbows! The landscape before us was ever fresh, ever graceful, ever changing." Like Palgrave, he believed that "innovation" had "made fearful progress in the child's library." Unlike Palgrave, however, the reviewer did not wonder at Nurse's becoming fastidious or criticize the Tabernacle for stuffing peddlers' baskets with righteous books. Instead, after praising those "graver studies of youthful readers," he attacked contemporary children's books as repositories of "nonsense, buffoonery, and ribaldry." They were "profligate productions" filled with "gross lampoons." The "gaudy glare" and "meretricious display" of the prints they contained vitiated the taste, the reviewer argued, "as much as the buffoonery of the letter-press" corrupted "the disposition of the youthful readers." As Duessa's scarlet appearance revealed her inner nature, so the dress of contemporary children's books revealed their value. "When our primers and storybooks," the reviewer recalled, "were enclosed in firm, compact, gilt covers, assurance seemed given externally, that there were golden stories within; but we cannot help regarding, as omens of sinister import, the flaming yellow, orange, green, and crimson wrappers, set off with a dandy, that are now in vogue. Those were good times, when the child regarded his book as a serious and precious affair,

—valuable as gold,—pure and bright as the metal with which it was ornamented."[2]

"Each risen generation," Charlotte Yonge shrewdly observed, "repeats to the *rising* one, that there was nothing like it in its departed childhood, and each mourns over the dissipation of mind created by the profusion of reading." The days when Palgrave's and the anonymous reviewer's hearts were young and gay may indeed have gone. But if there were a falling away, it was from the reviewers and not from children's literature. In 1820 smoke rising from literary cooks' shops streaked the skies above London. As he mistakenly called *Goody Two-Shoes* Tommy Two Shoes, so Palgrave mistakenly judged the trade in children's books. At the beginning of the nineteenth century, Darton wrote, the moral tale was proceeding somberly on its course, "but all around it was a cheerful bustle." Literary bakers like John Harris and Darton and Harvey rolled up their sleeves, bought carts of sugar and spice, laid in great supplies of kindling, and were cooking batches of children's books. Beside Mrs. Sherwood's wholesome moral tales, Mother Hubbard's mince pies and plum cakes for the *Butterfly's Ball* were bubbling noisily. If something had passed from children's books, it was not the visionary gleam of creativity. In fact, for some like the essayist in the *London Magazine,* there may have been too much creativity. Tossed amid the glaring colors splashed across the covers of contemporary children's books, he may have felt queasy and greeted Tabart's *Tales* enthusiastically simply because, like dry land, they were familiar. Criticizing children's books was easier in the eighteenth century. The number of books was smaller, and the writings of "the great Mr. *Locke*" not only influenced the form and content of children's books but they also provided the critic with handy analytical tools.[3] At the beginning of the nineteenth century, children's books, like an awkward child turning cartwheels, wobbled off in several directions at once, and it was difficult for a critic to predict which way they would go or to suggest how they could be improved.

From the turn of the century until 1830 or even 1840, children's books, Darton judged, went through "a period of apparent lack of central impulse."[4] By the end of the first quarter of the nineteenth century, Locke's direct influence had waned considerably. His indirect influence remained great, but it was not frequently acknowledged. Children's books had grown into the bright sunlight. The winter when their roots first took hold and during which they struggled upward was over. The snow had melted, and although children's books blossomed everywhere, tracing the footsteps of the gardener who nourished them would not be so easy in the nineteenth as it was in the eighteenth century. In Newbery's list, Watts's thought, Mrs. Trimmer's books, the *Cheap Repository Tracts,* Mrs. Barbauld's prose-poetry, and the books advertised by Marshall in 1785, Locke's fertilizing influence was clearly marked. By 1820 Locke had been absorbed and was taken for granted and often neglected. Like those "first-born affinities" described by Wordsworth, he lay influential but invisible under the surface of things.

Appendix A. John Locke and Innate Ideas

The biggest controversy involving Locke's educational ideas occurred over what Richard Hurd celebrated: Locke's "good sense" and constant "eye to the use and business of the world." Locke's thought was pervasively and persuasively rational. In *An Essay Concerning Human Understanding,* he denied the existence of innate ideas and innate principles, "primary notions . . . stamped upon the mind of man, which the soul receives in its first being and brings into the world with it." Throughout the seventeenth century, Anglican divines had generally held that man was endowed with an innate knowledge of God and of the fundamental principles of good and evil. "There are in our Minds Natural Impressions and Inbred Notices of True and False," John Edwards wrote, "which are as it were Streams issuing forth from the Uncreated and Everlasting Springs of Truth. And these Notions are not Indifferent and Arbitrary, but Fixed and Indelible, they being derived to us from That Immutable and Essential Truth." Belief in innateness stabilized religion and provided a foundation for a moral life. The doctrine stood, Richard Ashcroft wrote, "as a rock against the perilous and uncertain forces of political, social, and intellectual change." What some divines believed to be a boulder supporting the castle of truth, however, Locke saw as a remnant of rough-hewn old night, blocking out the sunlight of reason and keeping knowledge hidden in a subjective world of shadows. The "white paper" of a person's mind, Locke observed, was susceptible to "any characters." Many "*doctrines,*" he argued, which were originally derived from "the superstition of a nurse or the authority of an old woman," grew "by length of time and consent of neighbors . . . *to the dignity of principles* in religion and morality." These were impressed upon infants' minds. When they grew up and began to "reflect on their own minds," they could not find "anything more ancient there than those opinions" taught to them before "memory began to keep a register of their actions." As a result, they frequently concluded "*that those propositions of whose knowledge they can find in themselves no original, were certainly the impress of God and nature.*" By "these means," it was clear, Locke argued, to see how men came to worship idols and be fond of absurdities. Instead of accepting a scheme of thought as innate, Locke urged, men should reflect on their experiences and beliefs. It was possible, he stressed, for "any absurdity" to be taken "for innate principles."[1]

Although Locke emphasized throughout *An Essay* that he was religious, some theologians believed that his criticism of innate ideas constituted a covert attack upon religion, or at least smacked of Socinianism, a term loosely applied to those latitudinarian beliefs that discounted the Trinity and held that charity and good deeds were more important than doctrine. In *The Socinian Creed* (1697), John Edwards accused Locke of being a Socinian and then in *A Brief Vindication Of The Christian Faith* (1697) condemned Locke's writings out of hand. "Read *John Lock* who writ of *Humane Understanding,* and hath had little of it since, and not over much then," Edwards stated. "If you would *fill your Pupils heads* with Whimsies, there is a Book for you, If you would have *no Idea* of the Supreme Being, and a *false one* of Christianity, and a *fantastick one* of Good Manners, then *think it your great business* to fill your Studies with my *Essay,* and my *Reasonableness of Christianity,* and my *Thoughts of Education.*" Locke was readily defended against Edwards's crude accusations. In *Some Considerations On The Principal Objections And Arguments Which have been Publish'd against Mr. Lock's Essay of Humane Understanding* (1699), Samuel Bold declared that the *Essay* was the best book he knew "to serve the Interest of Truth, Natural, Moral, and Divine." Moreover, he thought it the "best Book" he "ever read, excepting those which were writ by Persons Divinely inspir'd."[2]

In a letter to Richard Hurd, Warburton compared the fate of

Malebranche's theories to that of Locke's. When they first appeared, Warburton noted, Malebranche's theories had been celebrated; now, however, Warburton said, they were neglected. In contrast, Locke's theories, which had not met with immediate critical approval, were now acclaimed. Locke had "at length worked his way," Warburton explained, because he was "every where clear, and every where solid." Locke's theory on the origin of ideas and his concomitant argument against innate ideas worked its way more rapidly than Warburton implied. By "the first years of the eighteenth century," John Yolton wrote, the "polemic against innate ideas had won general acceptance." In 1704 in *A Discourse Concerning the Happiness of Good Men, And The Punishment of the Wicked In The Next World,* William Sherlock, the dean of St. Paul's, attempted to answer Locke's criticism of innate ideas and principles. Locke was not the only writer to attack innateness. But he was the most prominent, and in a forty-page essay, "A Digression concerning Connate Ideas, or Inbred Knowledge," Sherlock concentrated on Locke's arguments. Locke's views, however, had worked their way; even Sherlock was influenced by them. "Whatever Ideas we have latent in our Minds," he wrote, "we gain no actual Knowledge of them, but as they are awakened in us by external Impressions, Observations, and a Chain of Thoughts." "Our Actual Knowledge," he said, was "acquired, and possibly much in the same way that Mr. *Lock* represents it." Sherlock opposed Locke's view of innateness, not so much, it seems, because it was untrue, but because it threatened religion. "Modern Atheists," he wrote, would magnify and use his "Hypothesis" to "confute those Principles of Religion and Virtue which he owns." After all, he continued, there was "not a more formidable Objection against Religion, than to teach, That Mankind is made without any Connate Natural Impressions and Ideas of a God, and of Good and Evil: For if all the Knowledge we have of God, and of Good and Evil, be made by our selves, Atheists will easily conclude, that it is only the Effect of Education, and Superstitious Fears; and satisfie themselves, that they can make other Notions, more for the Ease and Security of Life." "This is certain," Sherlock concluded, "no Man who believes that the Ideas of God, and of Good and Evil, were originally impress'd on our Minds when they were first made, can doubt whether there be a God, or an essential difference between Good and Evil. Those who believe these Notions were made, and not born with us, are more at liberty to question their Truth."

The denial of innate ideas did not turn eighteenth-century parents and educators into atheists, but it did help convince them that education had extremely important effects. Moreover, they now believed that they were able, if not to make "other Notions," at least to educate their children so that they would achieve "the Ease and Security of Life" and afterlife. Finally, the denial of innateness did put children more at liberty, if not to question the truth, at least to become what they wished. No longer were people's personalities partially determined by an omnipotent force over which man had no control, and "the right Method of *Education,*" as John Clarke put it, became "a Matter of the greatest Importance." Sherlock's critique of Locke had little effect. In 1728 Chambers's *Cyclopaedia* noted under *Ideas* that the controversy had died. Innate ideas, the encyclopedia asserted, were "mere Chimera's." "Our great Mr. *Locke,*" it stated, "put this Matter out of dispute, having made it appear that all our *Ideas* are owing to our *Senses.*"[3]

Appendix B. John Newbery's Predecessors

In *John Newbery And His Successors,* Sydney Roscoe gave Newbery less credit for creating the eighteenth-century children's book than did Harvey Darton. Newbery's achievement, Roscoe wrote, was not to invent or start a fashion for children's books "but so to produce them as to make a permanent and profitable market for them, to make them a class of book to be taken seriously as a recognized and important branch of the book-trade."[1] Newbery does not, however, seem to have had many predecessors in the children's book trade. If godly books and chapbooks are excluded from consideration, only a handful of his forerunners' publications are extant.

The works of two publishers, both of whom published a few children's books in the early 1740s, may, however, have had some influence upon Newbery. The first of these was Thomas Boreman. From 1740 to 1743, Boreman published a series of ten, minute four-penny volumes, nine of which described the sights of London. Measuring 1¾ inches by 2¼ inches, Boreman's first book was *The Gigantick History Of the two Famous Giants, And Other Curiosities In Guildhall, London.* Like Newbery's books, it appeared in boards covered with shiny Dutch floral paper. Despite their bright wrappings, however, Boreman's books were generally dull and often resembled handy pocket or finger guide books. The two volumes of *The History and Description of Westminster Abbey* mechanically described one hundred and three monuments within the abbey, after which "progress" was stopped by the "iron barricado" that prevented people from seeing the chapels and monuments of the kings and queens unless they paid threepence. Unfortunately, the person in charge of showing these monuments, Boreman explained, was "apt to run them over in so much hurry, that but little can be remember'd of what is seen." As a remedy for this problem, Boreman promised to publish another volume which he said would conclude "our *History of Westminster Abbey*; which gloomy subject we fear, has already well nigh tired the patience of our young readers."[2] *The History and Description of Westminster Abbey* was not unique among Boreman's books. Just as wearying were *The History And Description Of the Famous Cathedral Of St. Paul's* (two volumes) and *Curiosities In the Tower of London* (two volumes).

Boreman's most entertaining books described the giants and curiosities found in the Guildhall [I have not seen his *The History of Sejanus the Swedish Giant*]. On the reverse side of the title page of *The Gigantick History,* Boreman wrote that "during the Infant-Age, ever busy and always inquiring, there is no fixing the attention of the mind, but by amusing it." Newbery, of course, agreed with this statement. Unlike Newbery, however, who took his philosophy and methodology from Locke and who used amusement as a bait to lure children to learning, Boreman seems not to have had any clear educational purpose. In places *The Gigantick History* was amusing, but this amusement did not fix the attention of children on anything more substantial than the history and appearance of the Guildhall and its furnishings and decorations. Dedicated to "all the little masters and all the little misses" in London and in the country, *The Gigantick History* began with a long list of subscribers. All Boreman's books, as did Newbery's *Lilliputian Magazine,* contained a list of subscribers. Several of these were highly suspect. Corineus and Gogmagog, the two Guildhall giants, were down for a hundred volumes each. The giants' subscriptions paled, however, beside that of "Master Hercule Vinegar the 9th," who ordered six hundred sets of the volumes describing the Tower of London. In contrast, "Master Theoppy Cibber" ordered but one set for "self and Papa." Finding the Dutch floral paper inappropriate for more sober thought, the "*Vatican* Library at Rome" ordered a set of *The Gigantick History* bound in morocco. Aside from the list of subscribers, Boreman's playfulness was mostly confined to his introductions. He had published two four-penny volumes describing the

Guildhall rather than one larger volume, he explained, because Necessity had urged him to do so. "A huge volume," he wrote, "would come too dear for children, and be too heavy to carry in one pocket; it was therefore better to have two; one for each, which would ballance them so equally, there would be no fear of their growing lap-sided from the weight of such a gigantick work." Unlike Newbery's Woglog, who was a giant with some personality, the Guildhall's Corineus and Gogmagog were stony creatures. Only rarely did Boreman's description of them strike a spark capable of brightening children's fancies. On the subject of the giants' dining habits, however, Boreman did skip beyond the factual. "'Tis said," he wrote, "that when the giants hear the clock at noon strike twelve, they strait step down from off the shelve they stand upon, to eat their dinners, and when they hear the clock at one, they step from whence they come. Tho' this may seem very strange, yet 'tis well known that several gaping fellows have come to Guildhall on purpose to see 'em walk down to dinner; but were always disappointed, for either they happen'd to come on a fast-day, or the giants growing older, are more shy of company, and will sooner go without their meat, than be star'd and yawn'd at all the while they are eating it."[3]

Boreman's books are not without charm, but like the giants' dinner they provoke more yawns than they inspire interest. Boreman may have influenced Newbery; but just as the artist, according to Henry James, converted air-blown grains of suggestion into revelation, so Newbery transformed whatever Boreman's books suggested into something shiningly superior. The factual contents of Boreman's guide books were more suited to adults than to "little readers." In 1753 Newbery himself published *An Historical Account Of The Curiosities Of London and Westminster.* Written for adults, *An Historical Account* described many of the sights that Boreman examined in his diminutive books.[4]

Of more interest to the student of education and children's books than Boreman's publications were two books published by Mary Cooper of Paternoster Row. In 1743 appeared the second edition of *The Child's New Play-Thing: Being A Spelling-Book Intended To make Learning to Read, a Diversion instead of a Task.* Although it was larger than Newbery's books, measuring 3½ by 5¾ inches, and lacked the vibrant high spirits which marked Newbery's best books, the *Child's New Play-Thing* had much in common with Newbery's children's books. Not only did it blend profit and delight, but, like many of Newbery's books, it was a miscellany. It began with an alphabet. The letters were arranged in squares; each was framed by a Christian name above and noun beneath. On the page behind was a sentence identifying the letter. Thus above "Bb" was *Balaam,* below appeared *Bread,* while "B was a Butcher, and had a great Dog" was written on the back of the page. Similarly, "Oo" was bracketed by *Obadiah* and *Orange* while the reverse side informed readers, "O was an Oyster-wench, and a sad scold." Two copies of this alphabet appeared in the *Play-Thing,* so that children were able to cut out one and play with it. The book also contained a syllabary, lists of words of one, two, three, and four syllables, and fables and lessons in words containing a similar number of syllables. The story of Joseph and his brethren was, for example, told in words of three syllables, while one of the fables recounted the history of Samson. Sections of the book contained selections of moral and religious precepts and English proverbs. Like those found in *A Little Pretty Pocket-Book,* many of the proverbs were not particularly suited for children. "God help the Rich, the Poor can beg" and "He that lies down with Dogs must rise up with Fleas" were typical. Songs, riddles, moral dialogues, prayers, the numbers, and portions of chapbook accounts of Guy of Warwick, St. George, Fortunatus, and Reynard, each accompanied by a woodcut, were also in the *Play-Thing.*[5]

Although the contents of the *Play-Thing* resembled that of the typical Newbery children's book, Mary Cooper's publication was comparatively pedestrian. No Giles Gingerbread, Tommy Trip, or Woglog the giant cavorted in its pages. No balm of gaiety bound amusement to instruction, and they bumped bruisingly together. Unlike *A Pretty Play-Thing,* which was printed in Alexandria "for the booksellers of *Egypt* and *Palmyra*" and sold for "half a Shass," the *Child's New Play-Thing* was obviously printed for Paternoster Row and sold for mundane coin of the realm. On 22 March 1744, in *The London Evening-Post,* Mary Cooper advertised the publication of *Tommy Thumb's Song Book* by Nurse Lovechild. On 23 May 1744, in *The Daily Advertiser,* she announced the publication of *Nancy Cock's Song Book,* which she said was the companion to "to Tommy Thumb, and the Second Volume of that great and learned

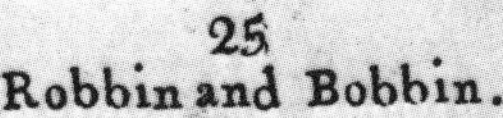
25
Robbin and Bobbin.

Robbin and Bobbin,
Two great Belly'd Men,
They eat more Victuals
Than threeſcore Men.

TIMOROSO.

From *Tommy Thumb's Pretty Song Book "Voll II."* By permission of the British Library.

and her PLUMB-CAKE. 51

all in the next Room drawing for King and Queen, and there aſſembled *Jemmy Dove, Billy Long, Tommy Hawes, Dicky Lovewell, Polly Grove, Betſy Sommers, Jenny Denham, Sally Brown,* and others whoſe Names I cannot at this Time recollect.

As ſoon as Mrs. *Williams* had ſerved the young Ladies, ſhe called

D 2

From *Nurse Truelove's New-Year's-Gift.* Copyright Bodleian Library Oxford.

Work." Like the first edition of *The Child's New Play-Thing,* these editions are not extant. A copy, however, of *Tommy Thumb's Pretty Song Book "Voll II"* is extant. The *Pretty Song Book* is interesting, for it conveyed the gaiety absent from the *Child's New Play-Thing.* With some of its pages printed in red and others in black, the *Song Book* contained forty nursery rhymes, most of which were accompanied by delightful woodcuts. Many of the rhymes were those which are now labeled "classic": "Lady Bird, Lady Bird," "Sing a Song of Sixpence," "The Mouse ran up the Clock," "London Bells," "Little Tommy Tucker," "Great A, little a," "Bah, Bah a Black Sheep," and "London Bridge." Instructions on how to sing them accompanied the rhymes. Thus "Piss a Bed" was to be sung in the "Grande" manner while "Blackamoor, Taunymoor" was to be sung "Vere Subito." "Replicao" was thought suitable for "Lady Bird"; "Pronto," for "Robin red breast," and "Timoroso" for "Robbin and Bobbin." Nurse Lovechild herself appeared in one of the illustrations and the book ended with a Newbery-like puff for *The Child's New Play-Thing.* "The Childs Plaything," Nurse Lovechild hymned, "I recommend for Cheating / Children into Learning / Without any Beating."[6]

Tommy Thumb's Pretty Song Book was a lively, happy book. In contrast to the children's books published by Newbery, however, it seemed slapdash. Comparatively little care had been taken in producing it. The print often drifted across the page; lines sometimes wandered crookedly, and letters bunched together like piles of ashes. Moreover, the *Song Book* only amused. Unlike Newbery's Tommy Trip or Jack the Giant-Killer, who were concerned about children's moral and educational growth, Tommy Thumb did not beat an instructive tune on his "Pipe & Drum." An advertisement at the end of the *Song Book* showed a child sitting down reading a book on which was written "*The Child's Plaything* 1744." Behind and to the child's right were a hobbyhorse and a drum. The picture was almost an emblem of Mary Cooper's two extant children's books. As the hobbyhorse and the drum were simply amusing toys, so the *Song Book* provided no instruction but only delighted. As the child had to put aside his toys when he read the book in his hand, so, despite its miscellaneous contents, *The Child's New Play-Thing* resembled a schoolbook filled with comparatively dull lessons. Newbery's success lay in his ability to do what Cooper did not do: blend amusement and instruction together in an appetizing and salable whole. Tommy Trip did not have a hobbyhorse, but he did have a hobby-dog, Jouler, which he rode not simply for pleasure but to lead children to learning. Newbery's children did not learn their letters in lonely studies or to the confusing beat of a tin drum, but in the company of a jovial Cuz and to the sounds of his melodious chorus.[7]

Appendix C. John Newbery's Advertising Methods

Many of Newbery's advertisements were delightful. From Locke he learned that a thimbleful of fun would lead more Lilliputians to learning than a cord of rods. Going a step beyond Locke as a businessman rather than a philosopher, he recognized that what attracted children would also probably attract adults. Since children themselves did not buy books, at least not their first books, he saw that he would have to attract adults before children. Consequently, he baited his advertisements with playfulness. Part owner of several London newspapers, Newbery often announced the publication of new books in their pages. Frequently, he declared that the book was being given away free. The publication of *Nurse Truelove's Christmas-Box; or, the Golden Plaything* was announced in *The General Advertiser* on 9 January 1749–50 under bold type as "GIVEN GRATIS, By J. NEWBERY, *at the Bible and Sun in St. Paul's Church-yard, over against the North Door of the Church, (only paying One Penny for the Binding)*." In March *The General Advertiser* announced that *Nurse Truelove's New-Year's-Gift* was also being given away free except for the binding, which cost twopence. Even if one had the twopence, this book could not be bought, Newbery told his prospective diminutive customers, "*unless you are good.*" Newbery was a stickler for good behavior. In *The London Chronicle* for 29 December 1764—1 January 1765, he announced the publication of four books for children, declaring: "The Philosophers, Politicians, Necromancers, and the Learned in every Faculty, are desired to observe, that on the First of January, being New

Year's Day (OH that we may all live new Lives!) Mr. NEWBERY intends to publish the following important Volumes, bound and gilt; and hereby invites all his little Friends who are Good, to call for them at the Bible and Sun, in St. Paul's Church Yard; but those who are naughty, are to have none."[1]

As a successful promoter, Newbery knew the value of an unsolicited testimonial. In publicizing the *Lilliputian Magazine* and his society of subscribers, he was fortunate enough to elicit broad support. From "MAB, Queen of the Fairies," who was holding court "in a Bean Blossom" in a "Corner of Hornsey Wood" on 22 January 1750, came an impeccable recommendation. "All my little Friends," Mab wrote to the *General Evening Post,* "who would be wise, happy, and never want Money, are desired to enter themselves Members of this my favourite Society." Although she was quite busy with "a Tragedy now in Rehearsal," Nurse Truelove thought the *Lilliputian Magazine* and society so valuable that she took time to write from her home in Grosvenor Square. "I have read," she said, "by Order of her Grace the Dutchess of *** the Pieces which are to be published by this Society, together with their Laws and Regulations: And I earnestly request all my little Friends to become Members thereof."[2]

The playfulness with which Newbery advertised his books drew attention not merely to the books but also to his methods. In 1755 "Adam Fitz-Adam," an essayist in *The World,* devoted almost an entire number to Newbery's generosity. Fitz-Adam first laughed at Newbery's advertising methods, then deftly used them to publicize the collected edition of *The World.* He began by comparing the present with the past. Contrary to popular opinion, the present, he wrote, was not a time of cultural or moral deterioration. In the past, men's actions often began and ended in self. Advertisements in the "public papers," he wrote proudly, showed that there were "instances of public-spiritedness in the present" which "put to shame every record" that could be produced in favour of the past. "*Practitioners in physic,*" he cited as proof, showed great "disinterested zeal" in "their labours" for "the good of mankind." In particular, an advertisement for "*Old Iron Pear-tree Water and its Salts*" testified to the virtuous spirit of modernity. A selfish desire for gain played no part in the appearance of this notice, for the inventor of Old Iron Pear-tree

Water stated unequivocally "that the UNHAPPY may know where to apply for relief, is the full end of this advertisement."

Influenced by this "noble and disinterested spirit," Fitz-Adam decided to direct Dodsley, his bookseller, to bind the past issues of *The World* into three neat pocket volumes. These would be sold for three shillings each, not of course for a profit, Fitz-Adam assured readers, but merely to relieve the unhappy. This benevolent scheme did not get beyond the planning stage, however, for Fitz-Adam was interrupted by a friend who informed him "that an author of his acquaintance had greatly out-done" him "in generosity." As proof, the friend produced Newbery's advertisement for *Nurse Truelove's New-Year's-Gift.* "I confess very freely," Fitz-Adam admitted, "that the generosity of this advertisement put me out a little of countenance; but as I pique myself upon nothing so much as my benevolence to mankind, I soon came to a resolution not to be out-done by this public-spirited gentleman; and I hereby give notice, that the abovementioned three volumes of the WORLD, together with a very elaborate index to each (all of which were, I confess, intended to be SOLD) will now be given GRATIS at every bookseller's shop in town, to all sorts of persons, *they only paying* NINE SHILLINGS *for the* BINDING."[3]

Although his generosity caught the fancy of the literary world, Newbery's most characteristic advertisements were in his books themselves. In the texts, he often inserted references to other publications. In the *Lilliputian Magazine,* he wrote, "Master *Peter Primrose* was a boy of such uncommon abilities, that he was admired by every body." This admiration had not fallen from the air unexpectedly, however, for Master Peter had read Newbery's *Circle of Sciences* (1745–1748), which gave him "some knowledge of men and things."[4]

The most outrageous of Newbery's inserted advertisements appeared in *The Valentine's-Gift* (1765). In the days of the first Christians, Mr. Simpson recounted, the first man and woman who saw each other on Valentine's Day were Valentines for the rest of the year and were responsible for admonishing each other if their conduct fell away from a high standard. The distinguished Mr. Worthy, Mr. Simpson said, had benefited greatly from the custom, for he had once been a very naughty boy. Early one Valentine's Day, as he walked sniffling past Sir Richard Lovewell's home, young Lucy Lovewell saw him and he automatically became her Valentine. Discovering that he was crying because he did not want to go to school, Lucy told him it was necessary that he like books. To encourage him, she showed him her closet, where "all Mr. Newbery's little books lay in a window." The effect on Master Worthy was galvanic.

> "Bless me!" he exclaimed, "I should like such books as these. Here is master Friendly carried in the chair; here is Miss Friendly in the lord-mayor's coach; here is Mrs. Two-and-again, and Lazy Robin, and the House that Jack built! Oh! mame, and here is Mrs. Williams and the Plumb-cake, Trade and Plumb-cake for ever! huzza! O dear! dear! and here is Woglog and Tommy Trip upon Joler, and Leo the great Lion, and Miss Biddy Johnson, and Jemmy Gadabout, and Miss Polly Meanwell, and Mr. Little Wit's Cock-Robin, and the Family of the Little Wits is a large Family. Oh, dear! mame, and here is the Cuz in his Cap with his Chorus, Ba, be, bi; and mame, here is Leapfrog. . . . And here is the Ball and pincushion, to make Miss Polly a good girl, and Master Tommy a good boy; and a Letter from Jack the Giant-killer. Your servant, Mr. Jack the Giant-killer; and here is a pretty Little Bible; oh, dear! I should love to read in such a Bible as this; and a little Dictionary, mame, the size of a snuff-box. This Dictionary won't come thump against my head like our great one at school; and here is the pretty Little Fables, written by Abraham Aesop, Esq; and Woglog the Great Giant. . . . And here, mame, is the Pretty Poems for the Children three feet high, that is me, mame, and here is the history of Little Goody Two-Shoes."

Young Master Worthy got carried away by the profusion of books, much as Newbery was carried away in listing his favorite characters and games. Lucy interrupted him, crying, "hold . . . I won't have my books tumbled over in this manner; but if you will promise to be a good boy, you shall begin with the first of them, and carry away as many as you can read." Astounded by her generosity, Master Worthy began reading and before dinner he had read *Nurse Truelove's Christmas-Box, The New-Year's-Gift, The Easter-Gift, The Whitsuntide-Gift,* and *The Fairing*. Even chocolate could not tempt him from such palatable learning, and he read *The Royal Primer* and *The Lottery-Book* aloud to Lucy.[5]

In all Newbery's books, the good child was the father of the successful man, and not surprisingly the foundation of Mr. Worthy's character was laid in Lucy Lovewell's closet as he flipped eagerly through many "little books." In his good fortune, Master Worthy was not alone. Master Friendly, who became "a Parliament-Man," began his education by getting "all the little Books by Rote that are sold at the *Bible* and *Sun* in *St. Paul's* Church-Yard, when he was but a very little Boy!" Because they read the books "*Sold at Mr.* Newbery's, *at the* Bible *and* Sun *in* St. Paul's Church-yard," Master Billy and Miss Kitty Smith changed from "the very worst Boy and Girl in the Parish" into "the very best Children in the whole country" and became happy, wealthy adults riding in coaches that carried them far beyond the pages of *The Whitsuntide-Gift* (1765) in which they first appeared. Master Billy and Miss Kitty became so good that Tommy Trip cultivated their acquaintance. Having learned that they were visiting the Duke of Galaxy, Tommy coupled Jouler to "*Tinker,* and *Towser,* and *Rockwood,* and *Ringwood,* and *Rover*" and set out to see them. Joined to "a little Chariot," Tommy's steeds pulled into *The Fairing* with a great hullabaloo. "Master Trip," YOU KNOW WHO reminded readers after the noise died down, "will ride an hundred Miles at any Time to see any little Boy or Girl, who is remarkably good. He is the little Gentleman, who used to go round with Cakes and Custards to all the Boys and Girls, who had learned Mr. *Newbery's* little Books, and were good; and having heard, that Master *Billy,* and Miss *Kitty Smith,* were on a Visit at the Duke's, he is come a long, long Way to see them."[6]

Newbery's activities were not, as has been mentioned before, limited to the book trade. He also sold patent medicines, dealing in some thirty nostrums at one time or another. His most successful were Dr. James's Powders and Greenough's Tinctures for Teeth. The former was one of the best-known cure-alls in England in the eighteenth century. Newbery claimed it was "a most effectual remedy" for colds, small pox, measles, St. Anthony's Fire, and "all internal inflammations, pleurises, quinsies, acute rheumatisms, and the lowness of spirits, and uneasinesses proceeding from the slow and latent fevers, which are generally mistaken for vapours and hysterics." A medicine of such curative powers was a rare discovery, one which no family should be without. And with concern for the physical health of his young readers rivaling his concern for their mental strength, Newbery poignantly drew attention to the miraculous powders in *Little Goody Two-Shoes.* The unfair and quasi-legal persecutions of Sir Timothy Gripe and Farmer Graspall forced

Goody's father, Farmer Meanwell, off his land. Forced to forsake his family and his medicine chest as well, Farmer Meanwell was "seized with a violent Fever in a Place where Dr. *James's* Powder was not to be had, and where he died miserably."[7]

Although her mother died a few days later and harsh necessity forced her to live in barns, Little Goody found adversity to be the staff of morality. If she had not, however, Newbery had a medicine ready for her: Dr. John Hooper's Female Pills. These were "the best Medicine ever discovered for young Women." Not only would two or three boxes at a shilling a box cure that affliction vulgarly known as "the Green Sickness," but the pills were "excellent for the Palpitation of the Heart, Giddiness, Loathing of Food, bad Digestion, Pains of the Stomach, a Beating of the Arteries of the Neck, short Breath upon every little Motion, sinking of the Spirits, a dejected Countenance, and Dislike to Exercise and Conversation; and likewise for the Scurvy." For these distempers, Newbery assured young women, they were "a never-failing Cure" and were "to be given from seven years old to seventy." Although she was just seven and her father's death must have led to a sinking of the spirits if not a palpitation of the heart, Goody Two-Shoes does not seem to have taken Dr. Hooper's pills. Perhaps she was too poor to purchase them. Instead, she put her trust in education. Realizing that education would enable her to better her lot in life, she borrowed the books of children when they went home from school, and "by this Means she soon got more Learning than any of her Playmates." Particularly useful to her was the "Cuzz's Chorus," a syllabary which taught spelling and the alphabet and which the publisher helpfully pointed out "may be found in the *Little Pretty Play Thing* published by Mr. NEWBERY." Armed with knowledge, Goody began visiting neighboring farmhouses and became "*a trotting Tutoress.*" After she had taught industriously for many years, Sir William Dove helped her find a less peripatetic post. "Mrs. *Williams,*" Newbery wrote, "of whom I have given a particular Account in my *New-Year's-Gift,* and who kept a College for instructing little Gentlemen and Ladies in the Science of A, B, C, was at this Time very old and infirm, and wanted to decline that important Trust." In the *New-Year's-Gift,* Mrs. Williams' pedagogical talents had been highly praised. Besides her professional knowledge, she was "well acquainted with the

World," and, although a widow, she knew "many Things" from "Experience, of which she had a larger Stock than any old Woman in either of the *European* Universities." This experience bore fruit in her good judgment, for her scholars studied eleven books, all of which were listed in the *Gift* and all of which were published by Newbery. Following in Mrs. Williams' footsteps, Goody Two-Shoes was an even greater success, for she had benefited from progressive educational developments—that is, the list of books "usually read" by her scholars had grown from eleven to forty-three. All of these were conveniently published by Newbery and were listed in an appendix. Moreover, in case any of her scholars became ill, twelve patent medicines were also listed, including Dr. James's Powders, Mr. Greenough's Tinctures, The Original Daffy's Elixir, The Balsam of Health, Dr. Boerhaave's Purging Pills, and Dr. Hooper's Female Pills.[8]

Newbery's successors imitated his advertising methods with varying degrees of skill. At Tom Thumb's birth, Mr. Theophilus Thumb was disappointed at the appearance of his son. "A very learned Gentleman" wearing "a great Pair of Spectacles," however, examined the minute infant and told his father that one day Tom would be a great man. It was "Wisdom and Virtue," he emphasized, which made a man great, not size. When Tom's father learned this, he "immediately bought for his Son all Mr. *Newbery's* little Books, having been informed, that they were published with no other View, but to make People wise and good." Among the exhibits in E. Newbery's *Tom Thumb's Exhibition* was a "MAHOGENY CONJURING BOX." This box had "the uncommon property of converting every thing" put under it "into the very thing it ought to have been." When Tom put one of "Mrs. Newbery's little books" under the box as a demonstration, the book became "a swinging folio, very magnificently gilt and lettered." "At the bottom of the title page," Tom pointed out, "was printed in large capitals, 'PRICE THREE GUINEAS.'" From this he concluded that Mrs. Newbery's "little performance" contained "more useful instruction, more real good sense" and was "of three times greater value than many a swaggering and unwieldy folio."[9]

Although he rarely matched Newbery's playfulness, John Marshall imitated Newbery's advertising methods. In *Anecdotes of A Boarding-School,* Dorothy Kilner warned parents against sending children away from home for education. When it became absolutely necessary, however, to send little Martha Beauchamp to a boarding school, her mother gave her Marshall's *Dialogues and Letters, Adventures of a Pincushion,* and *Memoirs of a Peg-Top,* stressing that Martha would "reap great improvement from them" if she read them carefully. Later, almost as an afterthought, Mrs. Beauchamp gave Martha a Bible and prayer book. In *Jemima Placid,* the young heroine visited London and read many of the "little books" which could "be bought at Mr. Marshall's." On her return to Smiledale, she brought her library, and her father the Rev. Placid was so pleased with these "mighty volumes" that he ordered "an additional supply for his friends."[10]

After Lady Kindheart's young husband was killed in battle, she devoted her energy to improving the poor in her parish. When she walked in the fields, she would ask a poor child to accompany her. If the child could say his catechism, she would present him with "one of those little books which are sold by Mr. *Marshall, No. 4, Aldermary Church Yard, Bow Lane, London.*" Lady Kindheart "likewise desired Mr. *Meanwell* her chaplain, and the parson of the parish, to hear them their catechise every Sunday morning; and I have known her," the kind lady's biographer recalled, "when a child said it all throughout without missing a word, give it a whole library of Mr. *Marshall*'s gilt books, among which were the following, *Timothy Ticklepitcher's* TALES and FABLES, the FRIENDS; or, the HISTORY of *Billy Freeman* and *Tommy Truelove*; The *Universal* PRIMER, where you have the History of Miss *Nancy Truelove.*" While she was living with Mrs. Bountiful, Goody Goosecap fashioned a pocket for her benefactor on which she sewed roses, lilies, and carnations. As a present and not as a reward, she received "a set of Mr. *Marshall*'s books." As soon as she saw how much Primrose Prettyface enjoyed her studies, Lady Worthy sent her "some of *Mr.* MARSHALL'S UNIVERSAL PRIMERS and BATTLEDORES." The first morning after Lydia Lively's mother decided she would write a story each day describing her daughter's behavior, Lydia began to read *The Footstep to Mrs. Trimmer's Sacred History.* Later, Lydia presented the poor-but-honest children of Mrs. Brush, a woman who kept a "little school" and took "in needle-work," with a selection of Marshall's books, including *Short Conversations, Familiar Dialogues, First Principles of Religion,* and *The Good Child's Delight.* In following Newbery's advertising methods, Marshall even discovered a successor to Mrs. Williams and Goody Two-Shoes: Mrs. Teachwell. Straightened circumstances forced Mrs. Teachwell to turn her comfortable country home into a school. Like her predecessors, she selected a library "for the use of the young people." But believing more in the "cram" method, her list was twice as long as that of Goody Two-Shoes, consisting of some eighty-five titles, all of which were probably sold by Marshall.[11]

Notes

Introduction

1. *Guardian of Education* 1 (1802), 8.
2. Thomas Bridges, *The Adventures of a Bank-Note* (London, 1771), IV, 24.
3. *The Foreign Travels of Sir John Mandeville* (London, 1760), 4.

Chapter 1

1. For those who have forgotten: Mrs. Tiggy-Winkle, Squirrel Nutkin, Old Brown, Peter Rabbit, the Flopsy Bunnies, Ginger, and Pickles are from the books of Beatrix Potter. Toad drives through Kenneth Grahame's *The Wind in the Willows,* and Uncle Wiggily Longears is Howard Garis's "rabbit gentleman." Pooh Corner is A.A. Milne's creation, and "Bred and bawn" is Brer Rabbit's comment to Brer Fox after he escaped the clutches of the Tar-Baby, in the stories by Joel Chandler Harris.

2. F.J. Harvey Darton, *Children's Books in England*, 2nd ed. (Cambridge, 1958), 1. Mrs. Jane West, *Letters To a Young Lady,* 2nd ed. (London, 1806), I, 139. John Richard Green, *History of the English People* (London, 1880), IV, 273–74. Sarah Trimmer, *Reflections upon the Education of Children in Charity Schools* (London, 1792), 13.

3. James Lackington, *Memoirs Of The First Forty-Five Years Of The Life Of James Lackington,* a new edition (London, 1792), 386–91. For a discussion of Newbery's predecessors, see Appendix B.

4. Henry Peacham, *The Compleat Gentleman* (1622), 1, 3, 11–15, 138.

5. *The Works of the late Right Honorable Henry St. John, Lord Viscount Boling-*

broke (London, 1754), III, 329. John Clarke, *An Essay Upon Study* (London, 1731), 229–30. John Locke, *The Educational Writings of John Locke,* ed. James L. Axtell (Cambridge, 1968), 325 (hereinafter cited as Locke in Axtell). Samuel Richardson, *Pamela* (London, 1742), IV, 152, 315–77. Pamela did not agree with all of Locke's ideas, and in her letters to Mr. B. she explained why. In doing this, she followed Locke's own suggestion. At the conclusion of *Some Thoughts,* Locke stated that his work was "far from being a compleat Treatise on this Subject." Instead, he hoped that it would merely serve as a teaching aid, giving, he wrote, "some small light to those, whose Concern for their dear little Ones makes them so irregularly bold, that they dare venture to consult their own Reason, in the Education of their Children, rather than wholly to rely upon Old Custom" (Locke in Axtell, 325).

6. *Guardian of Education* 1 (1802), 8, 62. Locke in Axtell, 114–15, 129. John Locke, *An Essay Concerning Human Understanding,* ed. John W. Yolton (London, 1965), I, 15–16, 77–80, 88–90, 130 (hereinafter cited as Locke in Yolton).

7. Locke in Yolton, I, 79–80. Locke in Axtell, 237. See Appendix A for more on Locke's denial of innate ideas.

8. Locke in Axtell, 146. Locke in Yolton, I, 335–38. David Fordyce, *Dialogues Concerning Education* (London, 1745), 270. Catharine Macaulay Graham, *Letters On Education With Observations On Religious And Metaphysical Subjects* (London, 1790), i–ii.

9. Gerald R. Cragg, *Reason and Authority in the Eighteenth Century* (Cambridge, 1964), 5–6. Lawrence A. Cremin, *American Education* (New York, 1970), 255. John Yolton, *John Locke And The Way of Ideas* (Oxford, 1956), 24–25. Richard Aaron, *John Locke,* 2nd ed. (Oxford, 1955), 292.

10. James Burgh, *The Dignity of Human Nature* (London, 1754), 119. Philip Doddridge, *Sermons on The Religious Education of Children* (London, 1732), 52. Locke in Axtell, 98–104. William Warburton, *Letters From A Late Eminent Prelate To One of His Friends* (Kidderminster, 1808), 208. Ephraim Chambers, *Cyclopaedia* (London, 1728), I, 279. *Gentleman's Magazine* 2 (1732), 917.

11. Isaac Watts, *Philosophical Essays On Various Subjects* (London, 1733), viii. James Talbott, *The Christian School-Master* (London, 1709), 24. John Clarke, *An Essay Upon The Education Of Youth In Grammer-Schools* (London, 1720), 4, 8–9; *An Essay Upon Study* (London, 1731), 21–22.

12. Thomas Sheridan, *British Education* (London, 1756), 8, 25. Richard Hurd, *Dialogues On The Uses of Foreign Travel* (London, 1764), 4–5, 83. Also see Burgh's *The Dignity of Human Nature* and George Chapman, *A Treatise On Education* (London, 1773).

13. Jean LeClerc, *The Life and Character of Mr. John Locke* (London, 1706),

26–27. *Gentleman's Magazine* 2 (1732), 917. James Whitchurch, *An Essay Upon Education* (London, 1772), 201.

14. Locke in Axtell, 225–26.

15. Darton, 11. Darton's chapter on the history of fables is good (10–32). Locke in Axtell, 259–60, 298.

16. *Guardian of Education* 1 (1802), 63. *Payne's Universal Chronicle* 20 (Aug. 12–Aug. 19, 1758), "The Idler, No. 19," p. 153. For Darton, the date (1744) of the publication of Newbery's *A Little Pretty Pocket-Book* was in terms of children's books "comparable to the 1066 of the older histories" (7). A new literary and educational era began, Frank Mumby wrote, as Englishmen started to study the literary needs of children and began to furnish them "with a special library and a light literature of their own." Frank Mumby and Ian Norrie, *Publishing and Bookselling,* 5th ed. (London, 1974) pt. I, 167. In part, the rapid growth in the number of children's books published from the time of Newbery's small beginning to the end of the century merely reflected the phenomenal growth of the publishing trade itself in the eighteenth century. For a discussion of Newbery's predecessors, see Appendix B.

17. Locke in Axtell, 325. The *Twelfth-Day-Gift* (London, 1770), 6–9. The dates given to Newbery's books in the text differ from those cited in the footnotes. Few early editions of Newbery's books are extant. However, in his superb bibliography *John Newbery And His Successors, 1740–1814,* Sydney Roscoe dates the first editions of Newbery's and his successors's children's books. In the text I cite his dates while in the footnotes I refer to editions I actually use. Roscoe, *John Newbery And His Successors* (Wormley, 1973).

18. *The Lilliputian Magazine* (London, 1751), 35–37. Tom Telescope, *The Newtonian System of Philosophy* (London, 1762), 99, 113–14. *The Valentine's Gift* (London, 1777), 37–70. *The History of Little Goody Two-Shoes* (London, 1765), 68–69. Oliver Goldsmith contributed to Newbery's children's books and may have been responsible for the Ambassador of Bantam's feelings. The Chinese philosopher Lien Chi Altangi, who was visiting London at the same time as the ambassador and whose letters home were published by Newbery, commented on the discrepancy between the natives' fondness for professing sympathy for animals and their delight in eating them. "The better sort here," he wrote, "pretend to the utmost compassion for animals of every kind; to hear them speak, a stranger would be apt to imagine they could hardly hurt the gnat that stung 'em. . . . And yet would you believe it, I have seen the very men who have thus boasted of their tenderness; at the same time devouring the flesh of six different animals tossed up in a fricasse." Oliver Goldsmith, "Letter 15," *The Citizen of the World* (London, 1762), 51.

19. Hezekiah Woodward, *Of The Childs Portion* (London, 1649), 15, 60. Arthur Dent, *The Plaine Mans Pathway to Heaven* (London, 1601), 17–18, 97. Samuel Crossman, *The Young Mans Monitor* (London, 1644), 18, 22.

20. For Sherlock's criticism of Locke, see Appendix A. Doddridge, *Sermons,* II, 51–52.

21. Isaac Watts, *A Treatise on the Education of Children and Youth,* 2nd ed. (London, 1769), 16–17, 110–11; *Catechisms* (London, 1730), 7. Locke in Axtell, 241. Doddridge, *Sermons,* 71.

22. *Monthly Review* 81 (1789), 371. Sara Trimmer, *An Easy Introduction To The Knowledge of Nature* (London, 1780), vii, xiii–xiv, 1, 208. Ellenor Fenn, *The Rational Dame* (London, 1790), vii–viii. Mrs. Trimmer believed that *Some Thoughts* greatly influenced the direction of religious education in the eighteenth century. By recommending that children learn the Lord's Prayer, the Creed, and the Ten Commandments "at an early age," Locke's "system" produced "great benefit to the Establishment." On Locke's reluctance to advocate intensive religious study, Mrs. Trimmer hedged slightly, writing: "There is not, indeed, much said expressly in Mr. Locke's book upon the subject of RELIGION, but more is implied; for all that related to the forming of the minds of children to *virtue* by checking the growth of unruly passions, and teaching them to govern appetities, may be referred to this head." *Guardian of Education* I (1802), 9. For Locke on the Lord's Prayer, see Locke in Axtell, 262.

23. Jerom Murch, *Mrs. Barbauld and Her Contemporaries* (London, 1877), 125. Burgh, *The Dignity,* 125. *Monthly Review* 70 (1784), 126; 72 (1785), 469.

24. Sarah Trimmer, *Fabulous Histories* (London, 1786), vii–xi. Throughout the eighteenth century, there was some discussion of the nature and abilities of animals and their differences from man. Descartes and the Cartesians did not grant animals the ability to think and classed them as machines. Although he wrote little about animals, Locke differed with Descartes and, in various parts of *An Essay*, said that animals possessed perception, memory, and reason. Their reasoning ability was, however, much inferior to that of man, whose capacity for reason was one of the primary ways in which he was "distinguished from the beasts." Moreover, unlike man, animals were incapable of religion. Unfortunately, Locke added, "religion, which should most distinguish us from beasts and ought most peculiarly to elevate us as rational creatures above brutes, is that wherein men often appear most irrational and more senseless than beasts themselves." Locke in Yolton, I, 116, 122, 127; II, 262, 287. Locke's position on animals seems to have been the generally accepted one. In *The Wisdom of God Manifested in the Works Of The Creation* (London, 1691), a popular book appearing in its tenth edition in 1735, John Ray pointedly differed with

the Cartesians, writing, "I should rather think Animals to be endued with a lower Degree of Reason, than that they are mere Machines" (38). In *The Religion Of Nature Delineated* (London, 1722), another popular book which reached an eighth edition in 1759, William Wollaston said that animals possessed the ability to reason (70). In *Observations On Man, His Frame, His Duty, and His Expectations* (London, 1749), David Hartley tentatively agreed with the Cartesians, writing, "I suppose, with Descartes, that all their Motions are conducted by mere Mechanism." Hartley ameliorated his statement, adding, "yet I do not suppose them to be destitute of Perception, but that they have this in a manner analogous to that which takes place in us" (I, 413). Mrs. Trimmer thought the question of whether animals were machines or not was too complex for children. In *Fabulous Histories*, a Mrs. Franks said that she had considered animals as "mere machines" actuated by "the unerring hand of Providence" until she saw the Learned Pig in London. This led to a conversation on the instinct of animals which Mrs. Trimmer did not include, she said, because young readers would not understand it. Mrs. Benson did tell Harriet later, however, never "to give countenance to those people who show what they call learned animals." Great barbarities, she said, were used to teach animals things foreign to their natures. The Learned Pig's abilities to spell and tell time, she thought, were shams, and she said the helper must have directed the animal by private signs (66–73). For more on the subject, see Kenneth MacLean, *John Locke and English Literature of the Eighteenth Century* (New Haven, 1936).

25. Trimmer, *Fabulous Histories*, 9, 35.

26. *Ibid.*, 55, 67.

27. *Ibid.*, 57, 60, 65, 221.

28. Maria and Richard Lovell Edgeworth, *Practical Education* (London, 1798), 285. Dorothy Kilner (M.P.), *The Life and Perambulation of a Mouse* (London, 1783), 24. Richard Johnson, *The Adventures of a Silver Penny* (London, 1787), 49–53. *The Two Cousins*, Cheap Repository Tracts (London, 1797), 7, 9–20. Scotch Cheap Repository Tracts, *The Apprentice*, 2nd ed. (Edinburgh, 1815), 82. Maria Edgeworth, *Moral Tales for Young People* (London, 1801), III, 144–46.

29. *The History Of Little King Pippin* (Glasgow, 1814), 20, 24–25. American children also learned the dangers of being cruel to animals. The seeds of Benedict Arnold's treachery were sown during his boyhood. George Canning Hill wrote, "he would go out into the orchards and fields and tear them from the trees with an inward chuckle of maliciousness, crushing the eggs he found, and pulling the helpless and unfledged young cruelly limb from limb." *Benedict Arnold* (Boston, 1858), 13.

30. Trimmer, *Fabulous Histories,* 66–67. Dorothy Kilner, *Dialogues and Letters* (London, 1785), 51. *The Mosaic Creation* (London, 1759), 83–84. Richard Johnson, *Letters Between Master Tommy and Miss Nancy Goodwill* (London, 1770), 6–8. *Biography of A Spaniel* (London, 1816), 91–93. John Wesley believed that the great difference between men and brutes lay in man's capacity for religion. "What," Wesley asked rhetorically, "is the barrier between men and brutes,—the line which they cannot pass? It is not reason. . . . But it is this: man is capable of God; the inferior creatures are not." Robert Southey, *The Life Of Wesley,* 2nd ed. (London, 1820), II, 189.

31. Trimmer, *Fabulous Histories,* 68–69, 101–8, 222–24.

32. *Ibid.,* 145–48, 153–54, 159, 164, 179.

33. *Ibid.,* 149, 172, 219.

34. Dorothy Kilner, *Perambulation,* 25. Sarah Trimmer, ed., *Sunday School Dialogues* (London, 1784), 59. Mary Wollstonecraft, *Original Stories, From Real Life* (London, 1788), 6. Trimmer, *Fabulous Histories,* 220–21. The *Original Stories* were influenced by *Fabulous Histories.* Mrs. Mason even presented *Fabulous Histories* to her charges and later asked them if they had read it (11, 52).

35. Stephen Jones, *The Life and Adventures of A Fly* (London, 1789), 29, 64–66, 90–92. Laurence Sterne, *The Life and Opinions Of Tristram Shandy* (London, 1760), II, 79. Anna Barbauld (born Aikin) and John Aikin, *Evenings At Home* (London, 1794), IV, 151.

36. William Hayley, *Ballads* (Chichester, 1805), 2–12. See also L.P., *The Life of a Bee* (London, 1790), and *The Hare* (London, 1799).

37. J.J. Rousseau, *Emilius and Sophia* (London, 1762), I, 1–2. Trimmer, *Fabulous Histories,* vii–viii.

38. Thomas Day, "The History of Little Jack" in *The Children's Miscellany* (London, 1788), 2–8, 11–12, 57–58. Although Day's choice of a mother for Jack was unique, other writers also envisioned a Rousseauistic world. On its translation in 1788, Joachim Campe's *The New Robinson Crusoe* (London) immediately became popular. Although he was often forced to eat animals to keep from starving, this new Robinson consciously tried not to despoil nature. His closest friends were a llama and her young. Whenever he returned from a trip across the island, they would rush out to greet him, and Robinson, Campe wrote, "would mix his joy with theirs as a father rejoices over his children when he clasps them in his arms once more after an absence of some time" (II, 40).

39. Trimmer, *An Easy Introduction,* 193. *Memoirs of Dick, The Little Poney* (London, 1800), 17–18, 31.

40. Mary Pilkington, *Pity's Gift* (London, 1798), v–vi, 69, 72–74, 111–18.

41. *Guardian of Education* 1 (1802), 304–6. Locke in Yolton, I, 336.

42. Thomas Young, *An Essay on Humanity To Animals* (London, 1798), 4–8.

43. E.A. Kendall, *Keeper's Travels In Search of His Master* (London, 1798), iv–vi.

44. *Guardian of Education* 1 (1802), 393–400. Trimmer, *An Easy Introduction,* 193.

Chapter 2

1. The best account of the appearance of fairy tales in Britain is found in Iona and Peter Opie, *The Classic Fairy Tale* (London, 1974). Mother Goose was associated with Perrault's tales. The frontispiece of Robert Samber's translation of Perrault showed three children and a cat sitting in front of a fire listening to an old woman. On the wall above them hung a card which read "Mother Goose's Tales."

2. *Monthly Review* 78 (1788), 531. Dorothy Kilner, *The Histories of More Children than One* (London, 1783), vi–viii. Edgeworth, *Practical Education,* 335. Lucy Aikin, ed., *Poetry For Children*, 2nd ed. (London, 1803), iii–iv. Criticism of fairy tales was not limited to England. In France, Madame deGenlis, whose books influenced Mrs. Trimmer and Maria Edgeworth, condemned them in her popular *Adelaide and Theodore.* Baroness d'Almane did not let her children read fairy tales or stories from *The Thousand and One Nights.* "There is scarcely one of them which has a moral tendency," she declared; "love is the subject in them all. . . . all these ridiculous ideas give them only false notions, stop the course of their reasoning, and inspire them with a dislike for instructive reading"—from the first English edition of *Adelaide and Theodore* (London, 1783), I, 57–58.

3. Hugh Rhodes, *The Book of Nurture for menservants and Children* (London, 1558), 2. Scot, *The discoverie of witchcraft* (London, 1584), 152–53. Ady, *A Candle in the Dark* (London, 1656), "The Reason of the Book," 167ff.

4. Locke in Axtell, 114, 242–44, 303. Locke in Yolton, I, 77–80, 338.

5. Watts, *A Treatise,* 19, 100. In the seventeenth century, George Wither published "A Rocking Hymn" as a sample of the kind of song nurses should sing to children. "*Nurses,*" he explained, "*usually sing their Children asleep; and through want of pertinent matter, they oft make use of unprofitable (if not worse) Songs. This was therefore prepared, that it might help acquaint them, and their* Nurse-Children, *with the loving Care and Kindness of their Heavenly Father.*" Wither, *Heleluiah* (London, 1641), 82. In *Tommy Thumb's Song Book,* first published by Mary Cooper in 1744, "A Letter for a Lady on Nursing" prefaced Nurse Love-

child's collection of rhymes. The lady thought Nurse Lovechild's "Design of compiling a Collection of Songs" fit for children was laudable. She urged her, however, not to sing too loud and frighten children. She also warned her against old wives' and fairy tales, "this in particular, I insist on, above all others, that you never mention a Bull Beggar, Tom Poker, Raw Head and Bloody Bones &c, lest you make such frightful Impressions on their tender Minds, as may never be eradicated." *Tommy Thumb's Song Book* (Worcester, Mass., 1788), 4–6.

6. *Guardian of Education* 2 (1803), 185–86.

7. Locke in Axtell, 255–61.

8. See Roscoe for the books published by Newbery's successors. In the United States, Isaiah Thomas reprinted many of Newbery's books. The most prominent publisher in the United States after the Revolution, Thomas published some forty-five children's books during a three-year period in the 1780s. Most of these had originally appeared in England. In 1786, at least five of Thomas's "Worcester" editions were reprints of Newbery's books. In 1787, he published four more, including the first American edition of *A Little Pretty Pocket-Book.* See Charles Lemuel Nichols, *Isaiah Thomas* (Boston, 1912).

9. *A Little Pretty Pocket-Book* (London, 1767), 13–20. Although they appeared in Sarah Fielding's *The Governess,* Mrs. Teachum assured her "little Friends" that giants, fairies, and magic were introduced only to amuse and divert. Children should take care, she warned, not to be "carried away, by these high-flown things." *The Governess*, 2nd ed. (London, 1749), 41–43.

10. *The History of Jack and the Giants* (London, 1760), pt. II, 9. Unlike Scot's bugs, Jack was not a demon, for he killed giants. But from the point of view of the late eighteenth century, he was dangerously amoral, and his triumphs seemed, like many fairy tales, to teach dishonesty rewarded. Abraham Aesop, *Fables in Verse, For the Improvement of the Young and the Old,* 5th ed. (London, 1765), 32, 35–36.

11. Opie, *The Classic Fairy Tale,* 33, 38, 40–44. *A Pretty Book of Pictures for Little Masters and Misses,* 9th ed. (London, 1767), iv–vii.

12. Bunyano, *The Prettiest Book for Children* (London, 1770), 8–15, 23, 25, 43, 52, 55, 60–61. J. Coote published the first edition of *The Prettiest Book.* In 1772, F. Newbery published an edition.

13. *The History of Little Goody Two-Shoes,* 56, 119, 121–22, 136–38. Also see *Nurse Truelove's New-Year's-Gift* (London, 1770), 16–17. Since they did not tell "Stories about Hobgoblins and such Nonsense" and were able to go to sleep without a candle, "Mrs. *To-and-again*" promised "our little ones" that she

would run home as fast as she could and send "*Robin* with the Cow, to make them a Syllabub."

14. Priscilla Wakefield, *Leisure Hours* (London, 1796), II, 9.

15. *The Entertaining History of Little Goody Goosecap* (London, 1780). *The Renowned History of Primrose Prettyface* (London, 1785). Although Mrs. Trimmer criticized *Goody Two-Shoes,* she did not condemn its fairy-tale elements. Instead of Goody and her brother's suffering at the hands of Gripe and Graspall, she thought it would be better if they were depicted as helpless orphans. At a time when pains were taken "to prejudice the poor against the higher orders, and to set them against parish officers," she wrote, "we could wish to have a veil thrown over the faults of oppressive 'squires and hard-hearted overseers." Mrs. Trimmer also believed that the references to witchcraft and the story of Lady Ducklington's ghost were objectionable. "*A pair of scissors,*" she suggested, could rectify the faults. According to Charlotte Yonge, Mrs. Trimmer was the "parent" of "the didactic age of youthful literature." Although Mrs. Trimmer was influential, Charlotte Yonge's statement was an exaggeration. Be that as it may, however, Lady Ducklington's ghost was often "exorcised" in the nineteenth century. *Guardian of Education* 1 (1802), 430–31. *Macmillan's Magazine* 20 (1869), 230–31.

16. *The Alphabet Of Goody two Shoes* (London, 1808). *Dame Parlet's Farm* (London, 1806), 5–6.

17. *Fables in Verse,* iii–vi. Locke in Axtell, 260–61.

18. Mary Ann Kilner, *The Adventures of a Pincushion* (London, 1784), viii. *Monthly Review* 70 (1784), 126. Fordyce, 363–64. Ellenor Fenn (Mrs. Teachwell), *Fables in Monosyllables* (London, 1783), ix–xi.

19. *Fabulous Histories,* x–xi. Edward Augustus Kendall, *The Canary Bird* (London, 1799), 35–36. Dorothy Kilner, *A Father's Advice to His Son* (London, 1784), 1–4.

20. *Mother Bunch's Closet Newly Broke Open* (Newcastle, 1760), 9–11, 16–17, 21–22. Francis Newbery published an edition of Mother Bunch's fairy tales in 1773.

21. *Dreams and Moles with their Interpretation and Signification* (London, 1760), 23.

22. Ellenor Fenn, *Cobwebs to Catch Flies* (London, 1783), I, ix. Locke in Axtell, 211. Watts, *A Treatise,* 37–38.

23. John and Anna Aikin, *Miscellaneous Pieces, In Prose* (London, 1773), 39–40, 42–43. Richardson, *Pamela,* IV, 440–41. The division between fairy and old wives' tales and romance was fuzzy. Medieval romances were the source of

popular chapbooks like *Guy, Earl of Warwick* and *The Four Sons of Aymon,* while fairy tales were filled with miraculous devices similar to those found in romances.

24. Maria Edgeworth, *Practical Education,* 332–33. Jane West, *The Advantages of Education,* 2nd ed. (London, 1803), I, 3. Hannah More, *The Two Wealthy Farmers,* Cheap Repository Tracts (London, 1795), pt. I, 18–20. Sarah Trimmer, *The Servant's Friend,* 2nd ed. (London, 1787), iii, 51.

25. Dorothy Kilner, *Dialogues and Letters,* xi.

26. Priscilla Wakefield, *Juvenile Anecdotes, Founded On Facts* (London, 1795), I, preface.

27. Rousseau, *Emilius and Sophia,* I, 184–85; II, 58, 84.

28. *Monthly Review* 28 (1763), 81. Both leading journals commented on Rousseau's criticism of fables. According to the *Critical Review,* his examination of the fable was "rather puerile and captious"—14 (1763), 268. The *Monthly Review* suggested that fabulists could escape "censure" if they adapted their fables to the capacities of children—27 (1762), 352–53. George Chapman, master of the grammar school at Dumfries, agreed with Rousseau's criticism of fables. "Unless very judiciously explained," fables, he wrote, were "improper" for children under ten. "Seduced by the fiction," such children, Chapman argued, saw "not the truth which the fables convey, or the moral which they contain." *A Treatise On Education* (3rd ed.), 159.

29. Maria Edgeworth, *Early Lessons,* 7th ed. (London, 1820), I, 103–4. While writing the *Lessons,* Maria Edgeworth was under the influence of her father and tried to make the *Lessons* embody the theories of *Practical Education.* Although she neglects Rousseau, Marilyn Butler is particularly good in sorting out Richard Lovell Edgeworth's influence upon his daughter. See *Maria Edgeworth, A Literary Biography* (Oxford, 1972).

30. Maria Edgeworth, *The Parent's Assistant,* 2nd ed. (London, 1796), part I, xi–xii. James Boswell, *Boswell's Life of Johnson* ed. George Birbeck Hill, rev. L.F. Powell (Oxford, 1971), II, 407–8; IV, 8.

31. E.V. Lucas, ed., *The Letters of Charles Lamb* (London, 1935), I, 326.

32. *Newbery's Catalogue Of Instructive And Amusing Publications For Young Minds* (London, 1800). For a clear account of Newbery's successors, see Roscoe. After Newbery's death in 1767, the period from 1768 to 1780 was "marked by schism and quarrelling between the rival establishments of Francis Newbery the son and Carnan (the step-son) on the one hand and Francis Newbery the nephew on the other." Francis the son stopped publishing during the year 1779–80, and Francis the nephew died in 1780. Carnan died in 1788. On the death of Francis the nephew in 1780, Elizabeth Newbery, his wife, took over

the firm. She published as E. Newbery until 1802, when she sold out to J. Harris. Roscoe, 2.

33. *Tom Thumb's Exhibition* (London, 1815), 5, 12–16.

34. *Tom Thumb's Folio* (London, 1768), 4–5, 14–17.

35. *The Lilliput ion Auction* (Philadelphia, 1802), 5, 9–10, 14, 18. Jacob Johnson's Philadelphia edition was taken from an earlier edition published by T. Carnan, probably the edition of 1783.

36. *Macmillan's Magazine* 20, (1869), 231. *Robin Goodfellow* (London, 1770), 7–8, 13, 17, 19.

37. *Monthly Review* 3 (1790), 223. Ellenor Fenn, *The Fairy Spectator* (London, 1789), 13–17, 27, 31, 51–52.

38. *The Fairy Spectator,* 59–61. Mobility and wealth did not bring happiness to Fortunatus. In Solomon Winlove's *Collection,* Fortunatus threw his purse and hat into the fire so that he could lead a quiet, contented life (39). Brought up morally, Miss Child did not have to experience sin before she rejected it.

39. Lilliputius Gulliver, *Instructive Lessons* (London, 1803), 32–36.

40. *Ibid.,* 39–42.

41. *The Ruby Heart* (London, 1802), v–vi.

Chapter 3

1. Priscilla Wakefield, *Mental Improvement* (London, 1794), II, 66. Wakefield was an educational theorist and writer of children's books.

2. Locke in Axtell, 157, 255–60, 273, 274.

3. *Guardian of Education* 1 (1802), 63. *Payne's Universal Chronical* 20 (1758), 153. Locke in Axtell, 273–74. *The Twelfth-Day Gift,* title page, 2–5, 24, 41–42, 127. *The Fairing* (London, 1767), vi–vii. See Appendix C for a discussion of Newbery's advertising methods.

4. *A Little Pretty Pocket-Book,* title page, frontispiece, 5–6, 20.

5. *Ibid.,* title page, 50, 53.

6. *Ibid.,* 71–72.

7. *Ibid.,* 73–76, 85–90.

8. Locke in Axtell, 256. The quotation from *Some Thoughts* used by Newbery in the advertisement is found on the same page. *The Penny London Morning Advertiser* 141 (March 21–23, 1744). Beginning with the June 18–20, 1744 (179) issue of *The Penny London Morning Advertiser,* the "Fifty Six Squares" and *A Little Pretty Pocket-Book* were frequently advertised together. The quotation from Locke appeared at the foot of these advertisements in italics. Newbery used the idea of the squares again and in 1759 published "A Set of *Geographical*

CARDS, containing MAPS of all the *Empires, Kingdoms,* and *States* in the World; and yet so contrived as to be played with as other Cards are." Unlike the squares, the cards were definitely for "young Gentlemen and Ladies," for a set cost six shillings. *The Universal Chronical* 40 (30 Dec. 1758–6 Jan. 1759), 8.

9. Richard Johnson, *Juvenile Sports and Pastimes,* 2nd ed. (London, 1776), 3–9.

10. Locke in Axtell, 256–57, 318. *A Little Lottery-Book* (London, 1768), 4–6.

11. Dorothy Kilner, *Anecdotes Of A Boarding School* (London, 1784), I, 102–3; II, 4.

12. Doctor Hurlothrumbo, *The Fortune-Teller* (Boston, 1798), 5, 23, 33, 50, 56. According to Sydney Roscoe in his *John Newbery And His Successors,* the first British edition of the *Fortune-Teller* was published in 1769. It seems to have remained in print throughout the latter part of the century. Elizabeth Newbery advertised it in a catalogue she published in 1800.

13. P. Des Maizeaux, *A Collection Of Several Pieces Of Mr. John Locke* (London, 1720). Locke in Axtel, 290. Locke, *Elements Of Natural Philosophy* (London, 1750). For an account of Locke and Newton, see James L. Axtell's "Locke, Newton and the Two Cultures" in John W. Yolton, ed., *John Locke: Problems and Perspectives* (Cambridge, 1969), 165–82.

14. Locke, *Elements of Natural Philosophy,* 1. *The Newtonian System,* 5, 26–27.

15. Locke, *Elements of Natural Philosophy,* 2. *The Newtonian System,* 6–7.

16. *The Newtonian System,* 98–102. The *Monthly Review* said *The Newtonian System* was "a very pretty book for Children," adding "Pretty *old Children* too, may read it with improvement"—24 (1761), 277. Although Locke's educational ideas and views on human development supplied much of the content and theory of his children's books, Newbery was able to treat Locke playfully. In *Six-Pennyworth of Wit* (London, 1767), a children's jest book containing puns, humorous anecdotes, epigrams, and the conundrums of Lancelot Loggerhead, Esq., someone, probably Tom Trapwit, recalled the "best Pun" of his "Friend *Tom Trott.*" "On seeing a Gentleman in *Garraway's* Coffee-House well dress'd, with his Hair tied behind, dictating to the Company," Trott "sat himself down on the same Bench, and taking hold on his tied-up Hair, Sir, says he, Is this *Lock upon Understanding?*" (xiii).

17. Francis Coventry, *The History of Pompey the Little,* 3rd ed. (London, 1752), iii–iv, 10–11, 50, 285–90. After having been washed and trimmed, *Pompey* reappeared in 1802 as a children's book, *Little Juba: or, The adventures and vicissitudes of a lap dog.*

18. Locke in Yolton, I, 335–36. Coventry, 54. Coventry was familiar with Locke's ideas. In the debate on the soul's immortality between Lady Sophister on one side and Doctor Rhubarb and Doctor Killdarby on the other, "Mr. *Locke*," Coventry wrote, "had the misfortune to be" Lady Sophister's "favourite" philosopher (57). Chambers's *Cyclopaedia*, I, 161.

19. Charles Johnson, *Chrysal* (London, 1760), I, 3; II, 273–74.

20. Thomas Bridges, *The Adventures of a Bank-Note* (London, 1770), II, 123. *The Adventures of a Hackney Coach* 7th ed., (Dublin, 1781), 5–7. *Monthly Review* 65 (1781), 389–90.

21. *Critical Review* 52 (1781), 477–80; 57 (1784), 234.

22. William Roberts, *The Looker-On*, "April 14, 1792," pp. 85–87.

23. Hannah More, *The Two Wealthy Farmers*, Cheap Repository Tracts, I, 20. *Critical Review* 60 (1785), 79. *Monthly Review* 72 (1785), 469.

24. Dorothy Kilner, *A Father's Advice to his Son*, 1–4.

25. *Guardian of Education* 1 (1802), 435–36. Mary Wollstonecraft, *Thoughts On The Education of Daughters*, 16–17.

26. Dorothy Kilner, *The Life and Perambulation of a Mouse*, I, 4–6. Yonge, "Children's Literature Of The Last Century," *Macmillan's Magazine* 20 (1869), 231.

27. Locke in Axtell, 221–23. *Perambulation*, I, 8.

28. Locke in Axtell, 225–27. *Perambulation*, I, 20, 24–25.

29. *Perambulation*, I, 29–31, 42, 48.

30. *Ibid.*, II, 39–40.

31. *The Dog of Knowledge* (London, 1803). *Memoirs of Dick* (London, 1800). Edward Augustus Kendall, *The Sparrow* (London, 1798); *The Canary Bird* (London, 1799). Elizabeth Helme, *Adventures of a Bullfinch* (London, 1809). *Biography of a Spaniel* (London, 1816). One of the better biographies of animals was Mary Pilkington's *Marvellous Adventures: or, The Vicissitudes of a Cat* (London, 1802).

32. *Guardian of Education* 2 (1803), 184–85; 4 (1805), 417. In Pilkington's *Marvellous Adventures*, Charles Langford put Grimalkin on an iron plate over a chafing dish of charcoal. While she danced on "this cruel contrivance" trying to keep her paws cool, Charles "always beat a drum" (13).

33. Mary Ann Kilner, *The Adventures of a Pincushion* (London, 1783?), vii–viii.

34. *Ibid.*, 15, 56–61.

35. *Ibid.*, 105–6.

36. Mary Ann Kilner, *Memoirs of a Peg-Top* (London, 1783), iv, 8, 23, 26. Newbery's books were written for boys and girls alike. And, so far as I can tell,

not until Marshall's publications in the 1780s was any significant differentiation made between books for little girls and for little boys.

37. In mentioning the plum cakes, the author evoked memories of Newbery. Although the *Whipping-Top* was published anonymously, it may have been written by Dorothy Kilner (M.P.). She and her sister-in-law were Marshall's leading authors of children's books. Moreover, the introduction to the book contained what may have been an anagrammatic clue. Having misread the title as "The adventrous whipping Tom," a boy who did not "mind" his book was ridiculed for not knowing *adventures* from *adventrous* "nor an M from a P" (vii.).

38. [Dorothy Kilner], *Whipping-Top* 11–15, 72–73. Despite the charm of this advertisement, there seems to have been no sequel and the *Whipping-Top* remained a threepenny book.

39. *Ibid.,* 76–78.

40. Richard Johnson, *The Adventures Of A Silver Penny,* 8, 125–26. Miss Smythies, *The History of A Pin, As Related By Itself* (London, 1798), 2.

41. *Monthly Review* 70 (1784), 126; 80 (1789), 88. *Guardian of Education* 1 (1802), 124.

CHAPTER 4

1. Darton, 72. Richard Steele in *The Tatler* 95 (15–17 Nov. 1709). Sterne, *Tristram Shandy,* VI, 127. *The History of Guy, Earl of Warwick* (London, 1760), 3. The origins of the stories appearing most frequently in chapbooks have been well documented. See Darton; Victor Neuburg, *The Penny Histories* (London, 1968); and John Ashton, *Chap-books of the Eighteenth Century* (London, 1882). In writing this chapter I have used, for the most part, chapbooks found in the Dicey Collection of the British Library. These seem to have been published sometime after the mid-eighteenth century, and I have dated them 1760. The titles which I cite were probably in print by 1700, and most had been in print for a considerable time before that date. At the back of one of the Bodleian's copies of *The Renowned History of the Seven Champions of Christendom* (c 1700) is a list of "*Books Printed for and Sold by* B. Deacon, *at the* Angel *in* Gilt-spur street, *without* Newgate." Although the books were longer and more expensive than those bought by and for children in the eighteenth century, Deacon's list shows the popularity of chapbooks at the beginning of the eighteenth century. It reads:

"The Arraignment of Lewd, Idle, Froward, and unconstant Women; or, The Vanity of them: (Chuse you whether.) With a Commendation of the

Wise, Vertuous, and Honest Women. To which is added, A Second Part, Containing merry Dialogues, witty Poems, and jovial Songs. Price Bound 1s.

The most Famous History of Amadis of Greece, sirnamed the Knight of the Burning Sword. Price 1s 4d.

Arcandam, that famous and expert Astrologian, to find the Fatal Destiny, Constellation, Complection, and Natural Inclination of every Man and Child by his Birth. Price 6d.

The Art of Legerdemain, with new Additions. Price 6d.

Sports and Pastimes for City and Country. Price 6d.

The most pleasant History of Tom-a-Lincoln, that ever-renowned Soldier, the Red Rose Knight. Price 6d.

Markham's Faithful Farrier, wherein the depth of his Skill is laid open in all those principle and approved Secrets of Horsemanship, in 8 vo. Price 4d.

Scogin's Jests: Full of witty Mirth, and pleasant Shifts. Price 4d.

A speedy Post, with a Pacquet of Letters and Complements: Useful for England, Scotland, and Ireland. Price 4d.

The Golden Garland of Princely Delight. Wherein is contained the History of many of the Kings, Queens, Princes, Lords, Ladies, Knights, and Gentlewomen of this Kingdom. Price 4d.

The Honour of the Cloathworking Trade: Or, The Pleasant and famous History of Thomas of Reading. Price 3d.

The Merchant-Taylors Renown: Or, The Famous and delightful History of Sir John Hawkwood, Knight. Price 3d.

The most Famous History of the Learned Fryer Bacon. Price 3d.

The Famous, Pleasant, and Delightful History of Ornatus and Artesia. Price 3d.

The History of the Valiant London 'Prentice. Price 3d.

The Noble Birth and Gallant Atchievements of that Remarkable Outlaw, Robin Hood. Together with a True Account of the many Merry and Extravagant Exploits he play'd; in Twelve several Stories. Price 3d.

The History of the Life and Death of that most Noble Knight, Sir Bevis of Southampton. Price 3d.

The Second Part of Mother Bunch of the West.

The History of Tom Tipler, the Merry Tinker of Banbury.

The Birth, Life, and Death of John Frank.

These Three last are but a Penny a piece."

For a similar list (found in the same volume of chapbooks—Douce R. 528), see *The Shooe-makers Glory.* On p. 24 is "A Catalogue of several Pleasant and Delightful Books, which are to be Sold by the Booksellers of *Pye-corner* and

London-Bridge." For the reference to these chapbooks, I am indebted to Louis B. Wright, *Middle-Class Culture in Elizabethan England* (London, 1964).

2. William Wordsworth, *The Prelude,* Ernest de Selincourt, corrected by Stephen Gill (Oxford, 1970), 77.

3. *The History of the Life and Death of that most Noble Knight Sir Bevis of Southampton* (London, 1760), title page. *No Jest like a True Jest* (London, 1760), title page. The merry life did not end so merrily. On 24 Sept. 1652, Capt. James Hind was hanged, drawn, and quartered at Worcester (24).

4. *The History of Jack Horner* (London, 1760), 6–9.

5. *Wanton Tom* (London, 1760), pt. I, 20–21. *The Friar and the Boy* (London, 1760), pt. I, 6–9.

6. *Poets Jest* (London, 1760), 5.

7. *The History of Four Kings, Their Queens and Daughters*... (London, 1760), 2–5. Also see *The Merry Tales Or the Wise Men of Gotham.*

8. *The Foreign Travels of Sir John Mandeville* (London, 1760), 4–5, 10, 15. *Bateman's Tragedy* (London, 1760), 24.

9. Watts, *A Treatise,* 100. Locke in Axtell, 243. *The Witch of the Woodlands* (London, 1760), 11–13, 16–17.

10. *The History of Mother Shipton* (London, 1760), 7. *Nixon's Cheshire Prophecy, At Large* (London, 1760), 3, 15–16. *Partridge and Flamsted's New and Well Experienced Fortune Book* (London, 1760), title page, and 13. *Dreams and Moles With their Interpretation and Signification* (London, 1760), 18–19.

11. *The Lover's Magazine* (London, 1760), 5.

12. Thomas White, *A Little Book For Little Children* (London, 1702), 17–18. Arthur Dent's *The Plaine Mans Path-way to Heaven* (1601) was a very popular book. At least twenty-five editions of it were published by 1640. Henry Crosse, *Vertues Common-wealth* (London, 1603), n.p. Dent, 408–9. *The History of Genesis,* 3rd ed. (London, 1708), vi–vii.

13. Francis Kirkman, *The Unlucky Citizen* (London, 1673), 7, 10–13. William London, *A Catalogue Of The most vendible Books in England* (London, 1657), "The Epistle Dedicatory." Thomas Fuller, *The Holy State* (Cambridge, 1642), 155. Sir William Corne-waleys, *Essayes* (London, 1600), essay 15, "Of the observation, and uses of things." Locke in Axtell, 114–15. Watts, *A Treatise,* 19. Sarah Trimmer, *The Oeconomy of Charity* (London, 1787), 2.

14. West, *Letters to a Young Lady,* I, 139. *The Family Magazine* 1 (1788), title page, iii–vi.

15. Sarah Trimmer, *The Servant's Friend* (London, 1787), 49–52. Doddridge, *Sermons* II.

16. *Evangelical Magazine* 3 (1795), ii, 388. William Roberts, *The Looker-On*

31 (8 Dec. 1792), 246. Arthur Roberts, ed., *Mendip Annals,* 2nd ed. (London, 1859) 6–7.

17. Henry Thornton, *Cheap Repository For Moral & Religious Publications* (London, 1796), 1–2. Thornton was secretary of the society, and this is the statement of the society for its first year of operation.

18. Hannah More, *The Carpenter* (London, 1795), 6. *The Contented Cobbler* (London, 1798?), 3–8. *The Judgment Awaiting Undutiful Children* (London, 1798?), 4. Throughout the sixteenth and seventeenth centuries, songs had been singled out for criticism. "The divell in elder ages in the blinde Papacie, fed blinde soules with fables and idle Friers inventions," Henry Holland wrote, "now mens wits be refined, they can no more feede on such dry stubble. He feedes daintie ears with choise of words, and uncleane hearts with the unchaste and wanton love-songs of Italian Poetrie. Such foode breedes many uncleane beasts in citie and countrie." Henry Holland, ed., *The Workes Of The Reverend And Faithful Servant of Jesus Christ M. Richard Greenham*, 3rd ed. (London, 1601), "The Preface To The Reader."

19. *Hints to all Ranks of People On the Occasion of the present Scarcity* (London, 1795), 14. *Ananias and Sapphira* (London, 1795), 16. *The Widow of Zarephath* (London, 1797), 15.

20. *The Sleeping Beauty In The Wood* (London, 1760), 16. *Betty Brown, The St. Giles's Orange Girl* (London, 1796), 3–16.

21. *Madge Blarney, The Gipsey Girl* (London, 1797), 3–6, 8–9, 12–15.

22. *The Two Soldiers* (London, 1797), 3, 10–12, 17, 24.

23. *The History of Parismus, Prince of Bohemia* (London, 1760), title page. *The Two Shoemakers* (London, 1795), pt. I, 12–13. *The Apprentice Turned Master* (London, 1796), 14–15.

24. *Sorrowful Sam* (London, 1795), 13, 21.

25. In *The History Of The Seven Champions of Christendom* (London, 1760), St. George killed a dragon and saved Sabra, while St. James of Spain killed a fire-drake and a boar (pt. I, 5–7, 12–14). More, *The Shepherd of Salisbury-Plain* (London, 1795), pt. I, 9, 11. *The Lancashire Collier Girl* (London, 1795), 8–14, 18, 21.

26. More, *The Cottage Cook,* (London, 1798), 13.

27. *The Deceitfulness of Pleasure* (London, 1798), 4–5, 5–6, 13–15.

28. *Robert and Richard* (London, 1796), 6.

29. *The Two Wealthy Farmers* (London, 1795), pt. I, 14. *The Hubbub* (London, 1797), 3–4.

30. *The Parish Nurse* (London, 1796), 5–6, 9–10.

31. More, *The Sunday School* (London, 1798), 10–15. Jest books abounded

and as a rule were filled with bawdy stories. See *Cambridge Jests Or, Wit's Recreation.* Akin to jest books were riddle books, the contents of which often depended on double entendre. See *A Whetstone For Dull Wits.* A candle was the answer to the following riddle: "I am white and stiff it is well known, / Likewise my nose is red: / Young Ladies will as well as Joan, / Oft take me to their bed" (*Whetstone,* 2). Children's riddle books were more polite than chapbooks. Occasionally, however, some of the ruder chapbook material appeared in riddle books published specifically for children. In *The Child's New Year's Gift,* one of the woodcuts depicted a small boy with his pants down, breaking wind and thereby putting out a candle. The riddle read, "Since the world first began, / I was never once seen. / Tho' every one knows, in their / presence I've been. / No sooner I'm born than I / give a loud cry, / And your noses inform you I / presently die"—7. J. Evans & Son published *The Child's New Year's Gift.* The last two numbers of the date of publication are obscured, but the date may be 181?.

32. *The Two Shoemakers,* pt. VI, 4–5.

33. More, *Tawny Rachel* (London, 1797?), 3–10, 14.

34. Religious Tract Society, *An Address to Christians, On the Distribution Of Religious Tracts* (London, 1799), 11.

35. George Crabbe, *The Poetical Works of George Crabbe,* ed. A.J. and R.M. Carlyle (London: Henry Frowde, 1908), 51–52. Wordsworth, *Prelude,* 73, 77, 80.

CHAPTER 5

1. Darton, 53. Woodward, 35. Abraham Chear, *A Looking-Glass For Children* (London, 1708), 30–31, 62, 66. John Bunyan, *A Book for Boys and Girls* (London, 1686), 62. Richard Baxter, *Compassionate Counsel To All Young-Men* (London, 1681), 5. In his *Children's Books In England & America In The Seventeenth Century* (New York, 1955), William Sloane wrote, "Seventeenth-century children's books fall into three large groups: the traditional or folk material, the books of good advice, and the religious books" (8). Sloane catalogued some 260 seventeenth-century children's books. Almost all are godly books or, if not godly books, conduct books filled with godly advice. The style of many of the books is hortatory, few make concessions to children's limited understandings, and almost none appeal to their delight in play and recreation.

2. Dent, 46. Locke in Axtell, 124–31. *A Little Pretty Pocket-Book,* 5. *The Pretty Play-Thing For Children of All Denominations,* new ed. (London, n.d.), 60. Trimmer, *Easy Lessons For Young Children,* 11th ed. (Paris, 1856), 30–33. *Payne's*

Universal Chronicle 39 (23–30 Dec. 1758), 312; 41 (6–13 Jan. 1759), 16. For Newbery's extravagant medicinal claims for Greenough's Tinctures, see *The Penny London Morning Advertiser* 144 (28–30 March 1744).

3. James Janeway, *A Token For Children* (London, 1671), "prefatory address," "preface," pt. I, 2–3, 11–12, 14–18, 28, 40–49; pt. II, 15, 18. James Burgh, *Youth's Friendly Monitor* (London, 1754), 7.

4. Watts, *Catechisms,* 27–28. Samuel Johnson, *The Lives Of The English Poets* (Dublin, 1781), III, 21. Despite the evangelical revival, godly books were not very popular as children's books at the end of the century. Many other books, of course, competed for children's attentions. Their contents, particularly the lugubrious biographies of young children, survived in the form of tracts used in Sunday schools or given away throughout Britain. Religious journals like the *Arminian,* later *Methodist, Magazine* and the *Evangelical Magazine* also printed biographies. In the preface to the first volume, the editors of the *Evangelical Magazine* explained that "the subjects . . . are calculated to please as well as to instruct, that the children of religious parents . . . may be allured, through pleasure, into the paths of true wisdom. Biography, Memoirs, Diaries, Authentic Anecdotes, Striking Providences, and the Expressions of Dying Christians, arrest the mind of the reader, and make a deep impression" — 1 (1793), 4. The biographies in the *Methodist* and *Evangelical* magazines provide fascinating period-piece reading. The holy innocents who triumphed over the arrows of outrageous fortune and inglorious temptation were the spiritual and literary ancestors of Dickens's youthful heroes and heroines, Oliver Twist, Little Nell, Florence Dombey, among others.

5. Isaac Watts, *Divine Songs* (London, 1715), "Preface." Locke in Axtell, 259. For other early books of religious poetry for children, see Nathaniel Crouch, *Youths Divine Pastime* (London, 1691). Crouch's poetry is poor. Moreover, his choice of subjects limited his audience; the book contained poems on Jezebel's being eaten by the dogs, David and Bathsheba, and "Joseph *and his Mistress.*" The woodcut for this last poem showed a full-breasted Potiphar's wife sitting half-nude in bed. Although it was written for older children, Benjamin Keach's *War with The Devil* (London, 1683) contained some good poetry. At the end, Keach included a section entitled "*Hymns and Spiritual Songs*" (116) that anticipated Watts's "Specimen of Moral Songs."

6. *Divine Songs,* "Preface," 12, 15, 16, 20, 23. Locke in Axtell, 146.

7. J.H.P. Pafford, *Isaac Watts* (London, 1971), 2, 70–71. Pafford's facsimile edition published in The Juvenile Library by the Oxford University Press is extraordinarily useful. *A Poem Sacred to the Memory of The Reverend and Learned Isaac Watts* (London, 1749), 6. David Jennings, *A Sermon Occasioned by the*

Death of the Late Reverend Isaac Watts (London, 1749), 28. Samuel Johnson, *Lives,* III, 23. Sarah Trimmer, *A Comment on Dr. Watts's Divine Songs for Children* (London, 1789), iii. In her "An Address to Parents" at the beginning of *The Parent's Assistant,* Maria Edgeworth quoted Johnson's tribute to Watts (iv).

8. Charlotte Barrett, ed., *Diary & Letters of Madame D'Arblay* [Fanny Burney] (London, 1905), V, 419. *Guardian of Education* 1 (1802), 63–64; 2 (1803), 43. Trimmer, *An Easy Introduction,* xi–xii. Edgeworth and Edgeworth, *Practical Education,* 317. Yonge, in *Macmillan's Magazine* 20 (1869), 234.

9. Anna Barbauld, *Lessons for Children, from Two to Three Years Old* (London, 1787), "advertisement"; *Lessons for Children of Three Years Old* (Dublin, 1789), pt. I, 16–18. Locke in Yolton, I, 77–78.

10. *Divine Songs,* 45–46.

11. Anna Barbauld, *Hymns in Prose for Children* (London, 1781), iii–vii.

12. *Ibid.,* 5–12.

13. Murch, 75. *Christian Reformer* 9 (1825), 141. Wollstonecraft, *Thoughts,* 16–17. William Hazlitt, *The Complete Works*, ed. P.P. Howe (London, 1930), V, 147. Samuel Taylor Coleridge, *Collected Letters*, ed. Earl Leslie Griggs (Oxford, 1956, 1971), I, 393; VI, 1013. Henry Crabb Robinson, *Diary, Reminiscences, and Correspondence,* ed. Thomas Sadler (London, 1869), I, 225.

14. Lamb, *Letters*, I, 326.

15. Although Mrs. Trimmer was a touchstone of educational thought in the late eighteenth century and accordingly is referred to often in this book, a detailed description of her career is beyond the scope of my study. A woman of great energy and high moral purpose, she labored hard on behalf of educational causes. From 1780 to 1785 she produced her six-volume *Sacred History,* an annotated Bible for children and families. During the 1780s, she was the Sunday school movement's most effective publicist, and in 1786 she wrote *The Oeconomy of Charity,* the most useful book published on the subject in the eighteenth century. Since few books were suitable for Sunday scholars, Mrs. Trimmer wrote a series during the late 1780s and early 1790s. During the 1790s she also wrote a series of books for charity schools and seems to have greatly influenced their curriculum. During 1788–1789, she wrote and edited *The Family Magazine,* whose "instructive tales" probably set the pattern for the *Cheap Repository's* "histories." From 1802 to 1806, she edited the *Guardian of Education,* most of which she wrote herself. In 1805, she attacked Joseph Lancaster's nonsectarian charity school and thus indirectly contributed to the founding of the National Society. Since the seventeenth century, few Britons have had as much influence upon the practical education of their own day as Mrs. Trimmer had

upon hers. Universities and public schools were beyond her scope, but she ranged broadly from infancy to adolescence and, in the case of the lower classes, from the cradle to the grave. When she died in 1810, several correspondents to the *Gentlemen's Magazine* suggested in their eulogies that a monument be erected to her memory in St. Paul's Cathedral–81 (1811), pt. I, 112–13, 203, 261. According to Rev. Thomas Haverfield, such an "exalted character" was "rarely to be met"—*A Sermon* (London, 1811), ix, 17. Despite the eulogies and her many genuine accomplishments, Mrs. Trimmer has rarely been praised in the twentieth century. Percy Muir thought her "a preposterous woman" who wrote "about children rather than for them"—*English Children's Books,* 87.

16. Locke in Axtell, 114, 285–87. Samuel Butler, *The Way of All Flesh* (London, 1903), 103. Wakefield, *Juvenile Anecdotes* I, 115. Wollstonecraft, *Thoughts,* 16–17. *Guardian of Education* 1 (1802), 124; 2 (1803), 46.

17. Locke in Yolton, I, 336. Ray, *The Wisdom Of God,* 1–2. Boyle, *The Christian Virtuoso* (London, 1690), 9. Also see Wollaston's *The Religion Of Nature Delineated,* 57, 60, and William Derham's *Physico-Theology* (London, 1714). By 1768, Derham's book had reached a thirteenth edition. In *A Treatise,* 87, Watts praised both Derham and Ray.

18. Paley, *Natural Theology* (London, 1802), 576. Wesley, *A Survey Of The Wisdom of God in the Creation,* 2nd ed. (Bristol, 1770), I, 229–30; II, 204–8. In "Nature Moralized: The Divine Analogy in the Eighteenth Century," *ELH* 20 (1953), 39–76, Earl Wasserman focused on the eighteenth-century urge to draw analogies and establish a network of correspondences between the natural world of God and the moral world of man. Although Wesley discussed "Divine Analogy" (II, 211ff.), he did little practical analogizing in *A Survey.* Instead, like John Ray whom he often quoted without acknowledgment, he concentrated on the miraculous variety of the universe and its inference of the existence of God. For more on analogizing, see A.J. Kuhn, "Nature Spiritualized: Aspects Of Anti-Newtonianism," *ELH* 41 (1974), 400–12.

19. Locke in Yolton, I, 116; II, 89.

20. Locke in Axtell, 241–42. Robert Boyle, *The Excellency Of Theology* (London, 1671/72), 118, 121–22. In *The Wisdom Of God,* John Ray urged people to "converse with Nature as well as Books." No knowledge, he wrote, could "satisfie and feed the Soul" better than "Natural History and the Works of the Creation." In comparison, the study "of Words and Phrases" was "insipid and jejune." Since words were "but the Images of Matter, to be wholly given up to the Study" of them was "*Pygmalions* Phrenzy," he wrote, falling "in Love with a Picture or Image"—123–24.

21. Locke in Axtell, 261, 301–5.

22. *Ibid.*, 114, 241, 305.

23. Although Ellenor Fenn stressed the importance of physico-theology and even included an extensive quotation from the introduction to *Hymns in Prose* in her preface (x–xv), *The Rational Dame* taught little about God. Illustrated by many good plates, the book was more factual than religious. The characteristics, habits, and uses of many animals were described. Children learned, for example, that ox blood made "a fine blue colour." From the ox's fat came candles; from its hide, shoes and boots; from its horn, combs, boxes, drinking cups, and handles for knives. Its hair was mixed with mortar, and its hooves were used in making glue. From its bones came spoons, knives, and buttons while the guts were "used in beating gold into thin leaf"(31). Despite its paucity of religious matter, Mrs. Trimmer praised the book in the *Guardian of Education,* saying, "A more useful companion of this kind the young mother will not easily find"—1 (1802), 200. *The Rational Dame* was popular, and its factual contents may explain its appeal to Mrs. Trimmer and others. Mrs. Trimmer's own *Easy Introduction* contained much factual matter, some of it fairly harshly put from our point of view. "Look at the pretty harmless Sheep, with their innocent Lambkins by their Sides," Henry's and Charlotte's mother exclaimed while the three took a walk. After discussing the uses of the sheep's wool, Henry's mother observed: "the poor Sheep would not be so merry if they knew that they will be sold to the Butchers too, but that must be the Case. —Their Flesh will be Mutton, and their Skins Parchment, such as Mr. Green, the Lawyer, brought to your Papa the other Day, and like what your Drum is covered with, Henry" (46–48).

Ellenor Fenn was an approved author, and in her review Mrs. Trimmer quoted the preface in which Ellenor Fenn said she hoped her book would assist mothers in leading children from nature to God. In the case of Lady Fenn, the stated intention was as good as the deed. Moreover, Marshall published *The Rational Dame.* In part, the book reflected the instructive bent of many volumes he published in the 1780s and the contemporary distrust of fiction for children or "prejudicial Nonsense"—a distrust Mrs. Trimmer shared. In the preface, Ellenor Fenn criticized fiction for children. "Children listen with avidity to tales," she wrote, "let us give them none but rational information . . . there is no need of invention; the world is full of wonders—banishing all fabulous narratives, let us introduce our little people to the wonders of the insect world." For Locke on lying to children, see Axtell, 230.

24. Trimmer, *An Easy Introduction,* vii. *The Mosaic Creation,* title page, iii. Priscilla Wakefield, *Mental Improvement* (London, 1794), I, i.

25. Locke in Yolton, II, 89. John Newton, *Letters and Sermons,* ed. T.

Haweis (London, 1787), 209–10. William Jones, *The Theological, Philosophical and Miscellaneous Works* (London, 1801), VII, 47–48. Ideally, revealed religion kept the imagination within proper bounds. However, the "magical effect" which discovered analogies between the natural world and revelation was liable to abuse. In Fordyce's *Dialogues,* Constant warned that there was "a strong Propensity in the Mind to find Similitudes and Analogies in Objects" where there were none. This inclination, he stated, was "very apt to lead the Judgment astray, especially when the Fancy is warm and luxuriant, as it generally is in young People"—212.

26. Mary Wollstonecraft, *A Vindication* (London, 1792); *Mary, A Fiction* (London, 1788), 12–13. Thomas Paine, *The Age Of Reason* (Paris, 1794), 2, 22, 27. Jane West, *Letters Addressed To A Young Man* (London, 1801), III, 344–46.

27. *Guardian of Education* I (1802), 415–16, 442. West, *Letters Addressed To A Young Man*, III, 386–88. Mrs. Trimmer was familiar not only with the abuses of natural theology but also with abuses of her own educational ideas on the subject. In 1786, E. Newbery published *Juvenile Rambles Through The Paths Of Nature;* put together by Richard Johnson, the book borrowed much of its matter from *An Easy Introduction.* Johnson's rambles and language frequently resembled Mrs. Trimmer's. Unlike Mrs. Trimmer, Johnson was not an educational theorist, and many of the incidents in *Juvenile Rambles* seem to have been included to help swell the book to six-penny size. As a result, it contained incidents that exposed natural theology to ridicule.

In 1802 Mrs. Trimmer reviewed the *Juvenile Rambles* and noted that authors "do not always follow the Golden Rule of *doing to others as they would wish others to do to them.*" "The *Rambles,*" she said, were "*borrowed*" from "a well known 'Introduction to the Knowledge of Nature' "—*Guardian of Education* I (1802), 508–9. Popularity and fame brought disadvantages. While Johnson borrowed the contents of one of Mrs. Trimmer's books, Tegg and Castleman borrowed her name in 1803 and published *A History of Quadrupeds, Adapted to the Capacities of Youth* by "Mrs. Mary Trimmer of Kentish Town." The liberty angered Mrs. Trimmer, and she stated in the *Guardian,* "This work which is very meanly executed in every respect, may be regarded as a COUNTERFEIT throughout—the very NAME of its pretended author is, in part, a PLAGIARISM"—3 (1804), 284. Tegg and Castleman did not limit their plagiarism to Mrs. Trimmer; on the title page of the book appeared the statement, "*Embellished with Twenty-nine Engravings on Wood after* BEWICK."

28. Richard Brantley, *Wordsworth's "Natural Methodism"* (New Haven, 1975), 12, 139–70. Brantley's fine book should be read by all interested in Wordsworth and romantic poetry.

29. Robinson, I, 226. Wordsworth's opinion of Mrs. Barbauld's verse was not always favorable. He did, however, read it. See Edith Morley, ed., *The Correspondence of Henry Crabb Robinson with the Wordsworth Circle* (Oxford, 1927), I, 53–54.

30. Walter Pater, *Appreciations. With an Essay on Style* (London, 1889), 45–48. Newton, 209–10. William Wordsworth, *Poetical Works,* ed. Thomas Hutchinson, revised by Ernest de Selincourt (Oxford, 1969), 735. Locke in Axtell, 325. Wordsworth, *Prelude,* 17, 18, 28.

31. Wordsworth, *Prelude,* 17.

32. Watts, *Philosophical Essays,* 74–113. Watts's modifications of Locke should not be overemphasized; he did not tear down Locke's theories but instead made small additions to accommodate his religious beliefs.

33. Wordsworth, *Prelude,* 1, 12–13, 124; *Poetical Works,* 460–61, 206, 735. Watts, *Philosophical Essays,* 101–2, 105–6, 112–13. Ralph Waldo Emerson, *Nature* (Boston, 1836), 36.

34. Barbauld, *Hymns,* iii–vii. Locke in Axtell, 114.

35. Wordsworth, *Prelude,* 1, 28. Newton, 209–10. Wordsworth, *Poetical Works,* 462. Barbauld, *Hymns,* 75, 83–86.

36. Wordsworth, *Prelude,* 17, 124–25. Barbauld, *Hymns,* 51, 59–61.

37. Wordsworth, *Poetical Works,* 735, 736, 737. Locke in Yolton, II, 89. Barbauld, *Hymns,* 13.

38. Wordsworth, *Prelude,* 9, 73, 77, 79. Barbauld, *Hymns,* 89–91.

39. Wordsworth, *Prelude,* 75, 76. Barbauld, *Hymns,* 36–40.

40. Matthew Arnold, *Essays in Criticism, Second Series* (London, 1888), 162.

CHAPTER 6

1. West, *Letters Addressed To A Young Man,* III, 386–88. Newton, 209–10. Locke in Axtell, 182. Dorothy Kilner, *A Father's Advice to His Son,* 68–69.

2. Warburton, 208. Sheridan, 8. Fordyce, 191. Parsons, *The First Book for English Schools* (Nottingham, 1787), i–iii.

3. Locke in Axtell, 148. Edgeworth and Edgeworth, 53–54. Related to criticism of amusement in children's books was criticism of such books' depictions of virtue and education rewarded on this earth. Disapproval grew particularly pronounced during the Napoleonic Wars, when conservatives thought that the French were trying not simply to defeat British armies but also to undermine both church and state. "The pilgrim CHRISTIAN, was the companion of our childhood," Mary A. Burges wrote in *The Progress of The Pilgrim Good-Intent, in Jacobinical Times* (London, 1800), until "the refinements of modern

education banished him from our nurseries" (viii). Some educators thought that "visionary" and French philosophers, in particular Rousseau, had carried Locke's malleability of man to a dangerous extreme. Mrs. West wrote that she rejected "the new tenet of human perfectibility" and declared that Christian humility was the "foundation of true knowledge"—*Letters to a Young Man*, I, 102. In an "Address to Parents" in *The Sorrows Of Selfishness* (London, 1802), a novel for adolescent girls, Mrs. West recounted that the book was objected to as "too dismal for children; and it was represented that the most suitable method of instructing youth was, to set before it the *certain* rewards and advantages of virtue, instead of depicting the pains and punishments of vice. Life, it was observed, should be dressed in gay and pleasing colours. . . ." If this "doctrine of the *ultimate temporal* prosperity of virtue was thoroughly canvassed," Mrs. West wrote, perhaps "it would be found to branch from that false philosophy which has infected every species of education, ever since Fashion determined it to be absurd, preposterous, fanatical, and even immoral, to give children an early knowledge of the Christian Religion." When children were familiar with the Bible, she said, they knew that vice often prospered and virtue often suffered in this world. The rewards for good actions, Mrs. West emphasized, were found in "the silent recesses" of one's heart. Considered from a general point of view, virtue was "*likely* to lead to honour and opulence," but the Christian, she urged, should always remember that God tried "his faithful servants." False philosophy preached "the possibility of an earthly paradise" and endeavored "to prevent young minds from being imbued with the wholesome truth, that man is born to suffer" (iii–ix, passim). Conservatives blamed Rousseau, not Locke, for banishing religious education from the nursery. In *Emilius,* Rousseau criticized early religious education, saying that at fifteen Emilius would hardly know whether or not he had a soul. If he were to draw "a picture of the most deplorable stupidity," it would show, Rousseau wrote, a pedant teaching children their catechism. The mysteries of Christianity, he thought, were beyond the limited understandings of children. "It were better to have no idea of God at all," he wrote, "than to entertain those which are mean, fantastical, injurious and unworthy"—*Emilius and Sophia,* II, 257–65.

4. Locke in Axtell, 138, 182, 283–84.

5. *Ibid.,* 150–53. *The Renowned History of Giles Gingerbread* (London, 1764), title page.

6. *Giles Gingerbread,* 6, 16, 23–30.

7. *Guardian of Education* 1 (1802), 63; 4 (1805), 98–99. *Mince Pies For Christmas* (London, 1805), title page.

8. Lamb, I, 326. A.C., *The Footstep to Mrs. Trimmer's Sacred History* (Lon-

don, 1785), advertisement at the end. In addition to the thirty books listed by title, Marshall said he had published "thirty-five more Books of various Prices, for the Instruction and Amusement of young Minds." I found the thirty books listed, but many in editions published after 1785.

9. *The History Of The Good Lady Kindheart* (London, 1780), 45–47.

10. *Gaffer Goose's Golden Plaything* (Exeter, 1808), letter at the front of the book. *The Whitsuntide—Gift* (London, 1767), *The Whitsuntide Present* (New Haven, 1813), 9–10, 25–26.

11. *The House That Jack Built* (Edinburgh, 1815). *Jackey Dandy's Delight* (Edinburgh, 1815). *Nurse Dandlem's Little Repository of Great Instruction* (Glasgow, 1815), title page, 19, 25. I have been unable to find copies of Marshall's editions of these books. These later editions, published in Edinburgh, Glasgow, and the United States, were probably not very different from the versions published by Marshall.

12. *Nurse Dandlem's Repository,* 6. Charlotte Yonge, *A Storehouse Of Stories* (London, 1870), vii.

13. *Poems On Various Subjects, For The Amusement Of Youth* (London, 1785), 63–65.

14. Mary Ann Kilner, *William Sedley* (London, 1783), 73–80. For a gayer but just as relentlessly instructive book, see Dorothy Kilner, *The Happy Family* (London, 1785).

15. *An History Of the Lives . . . of the most eminent Martyrs* (London, 1764), preface. *The New Testament* (London, 1764), title page, v. Locke in Axtell, 261. In the issue of *Lloyd's Evening Post* for 24–26 Dec. 1764, (1164:611), Newbery advertised the four volumes and *A Pleasant and Useful Companion to the Church of England: Or, A Short, Plain, and Practical Exposition Of The Book of Common Prayer* as "THE YOUNG CHRISTIAN'S LIBRARY." In 1710, J. Downing in London used the same label to advertise a long list of serious books. Consisting of collections of sermons, biographies of famous ministers, conduct books, studies of creeds and doctrines, catechisms, Latin texts, and even *Paradise Lost,* Downing's catalogue shows the kinds of books that children born in Calvinistic households at the beginning of the eighteenth century might have read. The gap between *A Little Pretty Pocket-Book* and Downing's "Library" was vast. Although Newbery used the same phrase to advertise his pedestrian religious books as did Downing, the chance of there being any connection between the two is very small. Downing's list is printed in facsimile in Sloane's study.

16. Locke in Axtell, 261–62.

17. *Ibid.,* 243. Trimmer, *The Servant's Friend,* 52.

18. Locke in Axtell, 243. Hannah More, *Strictures On The Modern System Of Female Education* (London, 1799), I, 237–38. Mrs. West, *Letters Addressed to A Young Man,* I, 255.

19. A Lady, *Short Histories Transcribed From The Holy Scriptures* (London, 1787), title page. Like Newbery's religious books, this volume cost a shilling. Also see *The History Of Our Saviour* (London, 1787). This book was also written by "A Lady" and was published by Marshall. Many comparisons can be made between biblical stories and fairy tales. Since many chapbooks were the degenerate remnant of medieval romances, many of whose heroes were Christian heroes, there are also many similarities between romances and biblical stories.

20. *The Holy Bible Abridged,* 7th ed. (London, 1768), v–vi. Locke in Axtell, 261.

21. *The Lilliputian Magazine,* 18–19, 133–34.

22. *The Newtonian System,* title page, 1, 4, 23, 68–69, 127.

23. *Nurse Truelove's New-Year's-Gift* (London, 1770), 45–46.

24. Dorothy Kilner, *Letters From A Mother* (London, 1784), vii. *The Newtonian System,* 17. Locke in Axtell, 152, 241. Oliver Goldsmith, Christopher Smart, and Griffith and Giles Jones may have helped Newbery with his children's books. Although his books were not so thematically unified as those advertised by Marshall, Newbery often implied that Locke's profit-and-delight formula lay behind the design of his books and unified them. In an advertisement listing twenty-eight of his books, eighteen of which were for children and ten for young gentlemen and ladies, he wrote, "At a Time when all complain of the Depravity of Human Nature, and the corrupt Principles of Mankind, any Design that is calculated to remove the Evils, and inforce a contrary Conduct, will undoubtedly deserve the Attention and Encouragement of the Publick. . . . It has been said, and said wisely, that the only way to remedy these Evils, is to begin with the rising Generation, and to take the Mind in its infant State, when it is uncorrupted and susceptible of any Impression; to represent their Duties and future Interest in a Manner that shall seem rather intended to amuse than instruct, to excite their Attention with Images and Pictures that are familiar and pleasing: To warm their Affections with such little Histories as are capable of giving them Delight, and of impressing on their tender Minds proper Sentiments of Religion, Justice, Honour, and Virtue." *The Universal Chronicle* 45 (3–10 Feb. 1759), 48.

25. *Monthly Review* 78 (1788), 73; 72 (1785), 216. Locke in Axtell, 261. A.C., *The Footstep* 3–6. Sarah Trimmer, *Sacred History* I, title page, preface. See Watts, *A Treatise,* 104–5, for his views on indiscriminate reading of the Bible.

26. *Critical Review* 56 (1783), 300. *Guardian of Education* 2 (1803), 302. Clara Lucas Balfour, *A Sketch Of Mrs. Trimmer* (London, 1854), 24.

27. Madame de Genlis, *Adelaide and Theodore* (London, 1783), I, 30–34, 47.

28. Sarah Trimmer, *A Description Of A Set of Prints Of Scripture History* (London, 1786), v–vi. *Guardian of Education* 2 (1803), 297.

29. Trimmer, *A Description Of . . . Scripture History,* vi. Trimmer, *Reflections Upon The Education Of Children In Charity Schools,* advertisement at the end. Locke in Axtell, 302.

30. *Guardian of Education* 2 (1803), 296–97. Locke in Axtell, 182. Dating the histories is difficult. The first was published in 1786 and the last before 1792. All five were described in an advertisement attached to Mrs. Trimmer's *Reflections Upon The Education Of Children In Charity Schools.* Some time after 1792, probably in 1795 or 1796, Mrs. Trimmer expanded the *Scripture History* to 239 pages. *A Description Of A Set Of Prints Of Ancient History,* 3rd ed. (London, 1795), pt. I, iii–iv, 40, 71, 98; pt. II, 64. *A Description Of . . . Roman History* (London, 1789), 42, 202. Although Baroness d'Almane allowed scenes from Ovid in the "eating parlour," Mrs. Trimmer avoided fiction. Mythology in particular, she remarked in the *Guardian of Education,* was "very unfit for the study of young children."

31. Ellenor Fenn, *A Spelling Book* (London, 1783), xii; *Fables in Verse,* 34.

32. Ellenor Fenn, *Cobwebs To Catch Flies,* I, xv, 28, 41; *Fables In Monosyllables,* xi. *The Newtonian System,* 95. *Critical Review* 57 (1784), 399. *Monthly Review* 69 (1783), 344. *Guardian of Education* 1 (1802), 124–25.

33. Locke in Axtell, 201–5. *Monthly Review* 70 (1784), 80. *Critical Review* 57, (1784), 479–80.

34. Dorothy Kilner, *Clear and Concise Account* (London, 1816), I, ix. Mrs. Trimmer abridged *The First Principles of Religion.* Marshall published the abridgement in 1784 as *Sunday School Dialogues.*

35. *Critical Review* 57 (1784), 480. Mary Ann Kilner, *Familiar Dialogues* (London, 1816), 14–15.

36. Mary Ann Kilner, *A Course of Lectures* (London, 1783), I, xv–xvi. Locke in Axtell, 204. Also see Ellenor Fenn, *Rational Sports* (London, 1823); *Juvenile Correspondence* (London, 1785); and Dorothy Kilner, *Short Conversations.*

37. Sarah Trimmer, *Sunday School Dialogues,* 18. The *Dialogues* differed so much from *The First Principles* that they seemed practically an independent work. In the introduction, Mrs. Trimmer explained that the book was written for children from "*the lower classes of life*"—iii. Hannah More, *Village Politics,* 2nd ed. (London, 1792), 4, 19–20.

38. Dorothy Kilner, *Letters From A Mother,* 20, 28, 30, 33; *Short Conversa-*

tions, 5–6; *The Holiday Present* (York, 1803), 5–10, 26–30; *The Histories Of More Children than One,* 10–18, 39. Locke in Axtell, 139, 145, 176–177. *Giles Gingerbread,* 28.

39. Ellenor Fenn, *School Occurrences* (London, 1783), vii, 15, 17, 28–29, 32–34; *The Female Guardian,* 2nd ed. (London, 1787), 16.

40. *School Occurrences,* 64–65. Marshall's imitations of *Goody Two-Shoes, Goody Goosecap* and *Primrose Prettyface* were more instructive and duller.

41. *The Wisdom Of Crop the Conjuror* (Worcester, 1786), title page, 10.

42. Dorothy Kilner, *Anecdotes Of a Boarding-School* (London, 1783), I, v, vii; II, 47. Locke in Axtell, 165–71. *School Occurrences,* 115.

43. *The Newtonian System,* 33. *Critical Review* 56 (1783), 480; 60 (1785), 240. *Monthly Review* 72 (1785), 235. Dorothy Kilner, *The Village School* (London, 1828), 5, 57.

44. *The Village School,* 88.

45. *Critical Review* 60 (1785), 240.

46. *Payne's Universal Chronicle* 20 (1758), 153. *Guardian of Education* 4 (1805), 98–99.

47. Locke in Axtell, 114, 255, 273. Locke in Yolton, I, 336. The French Revolution increased awareness of the social implications of education. See my *The Moral Tradition in English Fiction, 1785–1850* (Hanover, N.H., 1976). Hannah More, *Strictures On The Modern System Of Female Education,* I, 155–58, 164, 199. Despite disagreeing with Locke on this point, Hannah More believed Locke was "the great Author" on education. She recommended that after young ladies had had "a proper course of preparation," they "swallow and digest such strong meat" as "some parts of Mr. Locke's Essay on the Human Understanding." Sheridan, *British Education,* 4–5.

48. Hannah More, *Village Politics,* 4. Ellenor Fenn, *Fables, By Mrs. Teachwell* (London, 1783), vi–viii.

Afterword

1. *Popular Fairy Tales* (London, 1818), iii. *Quarterly Review* 21 (1819), 91–92.

2. *London Magazine* 2 (1820), 477–83.

3. *Macmillan's Magazine* 20 (1869), 229. *A Little Pretty Pocket-Book,* 6. Darton, 205. For a list of John Harris's books, see Marjorie Moon's fine bibliography, *John Harris's Books For Youth 1801–1843. The History of Tommy Two-Shoes* did exist. Taken mainly from the second chapter and the appendix of *Goody-Two-Shoes,* it was a much inferior work. In 1818 Mary Belson Elliot's *The Adventures of Tommy Two-Shoes* appeared. For more on Tommy Two-Shoes, see

d'Alté A. Welch, *A Bibliography of American Children's Books Printed Prior to 1821* (Worcester, Mass., 1972), 203. Palgrave was mistaken in writing that Marshall had been compelled to shut up his shop. Although Marshall was no longer located at 4 Aldermary Churchyard, the firm was still active.

4. Darton, 217.

APPENDIX A

1. Locke in Yolton, I, 9, 40–43. John Edwards, *A Free Discourse Concerning Truth and Error* (London, 1701), 28. Also see James Lowde, *A Discourse Concerning the Nature of Man* (London, 1694), and *Moral Essays* (York, 1699). Richard Ashcroft, "Faith and Knowledge in Locke's Philosophy" in Yolton, ed., *John Locke And The Way of Ideas,* 199.

2. John Edwards, *The Socinian Creed* (London, 1697); *A Brief Vindication* (London, 1697), 4. Samuel Bold, *Some Considerations* (London, 1699), 1.

3. William Warburton, *Letters* (Kidderminster, 1808), 208. Yolton, *John Locke and the Way of Ideas,* 25. For a longer account of the controversy and one which puts Locke's denial of innateness into historical perspective, see the *Way of Ideas.* William Sherlock, *A Discourse* (London, 1704), 104–5, 144, 161–62. Clarke, *An Essay Upon the Education of Youth,* 8–9. Chambers's *Cyclopaedia,* I, 368–69. Also see Temple Crocker, et al., *The Complete Dictionary Of Arts and Sciences* (London, 1765). "Mr. Locke," the *Dictionary* stated under *Idea*, "has made it appear that all our ideas are owing to our senses, and the reflections of our minds upon those ideas which the senses have at first furnished us with." All other theories were "mere chimera"—II, n.p.

APPENDIX B

1. Roscoe, *John Newbery,* 8–9.

2. *The History and Description of Westminster Abbey* (London, 1742), II, 122–25.

3. *The Gigantick History* (London, 1740), I, iv, x, xii, 19–20; II, xv, xx–xxi. *Curiosities In the Tower of London* (London, 1741), II, viii, xvii.

4. *The Gigantick History,* I, 11. *An Historical Account* (London, 1753). The *Historical Account* could be purchased as one book or "In Three Parts." The first part described the tower and its contents; the second part told the history of Westminster Abbey and described the tombs it contained; while the third part contained descriptions of St. Paul's Cathedral, the monument, and "other an-

tique Remains." In 1730 Boreman seems to have put together *A Description Of Three Hundred Animals; Viz. Beasts, Birds, Fishes, Serpents, And Insects.* In an address "To The Reader," he stated that "*most of the Books, which have been made to introduce Children into a Habit of Reading*" tended "*to Cloy than Entertain them.*" Consequently, he used animal pictures, he explained, "*to engage their Attention*" ("To the Reader," 19). The plates were poor, many being imitations ofTopsell's *Beasts,* and the prose was far too advanced for children. The best plates in the book depicted birds; those showing animals have at best a period-piece appeal. Boreman's natural history was out of date, and he included plates and descriptions of fabulous beasts like the lamia and the manticora. The latter had a triple row of upper and lower teeth "in bigness and roughness like a Lion's." Its feet, face, and ears resembled those of a human; its voice sounded "like a small Trumpet, or Pipe"; and its tail resembled a scorpion's and was "armed with a String, and sharp-pointed Quills." Swift as a hart and able to wound hunters with its tail, the manticora was difficult to tame. Indians, however, knew how to subdue it. When they "take a Whelp of this Beast," Boreman explained, "they bruise its Buttocks and Tail, to prevent its bearing those Sharp Quills; then it is tamed without danger." The description of the manticora was the high point of the book. Although the work was poorly done, numerous editions of *A Description* appeared in the eighteenth century. Francis Newbery was one of the many publishers of the eleventh edition.

5. *The Child's New Play-Thing,* 2nd ed. (London, 1743), 51, 53.

6. *A Pretty Play-Thing,* title page. *The London Evening-Post* 2555 (22–24 March 1744). *The Daily Advertiser* 4165 (23 May 1744). *Tommy Thumb's Pretty Song Book* "*Voll II*" (London, 1744), 62–64. John Marshall advertised an edition of *Nancy Cock's Song Book* in 1780. In 1788 Isaiah Thomas, the American publisher, published *Tommy Thumb's Song Book, For All Little Masters and Misses.* In reprinting English children's books, Thomas made few changes in the originals. The title of his "Worcester" edition was the same as that Mary Cooper advertised in March 1744, and it seems reasonable to assume that the contents of Thomas's book are those of vol. I of *Tommy Thumb's Song Book.* Thomas treated the rhymes in his book much the way Mary Cooper treated them in "Voll II" of the *Pretty Song Book.* Thus children learned to sing "Patty Cake," "Encore Ventesimo," while "Almain" suited "Magotty Pie"; "Giga," "Cat and a Fiddle," and "Adegio," "Fee, Faw, Fum." For more on Thomas's edition, see Iona and Peter Opie, *Three Centuries of Nursery Rhymes and Poetry For Children,* 11, and Welch, 263.

7. *Tommy Thumb's Pretty Song Book,* 62–64.

Appendix C

1. *The General Advertiser* 4748 (9 Jan. 1749–1750); 4797 (7 March 1749–1750). *The London Chronicle; or Universal Evening Post* 1253 (29 Dec. 1764—1 Jan. 1765), 3. For more on Newbery's advertisements, see Charles Welsh, *A Bookseller Of The Last Century* (London, 1885), 105–11, and John Dawson Carl Buck, "The Motives of Puffing: John Newbery's Advertisements 1742–1769," *Studies In Bibliography* 30 (1977), 196–210.

2. *General Evening Post* 2682 (9–12 Feb. 1751).

3. *The World* 115 (13 March 1755), 689–94. In this essay pp. 693 and 694 are misnumbered 687 and 688 and mistakenly called essay no. 114.

4. *The Lilliputian Magazine,* 24.

5. *The Valentine's-Gift,* 20–24.

6. *Nurse Truelove's Christmas-Box* (London, 1770), 20, 22. *The Whitsuntide-Gift* (London, 1767), advertisement, 4. *The Fairing,* 119–20.

7. *Payne's Universal Chronicle* 39 (23–30 Dec. 1758), 312. *The History of Little Goody Two-Shoes,* 13.

8. *Goody Two-Shoes,* 25, 28, 33, 61, 141. *Nurse Truelove's New-Year's-Gift,* 47–49. *The Penny London Morning Advertiser* 45 (30 March–2 April 1744).

9. *Tom Thumb's Folio,* 4–5. Newbery and Carnan published the *Folio. Tom Thumb's Exhibition,* 50–51.

10. Dorothy Kilner, *Anecdotes of a Boarding-School,* 20. Mary Ann Kilner, *Jemima Placid* (London, 1813), 12, 36, 61.

11. *The History Of The Good Lady Kindheart,* 18–20. *The Entertaining History of Little Goody Goosecap,* 19. *The Renowned History of Primrose Prettyface,* 25. *May Day* (London, 1787), 14, 43–45. Ellenor Fenn, *The Female Guardian,* 9.

Bibliography

Literature for Children and Servants

Chapbooks

Most are from the Dicey Collection in the British Library and seem to have been published betwen 1760 and 1770.

Bateman's Tragedy; Or The Perjured Bride Justly Rewarded.

Cambridge Jests Or, Wit's Recreation.

Dreams and Moles with their Interpretation and Signification.

The Foreign Travels of Sir John Mandeville. Containing, An Account of remote Kingdoms, Countries, Rivers, Castles, etc. Together with a Description of Giants, Pigmies, and various other People of odd Deformities.

The Friar and the Boy; Or, The Young Piper's Pleasant Pastime.

The History of Fortunatus.

The History of Four Kings, Their Queens and Daughters . . . Being The Merry Tales of Tom Hodge. And his School-Fellows.

The History of Guy, Earl of Warwick.

The History of Jack and the Giants.

The History of Jack Horner.

The History of the Life and Death of that most Noble Knight Bevis of Southampton.

The History of Mother Shipton.

The History of Parismus, Prince of Bohemia.

The History Of The Seven Champions of Christendom.

The Lover's Magazine; or Cupid's Decoy.

The Merry Tales, Or The Wise Men of Gotham.

Mother Bunch's Closet Newly Broke Open. Newcastle, 1760.

Nixon's Cheshire Prophecy, At Large. Published from Lady Cowper's correct Copy in the Reign of Queen Anne.
No Jest like a True Jest; Being a Compendious Record of the Merry Life and Mad Exploits of Capt. James Hind.
Partridge and Flamsted's New and Well Experienced Fortune Book.
Poets Jest, or Mirth in Abundance.
The Renowned History of the Seven Champions of Christendom.
The Shooe-makers Glory; Or, The Princely History Of The Gentle Craft. c 1700.
The Sleeping Beauty In The Wood.
Wanton Tom; Or, The Merry History of Tom Stitch, the Taylor.
A Whetstone For Dull Wits: Or A Poesy Of New and Ingenious Riddles.
The Witch of the Woodlands; Or The Cobler's New Translation.

Cheap Repository Tracts

Unless indicated otherwise, written by members of the Clapham Sect; many are by Hannah More (*q.v.*).

Ananias and Sapphira. 1795.
The Apprentice Turned Master; Or, the Second Part of the Two Shoemakers. 1796.
Betty Brown, the St. Giles Orange Girl: With Some Account of Mrs. Sponge, the Money-lender. 1796.
The Carpenter; Or, The Danger of Evil Company. 1795.
The Contented Cobbler. 1798.
The Cottage Cook, Or, Mrs. Jones's Cheap Dishes. 1798.
The Deceitfulness of Pleasure: Or, Some Account of my Lady Blithe. 1798.
Hints to all Ranks of People On the Occasion of the present Scarcity. 1795.
The Hubbub; Or, The History of Farmer Russel, the Hard-hearted Overseer. 1797.
The Judgment Awaiting Undutiful Children. Illustrated In The History of Absalom. 1798?
The Lancashire Collier Girl. 1795.
Madge Blarney, The Gipsey Girl. 1797.
The Parish Nurse. 1796.
Robert and Richard: Or, The Ghost of poor Molly, who was drowned in Richard's Mill Pond. 1796.
Scotch Cheap Repository Tracts. *The Apprentice.* 2nd ed. Edinburgh, 1815.
The Shepherd of Salisbury-Plain. 1795.
Sorrowful Sam; Or, The Two Blacksmiths. 1795.
The Sunday School. 1798.
Tawny Rachel: Or, The Fortune Teller. 1797.

Thornton, Henry. *Cheap Repository For Moral & Religious Publications.* London, 1796.
The Two Cousins; Or, Spare the Rod and Spoil the Child. 1797.
The Two Shoemakers. 1795.
The Two Soldiers. 1797.
The Two Wealthy Farmers; Or, The History of Mr. Bragwell. 1795.
The Widow of Zarephath. 1797.

Books

The Adventures of a Hackney Coach. 7th ed. Dublin: C. Jackson, 1781.
Aikin, Anna (Barbauld). *Hymns in Prose for Children.* London, 1781.
_______. *Lessons for Children, from Two to Three Years Old.* London, 1787.
_______. *Lessons for Children of Three Years Old.* Dublin, 1789.
_______, and John Aikin. *Evenings At Home; Or, The Juvenile Budget Opened.* London, 1792–96.
Aikin, Lucy, ed. *Poetry For Children, Consisting of Short Pieces To Be Committed To Memory.* 2nd ed. London: R. Phillips, 1803.
The Alphabet of Goody two Shoes. London: J. Harris, 1808.
Barbauld, Anna. *See* Aikin.
Baxter, Richard. *Compassionate Counsel To All Young-Men.* London: B. Simmons & J. Greenwood, 1681.
Biography of A Spaniel. London: A.K. Newman, 1816.
Bridges, Thomas. *The Adventures of a Bank-Note.* London, 1770–71.
Bunyan, John. *A Book for Boys and Girls: or, Country Rhimes For Children.* London, 1686.
Bunyano, Stephano. *The Prettiest Book For Children: Being The History Of The Enchanted Castle; Situated in one of the Unfortunate Isles, and governed by the Giant Instruction.* London: J. Coote, 1770.
Burges, Mary. *The Progress of the Pilgrim Good-Intent in Jacobinical Times.* London, 1800.
Burgh, James. *Youth's Friendly Monitor: Being a Set of Directions, Prudential, Moral, Religious, and Scientific.* London, 1754.
C., A. *The Footstep to Mrs. Trimmer's Sacred History For the Instruction and Amusement of Little Children.* London: John Marshall, 1785.
Campe, Joachim. *The New Robinson Crusoe.* London: John Stockdale, 1788.
Chear, Abraham. *A Looking-Glass For Children. Being A Narrative of God's gracious Dealings with some little Children, recollected by Henry Jessey, in his Life-Time.* 4th ed. London, 1708.
The Child's New Play-Thing: Being A Spelling-Book Intended To make Learning

to Read, a Diversion instead of a Task. 2nd ed. London: Mary Cooper, 1743.

The Child's New Year's Gift; A Collection Of Riddles. Adorned with Pictures. London: J. Evans. 181?.

Coventry, Francis. *The History of Pompey the Little; Or, The Life and Adventures of A Lap-Dog.* 3rd ed. London, 1752.

Crouch, Nathaniel. *Youths Divine Pastime, Containing Forty Remarkable Scripture Histories, turned into common English Verse. With Forty Curious Pictures proper to each Story.* 3rd ed. London, 1691.

Dame Partlet's Farm; Containing An Account Of The Great Riches She Obtained By Industry, The Good Life She Led, And Alas, Good Reader! Her Sudden Death. London: J. Harris, 1806.

Day, Thomas. "The History of Little Jack" in *The Children's Miscellany.* London: John Stockdale, 1788.

The Dog of Knowledge; or, Memoirs of Bob, the Spotted Terrier. London, 1803.

Edgeworth, Maria. *Early Lessons.* 7th ed. London: R. Hunter, 1820.

_______. *Moral Tales for Young People.* London: J. Johnson, 1801.

_______. *The Parent's Assistant; or, Stories for Children.* 2nd ed. London, 1796.

The Entertaining History of Little Goody Goosecap containing a Variety of Adventures calculated to Amuse and Instruct the Lilliputian World. London: John Marshall, 1780.

Fenn, Ellenor. *Cobwebs to Catch Flies; Dialogues in Short Sentences, Adapted to Children from the Age of Three to Eight Years.* London: John Marshall. 1783.

_______. *Fables, By Mrs. Teachwell: In Which The Morals Are Drawn Incidentally In Various Ways.* London: John Marshall, 1783.

_______. *Fables in Monosyllables By Mrs. Teachwell; To Which Are Added Morals, in Dialogues, Between A Mother and Children.* London: John Marshall, 1783.

_______. *The Fairy Spectator; or, the Invisible Monitor.* London: John Marshall. 1789.

_______. *The Female Guardian. Designed to Correct some of the Foibles Incident to Girls.* 2nd ed. London: John Marshall, 1787.

_______. *Juvenile Correspondence; Or, Letters, Suited to Children, From Four to above Ten Years of Age.* London: John Marshall, 1785.

_______. *The Rational Dame; Or, Hints Towards Supplying Prattle For Children.* London: John Marshall, 1790.

_______. *Rational Sports, or The Game of Trades and Commerce; In Dialogues Passing Among The Children Of A Family.* London: John Marshall, 1823.

_______. *School Occurrences: Supposed to have Arisen among A Set of Young Ladies Under the Tuition of Mrs. Teachwell.* London: John Marshall, 1783.

———. *A Spelling Book, Designed To render the Acquisition of the Rudiments of our Native Language Easy and pleasant.* London: John Marshall, 1783.

Fielding, Sarah. *The Governess; Or, The Little Female Academy.* 2nd ed. London, 1749.

The Friends. Hartford: John Babcock, 1801.

Gaffer Goose's Golden Plaything; Being A New Collection Of Entertaining Fables. Exeter: Norris & Sawyer, 1808.

Gulliver, Lilliputius. *Instructive Lessons, Conveyed To The Youthful Mind. Through The Medium of Tale and Dialogue.* London: E. Newbery, 1803.

The Hare; or Hunting Incompatible With Humanity. London: Vernor & Hood, 1799.

Hayley, William. *Ballads. Founded on Anecdotes Relating to Animals.* Chichester, 1805.

Helme, Elizabeth. *Adventures of a Bullfinch.* London, 1809.

Hill, George Canning. *Benedict Arnold: A Biography.* Boston: E.O. Libby, 1858.

The History of Little King Pippin; With An Account of the melancholy Death of Four Naughty Boys, who were devoured by Wild Beasts; And The Wonderful Delivery of Master Harry Harmless, by a Little White Horse. Glasgow, 1814.

The History Of The Good Lady Kindheart, Of Hospitable-Hall. Near The Village of Allgood. London: John Marshall, 1780.

The House That Jack Built. To Which is Prefixed The History Of Jack Jingle. Edinburgh: G. Ross, 1815.

Hurlothrumbo, Doctor. *The Fortune-Teller. By Which Young Gentlemen and Ladies may easily fortel a Variety of important Events that will happen both to Themselves and their Acquaintance.* Boston: John W. Folsom, 1798.

Jackey Dandy's Delight: Or, The History Of Birds And Beasts. Edinburgh: G. Ross, 1815.

Janeway, James. *A Token For Children: Being An Exact Account of the Conversion, Holy and Exemplary Lives, and Joyful Deaths of several young Children.* London, 1671.

Johnson, Richard. *The Adventures of a Silver Penny including Many Secret Anecdotes of Little Misses and Masters both Good and Naughty.* London: E. Newbery, 1787.

———. *Juvenile Rambles Through The Paths Of Nature; In Which Many Parts Of The Wonderful Works of the Creation are Brought Forward, And Made Familiar to the Capacity of every Little Miss and Master, Who Wishes To Become Wise And Good.* London: E. Newbery, 1786.

_______. *Juvenile Sports and Pastimes. To Which Are Prefixed, Memoirs of the Author, Including a New Mode of Infant Education. By Master Michel Angelo.* 2nd ed. London: T. Carnan, 1776.

_______. *Letters Between Master Tommy And Miss Nancy Goodwill.* London: T. Carnan & F. Newbery, Junior, 1770.

Johnston, Charles. *Chrysal; or, the Adventures of a Guinea. Wherein are exhibited Views of several striking Scenes, with Curious and interesting Anedotes of the most Noted Persons in Every Rank of Life, whose Hands it passed through in America, England, Holland, Germany, and Portugal.* London, 1760.

Jones, Stephen. *The Life and Adventures of A Fly.* London: E. Newbery, 1789.

Keach, Benjamin. *War with The Devil: Or, The Young Man's Conflict With The Powers of Darkness.* 7th impression. London, 1683.

Kendall, Edward Augustus. *The Canary Bird: A Moral Fiction.* London: E. Newbery, 1799.

_______. *Keeper's Travels In Search of His Master.* London: E. Newbery, 1798.

_______. *The Sparrow.* London: E. Newbery, 1798.

Kilner, Dorothy. *Anecdotes of A Boarding School; Or, An Antidote to the Vices Of Those Useful Seminaries.* London: John Marshall, 1784.

_______. *The Adventures of a Whipping-Top. Illustrated with Stories of many Bad Boys, who themselves deserve Whipping, and of some Good Boys, who deserve Plum-Cakes.* London: John Marshall, 1784.

_______. *Clear and Concise Account of the Origin and Design of Christianity.* London: John Marshall, 1816.

_______. *Dialogues and Letters On Morality, Oeconomy, And Politeness For The Improvement and Entertainment of Young Female Minds.* London: John Marshall, 1785.

_______. *A Father's Advice to His Son.* London: John Marshall, 1784.

_______. *The Happy Family; or, Memoirs of Mr. and Mrs. Norton, Intended to show the Delightful Effects of Filial Obedience.* London: John Marshall, 1785.

_______. *The History Of A Great Many Boys and Girls.* Boston: Samuel Hall, 1794.

_______. *The Histories of More Children than One.* London: John Marshall, 1783.

_______. *The Holiday Present: Containing Anecdotes of Mr. and Mrs. Jennet, And their Little Family.* York, 1803.

_______. *Letters From A Mother to Her Children, on Various important Subjects.* London: John Marshall, 1783.

_______. *The Life and Perambulation of a Mouse.* London: John Marshall. 1783.

_______. *Little Stories For Little Folks.* Boston: Samuel Hall, 1789.

———. *Poems on Various Subjects, For The Amusement Of Youth.* London: John Marshall, 1785.

———. *Short Conversations; or, an Easy Road to the Temple of Fame; which All May Reach who Endeavour To Be Good.* London: John Marshall, 1785.

———. *The Village School; A Collection of Entertaining Histories.* London: 1828.

Kilner, Mary Ann. *The Adventures of a Pincushion.* London: John Marshall, 1783.

———. *A Course of Lectures for Sunday Evenings Containing Religious Advice to Young Persons.* London: John Marshall, 1783.

———. *Familiar Dialogues for the Instruction and Amusement of Children.* London: John Marshall, 1816.

———. *Jemima Placid; or, The Advantages of Good-Nature.* London: John Marshall, 1813.

———. *Memoirs of a Peg-Top.* London: John Marshall, 1783.

———. *William Sedley: or, The Evil Day Deferred.* London: John Marshall, 1783.

Kirkman, Francis. *The Unlucky Citizen.* London, 1673.

Lady, A. *The History Of Our Saviour, Jesus Christ And His Apostles.* London: John Marshall, 1787.

Lady, A. *Short Histories Transcribed From The Holy Scriptures: Intended For The Use, Entertainment, and Benefit of Children.* London: John Marshall, 1787.

The Lilliputian Auction To Which All Little Masters and Misses Are Invited By Charly Chatter. Walk In Young Gentlemen and Ladies, A Going, a Going, a Going! Philadelphia: Jacob Johnson, 1802.

May Day; Or, Anecdotes Of Miss Lydia Lively. Intended to Improve And Amuse The Rising Generation. London: John Marshall, 1787.

Memoirs of Dick, The Little Poney. London: E. Newbery, 1800.

Mince Pies For Christmas: Consisting Of Riddles, Charades, Rebuses, Transpositions And Queries . . . By An Old Friend. London, 1805.

More, Hannah. *Village Politics. Addressed To All The Mechanics, Journeymen, And Day Labourers, In Great Britain. By Will Chip, A Country Carpernter.* 2nd ed. London, 1792.

Nurse Dandlem's Little Repository of Great Instruction, Containing The surprising Adventures of Little Wake Wilful. Glasgow: J. Lumsden, 1815.

P., L. *The Life of a Bee, Related by Herself.* London: John Marshall, 1790.

Pilkington, Mary. *Marvelous Adventures: or, The Vicissitudes of a Cat In which are Sketches Of The Characters Of The Different Young Ladies and Gentlemen Into Whose Hands Grimalkin Came.* London: 1802.

———. *Pity's Gift: A Collection of Interesting Tales, To Excite The Compassion of Youth for The Animal Creation.* London: E. Newbery, 1798.

The Renowned History of Primrose Prettyface, who By her Sweetness of Temper, & Love of Learning, was raised from being the Daughter of a poor Cottager, to great Riches, and the Dignity of Lady of the Manor. London: John Marshall, 1785.

Robin Goodfellow; A Fairy Tale. Written by a Fairy. For the Amusement of All the pretty little Faies and Fairies in Great Britain. London: Francis Newbery, 1770.

The Ruby Heart, Or, Constantio and Selima; And The Enchanted Mirror. A New Edition. London, 1802.

Smythies, Miss. *The History of A Pin.* London: E. Newbery, 1798.

Tabart, Benjamin. *Popular Fairy Tales; Or, A Lilliputian Library; Containing Twenty-Six Choice Pieces Of Fancy And Fiction, By Those Renowned Personages King Oberon, Queen Mab, Mother Goose, Mother Bunch, Master Puck, And Other Distinguished Personages At The Court Of The Fairies.* London, 1818.

Tom Thumb's Exhibition, Being An Account of Many valuable and surprising Curiosities Which he has collected In the course of his Travels. London: J. Harris, 1815.

Tom Thumb's Folio; Or, A New Penny Play-Thing For Little Giants. London: Newbery and Carnan, 1768.

Tommy Thumb's Pretty Song Book "Voll II". London: Mary Cooper, 1744.

Tommy Thumb's Song Book, For All Little Masters and Misses. Worcester, Mass.: Isaiah Thomas, 1788.

Trimmer, Mary. *A History of Quadrupeds.* London, 1803.

Trimmer, Sarah. *A Description Of A Set Of Prints Of Ancient History.* London: John Marshall, 1789.

_______. *A Description of a Set of Prints of English History.* London: Baldwin, Cradock, and Joy, 1817.

_______. *A Description of a Set of Prints Taken From the New Testament.* London: John Marshall, 1796.

_______. *A Description Of A Set of Prints of Roman History.* London: John Marshall, 1789.

_______. *A Description Of A Set of Prints Of Scripture History: Contained In A Set of Easy Lessons.* London: John Marshall, 1786.

_______. *An Easy Introduction To The Knowledge of Nature, And Reading The Holy Scriptures, Adapted to the Capacities of Children.* London, 1780.

_______. *Easy Lessons For Young Children.* Paris, 1856.

_______. *Fabulous Histories. Designed For the Instruction Of Children, Respecting Their Treatment of Animals.* London: T. Longman, 1786.

_______. *The Family Magazine.* London, 1788–89.

_______. *Sacred History Selected From The Scriptures, With Annotations and Reflections, Suited To The Comprehension of Young Minds.* 6 vols. London, 1782–86.

_______. *The Servant's Friend, An Exemplary Tale; Designed To Enforce The Reli-*

gious Instruction Given At Sunday and other Charity Schools. London, 1787.

_______. *Sunday School Dialogues; Being An Abridgement Of A Work, By M.P.* [Dorothy Kilner] *Entitled, "The First Principles Of Religion, and the Existence of a Diety, explained in a Series of Dialogues, adapted to the Capacity of the Infant Mind."* London: John Marshall, 1784.

Wakefield, Priscilla. *Juvenile Anecdotes, Founded On Facts.* London, 1795.

_______. *Leisure Hours: Or Entertaining Dialogues; Between Persons Eminent for Virtue and Magnanimity.* London: Harvey and Darton, 1794–96.

_______. *Mental Improvement: Or The Beauties and Wonders Of Nature And Art.* London, 1794.

Watts, Isaac. *Divine Songs, Attempted in Easy Language For The Use Of Children.* London, 1715.

West, Jane. *The Advantages of Education; Or, the History of Maria Williams.* 2nd ed. London, 1803.

_______. *Letters Addressed To A Young Man, On His First Entrance Into Life.* London, 1801.

_______. *Letters To A Young Lady, in which The Duties and Character of Women Are Considered.* 2nd ed. London: Longman, 1806.

_______. *The Sorrows of Selfishness; Or, The History of Miss Richmore.* London, 1802.

White, Thomas. *A Little Book For Little Children.* 12th ed. London, 1702.

The Whitsuntide Present. New Haven: Sydney's Press, 1813.

The Wisdom Of Crop the Conjuror, Exemplified In several Characters of Good and Bad Boys. Worcester, Mass.: Isaiah Thomas, 1786.

Wither, George. *Heleluiah, Or Britans Second Remembrancer.* London, 1641.

Wollstonecraft, Mary. *Mary, A Fiction.* London, 1788.

_______. *Original Stories, From Real Life.* London, 1788.

Books Originally Published by Thomas Boreman

Curiosities in The Tower of London. London, 1741.

A Description of Three Hundred Animals; Viz. Beasts, Birds, Fishes, Serpents, And Insects. London, 1730.

The Gigantick History. London, 1740.

The History and Description of Westminster Abbey. London, 1742.

Books Originally Published by John Newbery

Aesop, Abraham. *Fables In Verse For The Improvement Of The Young And The Old; by Abraham Aesop, Esq. To which are added, Fables in Verse and Prose; with the Conversation of Birds and Beasts, At their several Meetings, Routs, and Assemblies; by Woglog the great Giant.* 5th ed. London: John Newbery, 1765.

The Fairing: Or, A Golden Toy, For Children of All Sizes and Denominations. London: John Newbery, 1767.

An Historical Account Of The Curiosities Of London and Westminster. London: John Newbery, 1753.

An History Of The Life Of Our Lord and Saviour Jesus Christ. To which is added, The Life of the Blessed Virgin Mary. London: John Newbery, 1764.

The History of Little Goody Two-Shoes; Otherwise called, Mrs. Margery Two-Shoes. London, John Newbery, 1765.

The History Of the Lives, Actions, Travels, Sufferings and Deaths Of The Apostles And Evangelists. London: John Newbery, 1763.

An History Of the Lives, Actions, Travels, Sufferings, and Deaths of the most eminent Martyrs and Primitive Fathers of the Church, in the first four Centuries. London: John Newbery, 1764.

The Holy Bible Abridged. 7th ed. London: Newbery and Carnan, 1768.

The Lilliputian Magazine: or the Young Gentleman & Lady's Golden Library, being An Attempt to Amend the World, to render the Society of Man more Amiable. London: John Newbery, 1751.

A Little Lottery-Book For Children: Containing A "new" Method of "playing" them into a Knowledge of the Letters, Figures, Etc. London: "all the Booksellers," 1768.

A Little Pretty Pocket-Book. London: John Newbery, 1767.

The Mosaic Creation: Or, Divine Wisdom Displayed. London: John Newbery, 1759.

The New Testament of Our Lord and Saviour Jesus Christ, Abridged and harmonized in the Words of the Evangelists. London: John Newbery, 1764.

Nurse Truelove's Christmas-Box. London: Newbery and Carnan, 1770.

Nurse Truelove's New-Year's-Gift: Or, The Book of Books for Children. London: Newbery and Carnan, 1770.

A Pleasant and Useful Companion to the Church of England. London: John Newbery, 1764.

A Pretty Book Of Pictures for Little Masters and Misses: Or, Tommy Trip's History of Beasts and Birds. 9th ed. London: John Newbery, 1767.

The Pretty Play-Thing For Children of All Denominations. New ed. London: Francis Newbery, Jr., 1770.

The Renowned History of Giles Gingerbread. London: John Newbery, 1764.

The Royal Primer; Or, an easy and pleasant Guide to the Art of Reading. London: John Newbery and B. Collins at Salisbury, n.d.

Six-Pennyworth of Wit; Or, Little Stories for Little Folks, Of all Denominations. London: John Newbery, 1767.

Telescope, Tom. *The Newtonian System of Philosophy.* 2nd ed. London: John Newbery, 1762.

Trapwit, Tom. *Be Merry and Wise.* 5th ed. London: John Newbery, 1761.
The Twelfth-Day Gift: Or, the Grand Exhibition. 2nd ed. London: Carnan and Newbery, 1770.
The Valentine's Gift: Or, A Plan to enable Children of all Sizes and Denominations To Behave with Honour, Integrity, and Humanity. London: Carnan and Newbery, 1777.
The Whitsuntide-Gift: Or, The Way to be very happy. London: John Newbery, 1767.

Contemporary Periodicals

The Christian Reformer. 1825.
Critical Review.
The Daily Advertiser. 1744.
Evangelical Magazine. 1793.
The General Advertiser.
The General Evening Post. 1751.
Gentleman's Magazine.
Lloyd's Evening Post. 1764.
The London Chronicle. 1764.
The London Evening-Post. 1744.
London Magazine. 1820.
Macmillan's Magazine.
Monthly Review.
Payne's Universal Chronicle. 1758.
The Penny London Morning Advertiser. 1744.
Quarterly Review. 1819.
The Tatler.
The Universal Chronicle. 1759.
The World. 1755.

Contemporary Criticism, Philosophy, and Biography

Ady, Thomas. *A Candle in the Dark: Or, A Treatise Concerning the Nature of Witches & Witchcraft.* London: Tho. Newberry, 1656.
Aikin, Anna (Barbauld), and John Aikin. *Miscellaneous Pieces, In Prose.* London: J. Johnson, 1773.
Bold, Samuel. *Some Considerations On The Principal Objections And Arguments Which have been Publish'd against Mr. Lock's Essay of Humane Understanding.* London, 1699.

Bolingbroke, Viscount. *The Works of the late Right Honorable Henry St. John, Lord Viscount Bolingbroke.* London, 1754–98.

Boyle, Robert. *The Christian Virtuoso: Shewing That by being addicted to Experimental Philosophy, a Man is rather Assisted, than Indisposed to be a Good Christian.* London, 1690.

———. *The Excellency of Theology, Compar'd With Natural Philosophy, (as both are Objects of Men's Study).* London, 1671/72.

Boswell, James. *Boswell's Life of Johnson,* ed. George Birkbeck Hill, revised L.F. Powell. Oxford: Oxford Univ. Press, 1971.

Burgh, James. *The Dignity of Human Nature.* London: J. & P. Knapton, 1754.

Chambers, Ephraim. *Cyclopedia: Or, An Universal Dictionary of Arts and Sciences.* London, 1728.

Chapman, George. *A Treatise On Education.* London: T. Cadell, 1773. 3rd ed. London, 1784.

Clarke, John. *An Essay Upon The Education Of Youth In Grammar-Schools.* London: John Wyat, 1720.

———. *An Essay Upon Study.* London: Arthur Bettesworth, 1731.

Coleridge, Samuel Taylor. *Collected Letters of Samuel Taylor Coleridge,* ed. Earl Leslie Griggs. Oxford: Oxford University Press, 1956, 1971.

Corne-waleys, Sir William. *Essayes.* London: Edmund Mattes, 1600.

Crocker, Temple, et al. *The Complete Dictionary Of Arts and Sciences. In Which The Whole Circle Of Human Learning Is Explained.* London, 1765.

Crosse, Henry. *Vertues Common-wealth; Or The Highway to Honour.* London, 1603.

Crossman, Samuel. *The Young Mans Monitor.* London: J.H., 1644.

Dent, Arthur. *The Plaine Mans Path-way to Heaven.* London: Robert Dexter, 1601.

Derham, William. *Physico-Theology: Or, A Demonstration Of The Being and Attributes of God, from his Works of Creation.* London: W. Innys, 1713.

Des Maizeaux, P. *A Collection Of Several Pieces Of Mr. John Locke.* London: 1720.

Doddridge, Philip. *Sermons on The Religious Education of Children.* London: R. Hett, 1732.

Edgeworth, Maria, and Richard Lovell Edgeworth. *Practical Education.* London, 1798.

Edwards, John. *A Brief Vindication Of the Christian Faith.* London, 1697.

———. *A Free Discourse Concerning Truth and Error, Especially in Matters of Religion.* London, 1701.

———. *The Socinian Creed: Or, A Brief Account Of the Professed Tenets and Doctrines Of Foreign and English Socinians.* London, 1697.

Fordyce, David. *Dialogues Concerning Education.* London, 1745.

Fuller, Thomas. *The Holy State,* Cambridge: Roger Daniel, 1642.

Genlis, Madame de. *Adelaide and Theodore; of Letters on Education: Containing All the Principles relative to three different Plans of Education; to that of Princes and to those of Young Persons of both Sexes.* London: T. Cadell, 1783.

Goldsmith, Oliver. *The Citizen of the World.* London, 1762.

Graham, Catharine Macauley. *Letters on Education With Observations On Religious And Metaphysical Subjects.* London, 1790.

Hartley, David. *Observations On Man, His Frame, His Duty, And His Expectations.* London, 1749.

Haverfield, Thomas. *A Sermon, Occasioned by the Death of Mrs. Trimmer.* London, 1811.

Hazlitt, William. *The Complete Works of William Hazlitt,* ed. Percival Preland Howe. London, 1930.

The History of Genesis. 3rd ed. London, 1708.

Holland, Henry, ed. *The Workes Of The Reverend And Faithful Servant of Jesus Christ M. Richard Greenham.* 3rd ed. London: Felix Kyngston, 1601.

Hurd, Richard. *Dialogues On The Uses Of Foreign Travel,* London, 1764.

Jennings, David. *A Sermon Occasioned by the Death of the Late Reverend Isaac Watts.* London, 1749.

Johnson, Samuel. *The Lives of the English Poets; And A Criticism On Their Works.* Dublin: Wm. Wilson, 1780–81.

Jones, William. *The Theological, Philosophical and Miscellaneous Works of The Rev. William Jones.* London, 1801.

Lackington, James. *Memoirs Of The First Forty-Five Years Of The Life Of James Lackington.* new ed. London, 1792.

Lamb, Charles. *The Letters of Charles Lamb to which are added those of his sister Mary Lamb,* ed. E.V. Lucas. London, 1935.

LeClerc, Jean. *The Life and Character of Mr. John Locke.* London: J. Clark, 1706.

Locke, John. *The Educational Writings of John Locke: A Critical Edition with an Introduction and Notes,* ed. James L. Axtell. Cambridge: Cambridge Univ. Press, 1968.

———. *Elements of Natural Philosophy. By John Locke.* London: J. Thomson, 1750.

———. *An Essay Concerning Human Understanding,* ed. John W. Yolton. London: Dent, 1965.

Lowde, James. *A Discourse Concerning the Nature of Man.* London, 1694.

———. *Moral Essays: Wherein some of Mr. Locks and Monsir. Malbranch's Opinions are briefly examin'd.* York, 1699.

More, Hannah. *Strictures On The Modern System of Female Education. With A View Of The Principles And Conduct Prevalent Among Women Of Rank And Fortune.* London, 1799.

Newton, John. *Letters and Sermons. With a Review Of Ecclesiastical History, and Hymns,* ed. T. Haweis. London, 1787.

Paine, Thomas. *The Age Of Reason: Being An Investigation of True And Fabulous Theology.* Paris, 1794.

Paley, William. *Natural Theology: or, Evidence of the Existence and Attributes of The Diety, Collected from the Appearances of Nature.* London: R. Faulder, 1802.

Parsons, John. *The First Book for English Schools; Or The Rational Schoolmaster's First Assistant.* Nottingham, 1787.

Peacham, Henry. *The Compleat Gentleman.* London: F. Constable, 1622.

A Poem Sacred to the Memory of The Reverend and Learned Isaac Watts. London, 1749.

Ray, John. *The Wisdom of God Manifested in the Works of the Creation.* London, 1691.

Religious Tract Society. *An Address to Christians, On the Distribution of Religious Tracts.* London, 1799.

Rhodes, Hugh. *The Book of Nurture for manservants and Children.* London, 1558.

Roberts, William. *The Looker-On.* London, 1792.

Robinson, Henry Crabb. *Diary, Reminiscences, and Correspondence of Henry Crabb Robinson,* ed. Thomas Sadler. London, 1869.

Rousseau, Jean Jacques. *Emilius and Sophia; or, A New System of Education.* London: R. Griffiths, 1762–63.

Scot, Reginald. *The discoverie of witchcraft, Wherein the lewde dealing of witches and witchmongers is notablie detected.* London: W. Brome, 1584.

Sheridan, Thomas. *British Education: Or, The Source of the Disorders of Great Britain.* London, 1756.

Sherlock, William. *A Discourse Concerning the Happiness of Good Men, And The Punishment of the Wicked In The Next World.* London, 1704.

Southey, Robert. *The Life of Wesley; And The Rise and Progress of Methodism.* 2nd ed. London, 1820.

Talbott, James. *The Christian School-Master.* London, 1707.

Trimmer, Sarah. *A Comment on Dr. Watts's Divine Songs for Children.* London, 1789.

_______. *The Guardian of Education.* London, 1802–1806.

_______. *The Oeconomy of Charity; or, an Address to Ladies concerning Sunday Schools.* London: T. Longman, 1787.

_______. *Reflections upon the Education of Children in Charity Schools.* London, 1792.

Warburton, William. *Letters From A Late Eminent Prelate To One of His Friends.* Kidderminster, 1808.

Watts, Isaac. *Catechisms: Or, Instructions in the Principles of the Christian Religion.* London, 1730.

_______. *Philosophical Essays On Various Subjects.* London, 1733.

_______. *A Treatise on the Education of Children and Youth.* 2nd ed. London, 1769.

Wesley, John. *A Survey Of The Wisdom of God in the Creation.* 2nd ed. Bristol, 1770.

Whitchurch, James. *An Essay Upon Education.* London, 1772.

Wollaston, William. *The Religion Of Nature Delineated.* London, 1722.

Wollstonecraft, Mary. *Thoughts On The Education of Daughters.* London, 1787.

_______. *A Vindication Of The Rights Of Woman.* London, 1792.

Woodward, Hezekiah. *Of The Childs Portion, viz: Good Education. Or, The Book of the Education of Youth.* London, 1649.

Young, Thomas. *An Essay on Humanity To Animals.* London, 1798.

Contemporary Book Catalogs

London, William. *A Catalogue Of The most vendible Books in England.* London, 1657.

Newbery's Catalogue of Instructive And Amusing Publications For Young Minds, Sold At The Corner Of St. Paul's Church-Yard. London: E. Newbery, 1800.

Belles Lettres

Butler, Samuel. *The Way of All Flesh.* London, 1903.

Crabbe, George. *The Poetical Works of George Crabbe,* ed. A.J. Carlyle and R.M. Carlyle. London: Henry Frowde, 1908.

Richardson, Samuel. *Pamela; Or, Virtue Rewarded.* London: 1741–42.

Smollett, Tobias. *The History and Adventures of an Atom.* London: Robinson, 1749.

Sterne, Laurence. *The Life and Opinions of Tristram Shandy.* London: R. & J. Dodsley, 1760–67.

Wordsworth, William. *The Prelude, Or Growth Of A Poet's Mind (Text of 1805),* ed. by Ernest de Selincourt, corrected by Stephan Gill. Oxford: Oxford University Press, 1970.

———. *Wordsworth's Poetical Works,* ed. Thomas Hutchinson, revised Ernest de Selincourt. Oxford: Oxford Univ. Press, 1969.

Modern Criticism and History

Aaron, Richard. *John Locke.* 2nd ed. Oxford: Oxford Univ. Press, 1955.

Arnold, Matthew. *Essays in Criticism, Second Series.* London: Macmillan, 1888.

Ashton, John. *Chap-books of the Eighteenth Century,* London: Chatto & Windus, 1882.

Balfour, Clara Lucas. *A Sketch of Mrs. Trimmer.* London: W. & F.G. Cash, 1854.

Barrett, Charlotte, ed. *Diary & Letters of Madame D'Arblay* [Fanny Burney]. London, 1905.

Brantley, Richard. *Wordsworth's "Natural Methodism."* New Haven: Yale Univ. Press, 1975.

Buck, John Dawson Carl. "The Motives of Puffing: John Newbery's Advertisements 1742–1769," *Studies In Bibliography* 30 (1977), 196–210.

Butler, Marilyn. *Maria Edgeworth, A Literary Biography.* Oxford: Oxford Univ. Press, 1972.

Cragg, Gerald R. *Reason and Authority in the Eighteenth Century.* Cambridge: Cambridge Univ. Press, 1964.

Cremin, Lawrence A. *American Education: The Colonial Experience, 1607–1763.* New York: Harper & Row, 1970.

Darton, F.J. Harvey. *Children's Books in England.* 2nd ed. Cambridge: Cambridge Univ. Press, 1958.

Green, John Richard. *History of the English People.* London: Macmillan, 1877–80.

Kuhn, A.J. "Nature Spiritualized: Aspects Of Anti-Newtonianism," *ELH* 41 (1974), 400–12.

Maclean, Kenneth. *John Locke and English Literature of the Eighteenth Century.* New Haven: Yale Univ. Press, 1936.

Moon, Marjorie. *John Harris's Books For Youth 1801–1843.* Cambridge: A. Spilman, 1976.

Morley, Edith, ed. *The Correspondence of Henry Crabb Robinson with the Wordsworth Circle.* Oxford: Oxford Univ. Press, 1927.

Muir, Percy. *English Children's Books 1600–1900.* London: B.T. Batsford, 1954.

Mumby, Frank, and Ian Norris. *Publishing and Bookselling.* 5th ed. London: Jonathan Cape, 1974.

Murch, Jerom. *Mrs. Barbauld and Her Contemporaries.* London, 1877.

Neuburg, Victor. *The Penny Histories.* London: Oxford Univ. Press, 1968.

Nichols, Charles Lemuel. *Isaiah Thomas: Printer, Writer & Collector.* Boston: The Club of Odd Volumes, 1912.

Opie, Iona, and Peter Opie. *The Classic Fairy Tale.* London: Oxford Univ. Press, 1974.

_______. *Three Centuries of Nursery Rhymes and Poetry for Children: An Exhibition Held at the National Book League May 1973.* London: Oxford Univ. Press, 1973.

Pafford, J.H.P. *Isaac Watts: Divine Songs.* London: Oxford Univ. Press, 1971.

Pater, Walter. *Appreciations. With an Essay on Style.* London: Macmillan, 1889.

Pickering, Samuel. *The Moral Tradition in English Fiction, 1785–1850.* Hanover, N.H.: Univ. Press of New England, 1976.

Roberts, Arthur, ed. *Mendip Annals: or, A Narrative of the Charitable Labours of Hannah and Martha More.* 2nd ed. London, 1859.

Roscoe, Sydney. *John Newbery And His Successors, 1740–1814.* Wormley: Five Owls Press, 1973.

Sloane, William. *Children's Books in England & America in the Seventeenth Century.* New York: Columbia Univ. Press, 1955.

Wasserman, Earl. "Nature Moralized: The Divine Analogy in the Eighteenth Century," *ELH* 20 (1953), 39–76.

Welch, d'Alté. *A Bibliography of American Children's Books Printed Prior to 1821.* Worcester, Mass.: American Antiquarian Society, 1972.

Welsh, Charles. *A Bookseller Of The Last Century Being some Account of the Life of John Newbery, and of the Books he published, with a Notice of the later Newberys.* London, 1885.

Wright, Louis B. *Middle-Class Culture in Elizabethan England.* London: Methuen, 1964.

Yolton, John W., ed. *John Locke and the Way of Ideas.* Oxford: Oxford Univ. Press, 1956.

_______. *John Locke: Problems and Perspectives: A Collection of New Essays.* Cambridge: Cambridge University Press, 1969.

Yonge, Charlotte. "Children's Literature of The Last Century." *Macmillan's Magazine* 20 (1869), 229–37.

_______. *A Storehouse of Stories.* London, 1870.

Index